TALKING BACK, TALKING BLACK

TALKING BACK, TALKING BLACK

Truths About America's Lingua Franca

JOHN McWHORTER

Bellevue Literary Press
NEW YORK

First published in the United States in 2017 by
Bellevue Literary Press, New York

For information, contact:
Bellevue Literary Press
NYU School of Medicine
550 First Avenue
OBV A612
New York, NY 10016

Library of Congress Cataloging-in-Publication Data
is available from the publisher upon request

Bellevue Literary Press would like to thank all its generous donors
—individuals and foundations—for their support.

 This publication is made possible by the New York
State Council on the Arts with the support of Governor
Andrew Cuomo and the New York State Legislature.

 This project is supported in part
by an award from the National
Endowment for the Arts.

Book design and composition by Mulberry Tree Press, Inc.
Manufactured in the United States of America.

First Edition

1 3 5 7 9 8 6 4 2

hardcover ISBN: 978-1-942658-20-7
ebook ISBN: 978-1-942658-21-4

For Vanessa Hamilton McWhorter, who came into this world, born reflective, while I was writing this book. I hope that she will read this as soon as she is old enough to take it in, to make sure she never for a second thinks black people's speech is full of mistakes.

And for my cousin Octavia Thompson, who speaks what I think of as the perfect Black English, which I dare anybody to diss.

Contents

TALKING BACK, TALKING BLACK

Introduction

I N HAITI, THE LANGUAGE OF PRINT, school, and the media is French, but when speaking outside of formal settings, people use another form of speech: Haitian Creole.

In Sicily, the language of print, school, and the media is standard Italian, but when speaking outside of formal settings, many people use another form of speech: Sicilian.

In Switzerland, the language of print, school, and the media is High German, but for German speakers in that country, outside of formal settings they use something other than High German: Swiss German, which is quite different in sound, vocabulary, and structure from the German one learns from a book.

In the United States, the language of print, school and the media is Standard English, but when speaking outside of formal settings, black American people use . . . a lot of slang and bad grammar.

At least that is the general American take on the matter. However, comparing the situation here with that in other nations, it becomes clear that we may be missing something. Why would it be that in so many places, casual language is an alternative to the standard one, treated as perfectly normal, while here in the United States, the casual speech of millions of people is thought of as a degradation of the standard form, rather than simply something different?

Certainly, racism is part of the answer. However, black Americans themselves lack the clear conception of their speech as an alternate form of language that Haitians, Jamaicans, and Swiss Germans have. They, as well as whites, tend to be perplexed at the notion of themselves as speaking Black English in the way that a Haitian speaks something in addition to French, or a Germanophone Swiss speaks something in addition to High German. To America as a whole, Black English is rather like ultraviolet light. Scientists (linguists, in this case) discuss it, but for almost everybody else it is an unperceived abstraction despite permeating our very existences.

THE RESULT IS DISSONANCES such as one that I experienced twenty years ago. I had the unexpected experience of being taken up for fifteen minutes of modest media notoriety. Suddenly, America's television shows and newspapers wanted to know what I thought about, of all things, Black English. The matter was actually more specific: Oakland, California's school board had proposed using Black English as an aid to imparting Standard English to black kids. The idea was to address black students' lagging scholastic performance, with a hypothesis that part of the reason for it was that the English they encountered on the page was different from the English they spoke as a home language. I happened to be the black linguist—or maybe the linguist who studied black speech varieties—closest by, since I then was teaching at UC Berkeley.

From our vantage point today, it seems almost odd that there was a weeks-long media firestorm over whether a smallish city would be using Black English as a teaching tool. Similar proposals that had popped up in other cities over the twenty-five years before are today recalled only by those involved. It was partly that Oakland made its announcement during a slow news cycle before Christmas, and partly that this was at the dawn of the twenty-four-hour cable/Internet news era. If it had happened just a couple of years before, the whole affair would barely have registered beyond California.

However, the issue also resonated to such a degree because it entailed a judgment not only about black language but about black people. The Oakland school board was roundly disparaged as opportunistic, chasing bilingual education funds with a crackpot proposal that Black English is an "African" language. Jokes about Ebonics in the wake of the fracas circulate online to this day (Ebonics dictionary entry: PENIS—I went to da doctor and he handed me a cup and said penis [pee in this]). Many wondered why black people were supposed to be exempt from leaving the speech of the ghetto behind the way other immigrant groups have done, and saw the whole Oakland proposal as a kind of unreasoning identity politics.

FOR MOST LINGUISTS AND EDUCATORS involved in this saga or observing it, the racist element in all this vitriol and japery was what they carried away. The assumption was, therefore, that the academic's responsibility in commentary on the issue was to focus on calling attention to the role of racism in how people feel about Black English. That assumption was considered so unassailable that I actually found myself deemed un-PC on the issue by other linguists and educators specializing in Black English, for arguing that the reason black kids have trouble in school is not Black English but the quality of the schools themselves, as well as the problems that life in disadvantaged communities can saddle students with. Yes, indeed: That was considered a disloyal position for a linguist to take.

There was, in fact, something beyond societal inequality that motivated my position, however. Racism is hardly the only thing standing between how linguists see Black English and how the public sees it. What most struck me in 1996, and what I carried away from the whole business, was that America—black as well as white—had no idea that there was even a Black English worthy of discussion.

Linguists talked of grammar. The public talked of slang and mistakes. This never changed. But crucially, even acknowledging racism as an element in the debate, no one could deny that if the dustup had been about teaching white "redneck" in the schools in Mississippi, there would have been very similar anger and ridicule. Racially or not, linguists and the general public see speech very differently.

AMERICANS HAVE TROUBLE comprehending that *any* vernacular way of speaking is legitimate language. Given this situation, during the Oakland controversy linguists seemed unhinged. "Is Ebonics a language?" people would ask, with the quietly acrid skepticism with which one would ask whether Elmo is a philosopher. Television commentator Tucker Carlson derided Ebonics as "a language where nobody knows how to conjugate the verbs," as if it is unquestioned that Standard English's verb conjugations are logically inseparable from any English conceivable as coherent. And the Oakland episode was just one step on a time line. It has now been almost fifty years since linguistic experts began studying Black English as a legitimate speech variety, arguing that black Americans' colloquial English is not a degradation of English but one of many variations upon English. This effort has been largely in vain.

EVEN NOW, I FEEL MOVED to specify to some degree what I mean by Black English, given that so many factors cloud our vision as to just what the term might refer. There are two main ways that various dialects of a language differ: the sound (or accent) and the sentence structure.

For example, for an American, British people's English is different in its accent: that *pot* sounds more like "pawt," et cetera. The main task that faces an American actor playing the part of a British character is to change the way he articulates the sounds of the words. Black English, in the same way, has some sounds that are different from those in Standard English. It is these different sounds that give Americans the impression that someone can sound black, an intuition often harbored with a certain ambivalence, but based on a genuine difference in accent that linguistic research has confirmed the existence of.

British English also has some sentence structures different from those in American English. In the United States, one says "If she had smelled it, then I would have," whereas in England, one might more likely say "If she had smelt it, then I would have done." The past tense of *smelled* is formed differently, and in British English the *do* verb is often used differently than in American English. Black English, in this same way, has some sentence structures different from those in Standard English. For example, "If she had smelled it might in Black English be "If she had done smelt it."

Here is an example of perfect Black English in which we can see how sentence structures differ from those in Standard English:

> **It** a girl name Shirley Jones **live** in Washington. Most everybody on the street like her, 'cause **she a** nice girl. Shirley treat all of them just like they was her sister and brother, but most of all she like one boy name Charles. But Shirley keep away from Charles most of the time, 'cause she start to liking him so much she **be** scared of him. So Charles, he don't hardly say **nothing** to her neither. Still, that girl got to go 'round telling everybody Charles s'posed to be liking her. But when Valentine Day start to come 'round, Shirley get to worrying. She worried 'cause she know the rest of **them** girls going to get Valentine cards from they boyfriends.

Some basic features of Black English structure are in bold. **It** is used instead of the presentational *there*; **live**: the third-person singular *s* is not necessary; **she a**: the linking verb *be* can often be omitted; **be**: however, this usage of *be* signals that something goes on over a long period of time, such as Shirley's fright; **nothing**: double negatives do not make a positive in Black English; **them**: often replaces *those*.

Notice that there is no slang in this passage. Slang is one part of Black English, but then, slang is also rife in anyone's English, and there is much more to Black English than argot. Slang comes and goes; the Black English I refer to is more long-lived—this dialect is centuries old.

YET DESPITE PEOPLE LAYING OUT DATA about Black English for decades, the perception of the dialect has remained largely unchanged since the first articles on what was then termed *Negro English* in now-yellowing issues of academic journals in the 1960s. A small community of scholars study Black English intensely, discoursing enthusiastically about African-American Vernacular English, or AAVE, code switching, and identity, it being second nature to them to analyze the speech of black Americans with the same tools other linguists use to study Hungarian and Japanese. Since the 1970s, these scholars have transferred this conception to educators with a certain amount of success. However, even among them, one still encounters teachers attesting that Black English is okay but still harboring a sense of it as a passel of mistakes—only okay, then, in the sense that it's okay to belch openly at home. And beyond this, other than to occasional self-taught aficionados, Black English specialists' sense of Black English seems counterintuitive and possibly kooky, like the idea of multiverses or qi. The impression remains that Black English is simply a collection of streety expressions, rather than also a system of grammar and an accent, requiring native mastery to control fully.

I experience one manifestation of this in the classroom. Once, a regular result of teaching a class about Black English as having a grammar was that black students would notice that they spoke this "language" you were putting on the board. These days, not uncommonly, I am noting white students similarly excited that they "speak Black English." These people are the first generation raised entirely within the era of hip-hop as mainstream music, and there are indeed some white people who truly control the structures of the dialect and would sound black on an audio recording. Most of the time, however, what young white Americans thinking of themselves as Black English speakers are referring to is not the grammatical apparatus that linguists study, but black slang expressions. That is, they, too, have had no way of knowing that Black English is anything but slang. How, in current American discourse, could they have learned the rest of the story?

Meanwhile, something else that encourages ignorance of Black English's existence is, ironically, a desire not to stereotype. Namely, one is often taught that the only reason we might think there is a "black" way to talk is that we are essentializing black people, and that actually black people simply speak southern English. Back in 1971, Civil Rights leader Bayard Rustin argued that "'Black English,' after all, has nothing to do with blackness but derives from conditions of lower-class life in the South (poor Southern whites also speak 'Black English')." Rustin's perspective lives on today.

Yet while there is an obvious overlap between Black and southern English, few would say that Jeff Foxworthy and Samuel L. Jackson speak the same dialect. The differences are significant, documented by linguists, and immediately apparent to an American ear. When someone says "He the one" instead of "He's the one," uses *ain't* for *didn't* as in "He ain't told me," or uses *be* in that ongoing sense that Shirley did, they are speaking Black, not southern, English. No one goes about consciously aware of such things, but they are part of the sense we have that there is indeed a "black" way of talking.

Yet there have been remarks that Hillary Clinton adopts a southern accent when talking to black audiences. But does anyone think black people in Pittsburgh would really feel a special connection to the speech style of Dolly Parton or Jim Nabors? People are using *southern* as a stand-in for *black* out of a wariness of being criticized—"What do you mean, 'talking like a black person?'"—and crucially, that wariness is entirely justified. In after-talk question sessions, online chat forums, and even general conversation, speculation persists that Black English is really just southern dialect.

In yet another way, then, people miss a key component in America's speech repertoire. Since 1996, the media has further sought my opinions about Black English now and then, and each time I confront the very same conception of the dialect that reigned in the middle of the Clinton administration and before: that Black English is simply a flippant lingo. As recently as 2013, media commentators were baffled by the ordinary Black English used on the witness stand by Rachel Jeantel during the trial of the killer of her friend, teenager Trayvon Martin. Jeantel was simply using the grammatical patterns of Black English used all over the United States, and yet intelligent people actually consulted with me as to whether she was more comfortable in her parents' Haitian Creole than in English.

Before that, in 2010, the media had reported that the Drug Enforcement Administration had called for translators to help understand what surreptitiously recorded black criminals were saying. Black English, with its different accent from Standard English and different ways of putting sentences together, proved hard for nonspeakers to understand on a recording made under less than ideal conditions, where people were speaking rapidly, their voices often overlapping one another, as typically occurs in actual conversation. In Italy, no one would bat an eye if translators were called in to make sense of recordings made under equivalent conditions of Sicilian or Milanese. Here in the United States, however, that Black English could require such treatment seemed absurd to many, baffled at the idea that Black English is anything but lingo and grammatical mistakes. Seen only in part, looked past, or mistaken as something else, Black English in the American mind remains a phantom.

It doesn't have to be this way, and the goal of this book is enlightenment. Linguists (including me) are responsible for the fact that almost nobody knows that there exists something called Black English, which is complex enough to require books and academic articles to analyze, and which has its own grammatical structure, just as Standard English does, or Finnish, or Japanese. Certainly plenty of books have been written outlining and celebrating Black English, demonstrating that it is systematic in its structure and also the vehicle of a rich culture. However, the sad and simple fact is that *a dialect can be seen as both systematic and culturally rich while processed as "bad grammar" nevertheless.*

I see four main barriers to understanding:

1. When the public encounters the assertion that Black English is more than gutter talk, the argument usually depicts Black English as largely a matter of discarding or distorting standard language forms.

2. Partly because of the above perception, many Americans worry that even to acknowledge that there is a "black" way of talking may be racist.

3. The relatively uniform linguistic landscape of Anglophone America encourages a sense that people can't speak both a standard and a nonstandard form of a language in a complimentary relationship.

4. Many equate Black English with the distorted dialect that minstrel-show performers used, and suppose that the cartoonish quality of the latter requires treating the former as equally dismissible.

I'm aware that some feel that racism is *the* reason people disparage Black English, and that issues like those mentioned above may be considered "worth talking about" but that they essentially skirt the point. However, I would request those who feel that way to bear with me. Racism, after all, isn't going away anytime soon, but in my experience, people can be made to see Black English in a new way regardless. I present approaches here that I have found effective in imparting to reasonable skeptics, unconverted but open-minded—that is, the typical rational person—that Black English is not bad grammar, but alternate grammar.

The book is very directly targeted. I intend these chapters as didactic, and sometimes exploratory, essays. One may come away from them with a sense of having been introduced to the dialect, but for formal and comprehensive introduction to the structures and usage of Black English, the reader must seek other teachers, such as Geneva Smitherman, William Labov, John Rickford, and Lisa Green. This book is intended as building on the groundwork such scholars have established.

A note on terminology. To some, the term *Black English* may have a musty air. Specialists have long moved on to *African-American Vernacular English*, while among laymen, the term *Ebonics* gained a foothold in the wake of the Oakland controversy, which revived it, although it had otherwise fallen out of usage after a brief vogue in the 1970s. I am eschewing *African-American Vernacular English* partly because in this book I am addressing not only vernacular speech but also standard speech. Black Americans can sound identifiably black even when using neither slang nor grammatical features of the dialect. *African-American English* could be a possible substitute, but, along with *African-American Vernacular English*, it runs up against the fact that the dialect has very little identifiable African influence in it. Also, since the 1990s, the number of immigrants from Africa in the United States has grown so much that the very term *African-American* is becoming increasingly confusing. White South African immigrants are genuinely perplexed that they do not qualify as African-Americans, for example.

Meanwhile, the term *Ebonics*, although I have given in to it somewhat over the years, is unfortunate. Its reference to dark skin makes it much too general to apply only to black people in the United States. In fact, it was originally coined to refer to all languages of the African diaspora. Then also, the *ics* suffix is modeled on the word *phonics* out of a sense that phonics involves language. However, the *ics* suffix is not properly applied to the name of a language or dialect, as opposed to, say, a reading program. For our purposes, then, Black English it will be. I have always thought the term does the job quite well.

The concept here is more important than the label. It's time the dialect was discussed as something both interesting and normal. America hasn't known how to do that. This book attempts to show the way.

CHAPTER ONE

It's Complicated

A Toy Piano Isn't a Steinway, Right? The Real Story About Black English Grammar

I'll never forget the time a woman from Japan, who had been in the United States for a long time and spoke very good English, casually said to me that I was different from other black Americans in that "you don't use bad grammar." Her being from another country and culture made her comfortable spelling that out to me so bluntly, but her judgment as to how black Americans talk was, let's face it, representative of how most Americans feel—including quite a few black ones. For example, James Meredith, who was the first black person admitted to the University of Mississippi, has, later in his life, handed out a flyer before talks to young black audiences that includes this advice:

BLACK ENGLISH LANGUAGE
PROPER ENGLISH LANGAGE

Which one do you use? Most people in this room use a lot of Black English and a little Proper English.

Anyone who wants to become an intellectual giant must learn and use a lot of Proper English and as little Black English as possible.

I am not going to argue with anyone about the matter. You can do what you want to do.

However, I will tell you that anyone who continues to use a lot of Black English will never become an intellectual giant.

To me, Black English is like a clockwork or an engine, a system every bit as coherent as Latin or Chinese. But to most Americans, Black English means error.

Typically, it is thought that the reason the public fails to understand that Black English is coherent speech is racism. A typical reaction to this failure is: "No matter what we say, they just don't get it! Of course, it's because they don't *want* to get it." And surely racism plays a part in how Black English is heard. However, here's a thought: If it happened to be white people from a remote part of the country who spoke exactly the way black people can, do we really think people would in that case just accept their speech as okay? We barely have to wonder, because the speech of uneducated southern whites comes under a lot of fire, as well. The speech of Appalachian whites is condemned to an even greater degree: there are ample testimonials in that community to linguistic self-consciousness and discrimination similar to the kind that black people can attest to.

The truth is that the reason many people think Black

English is gutter talk is not all their fault; it's partly linguists' fault. We have not made the case to the public in a way that actually convinces, even when we think we have. And racism or not, there are ways of getting across the truth to even skeptical audiences. I've seen it, and I want to share what I have learned here. It's easy for a linguist to forget what language seems like to everyone else. But I feel a responsibility to try my hardest in order to, if I may, bring America out of Plato's cave.

What I'm Not Going to Do and Why

FIRST, LET'S TAKE A LOOK at what seems not to work, which will also be useful in gaining a sense of what linguists even mean when they say Black English is more than slang. Linguists and fellow travelers often teach people about Black English by discussing how the verb *to be* is used. In a sentence like "She be passin' by," what almost anyone hears most immediately is that the *be* verb isn't conjugated, as opposed to Standard English: "She is passing by." However, there is more going on in a sentence like "She be passin' by" than it might seem. This usage of *be* is very specific; it means that something happens on a regular basis, rather than something going on right now. As counterintuitive as it seems, no black person would say "She be passin' by right now," because that isn't what *be* in that sentence is supposed to mean. Rather, it would be "She be passin' by every Tuesday when I'm about to leave."

In other words, that unconjugated *be* is, of all things, grammar. In Standard English, it's easier to get a sense of what *habitual* refers to in language by thinking about how we express it in the past: "She used to pass by every Tuesday" means that it happened regularly. If you were referring to something that happened just once, you would use the simple past: "She passed by just now." In Black English, you can make that same differentiation in the present: "She's passin' by right now;" "She be passin' by every Tuesday."

That's neat, in that you would never think of this from just listening to black people talking, especially since we don't expect anything elegant or complex when people are just chatting. But linguists are trained to think that explaining this "habitual *be*," as it's called in the "biz," will teach people that Black English is okay. Specifically, we are taught to argue that the habitual *be* shows that Black English is *systematic*. If how the habitual *be* works is not just random, but based on rules, as in something I had to carefully explain just now, then that means that Black English is as good as Standard English, right?

Wrong. Linguists have been telling people that Black English is systematic for almost fifty years now, and it's safe to say that the argument has made not a dent in public feelings about the dialect. There's a reason. As long as the *be* verb is still unconjugated, the habitual *be* still sounds "wrong." People think to themselves, Yeah, it's systematic—systematically wrong!

It's the same with other things presented as examples of why there's nothing wrong with Black English. The layman can hear that in Black English the verb *to be* is often left out entirely: "She my sister," "They my friends." Now, an expert will tell you that, leaving out *to be* in Black English is not random, but systematic. So, you say "She my sister," but not "I your sister"—with *I*, you have to have the *am*. So, a linguist might couch this as "omission of the copula is ungrammatical in the first-person singular"—*copula* is a fancy word for (certain uses of) the verb *to be*, and *ungrammatical* means that if you say such a thing, you are breaking the rules of the dialect. But a perfectly reasonable person will think, Okay— but the fact that they don't use the *be* in the other persons is still wrong. This may be a system, but it's a broken one!

Quite simply, the systematicity argument doesn't change minds, as compelling as it can seem to the tiny guild known as linguists, who spend their lives examining the minutiae of how languages and dialects work. To ordinary people, language is two things. One is words. The other is grammar, but grammar in the sense taught in school: as rules one is warned about breaking. To me, grammar means things like the habitual *be* or the ablative absolute in Latin. But grammar as taught to most people in school means "Don't say *less* books, say *fewer* books" and "Say Billy and *I* went to the store, not Billy and *me* went to the store." Black English cannot help but look bad under this lens, where the words are slang and the grammar faulty. As to systematicity—well, there are plenty of things that are systematic but dismissable.

Think about it: Toy pianos are adorable, and systematic enough that I couldn't build one at gunpoint, but no one would want to hear Schubert played on one. There's a reason Andrés Segovia didn't perform on a ukulele; four strings going plink-a-plink is cute, but no one clamors for a ukulele recital at Carnegie Hall. The Mafia has been awesomely systematic; none of us would choose them to run a town, however. One reads in awe about how viruses thrive and replicate themselves—yet we'd happily never encounter one again. Sadly—and it is sad—systematicity does not score for nonlinguists as an argument in favor of Black English, except among the already converted. Surely we want to reach beyond that small circle.

On that note, it also moves few to say that Black English's floutings of Standard English rules have parallels in the way other languages work. We often say—and I mean "we," as I have made this argument often—that Russian doesn't use a *be* verb in sentences like "She my sister" either, and so it's okay that Black English doesn't. But the response for many is, "But this isn't Russian; it's English. Why can't they talk like everybody else?" Upon which we're back to systematicity, and well . . .

Further Reasonable Objections

SYSTEMATICITY ISN'T THE ONLY ARGUMENT linguists are taught to present in defense of Black English, but the other ones frankly haven't cut much more ice with the general public. Take, for example, "Different people speak in different ways," as it is sometimes put. However, the idea that Black English is simply different feels fake to most people. For them, if different includes not conjugating the *be* verb or leaving it out entirely, not to mention double negation ("She don't see nothin'") and pronunciations like *aks,* then one thinks of the fact that Lennie in Steinbeck's *Of Mice and Men* is "different" from George. "Special," perhaps?

Then there is a more sociopolitically charged argument. "After all, as much linguistics and anthropological research has shown, how we feel about a given language, more often than not, reflects how we feel about its speakers," two Black English specialists have written. In other words, as I once heard this observation most resonantly put—the speaker had one of those lovely educated British accents—"to criticize a dialect is to criticize its speakers." He was right, and the room applauded. But it was a room full of linguists, education experts, and speech pathologists—part of that small group of the converted. Such a group may assume that to associate criticism of Black English with racism is a smackdown argument. However, it only qualifies as such in that some people upon hearing the argument will clam up.

That's all, though, and in my experience, many people in private settings have a reasoned and even concerned riposte to the racism argument. That is, someone might say, "What would be racist is if we didn't teach them *not* to talk that way!" People of this mind-set are often as aware of racism in black Americans' past and present as anyone would want them to be, and yet this awareness leads them to statements such as "I know that they talk that way because of segregation and lack of education. But part of us making up for all of that is to teach them not to use broken language."

In the eighties, I knew a white, educated, urban northeastern woman who, upon reading about efforts to explore and destigmatize Black English in schools with large numbers of black students, fumed at the idea that teachers were going to make already-burdened kids' lives worse by teaching them that grammatical mistakes were okay. No one listening to her sentiments on this could reasonably have tarred her as a bigot, or even as regrettably ignorant. She was someone one could easily imagine in a film written by Nora Ephron or writing a smart letter to the *New York Times*. She was a racially enlightened, concerned citizen, raised in New York in the 1970s, who had no way of understanding Black English the way a few thousand experts on language or education do. And that's because she hadn't been given the message in a way that could have reached her.

Leaving Things Out Is Legitimate?

THE CORE OF THE PROBLEM is that people have been asked to accept Black English as legitimate when it is presented as a series of exemptions to using Standard English rules. Systematic or not, to any intelligent reader or listener, a defense of Black English based on what looks like a list of transgressions comes off as a shabby political exercise.

And yet, Black English is indeed presented to the public as a list of subtractions from Standard English. If two consonants are next to each other, you can drop one—*desk* to *des'*. You can leave verbs unconjugated: "I like the way she talk." You can omit the *be* verb. These examples are representative of how Black English was introduced to, say, people like my dismayed friend in 1987, or was introduced during the 1996 Ebonics controversy, when so many of my fellow linguists were distressed that the public didn't seem to be heeding our message. It can seem almost strange that people expect the public to embrace a dialect portrayed this way—until you remember that the systematicity argument is supposed to make up for all of the flouting.

However, systematic flouting sounds like something one could alternately call "linguistic delinquence," which puts into a sad perspective a defense of Black English founded on lists of rules it breaks. As I write this, the Wikipedia entry for Black English lists twenty-three grammatical traits, of which twelve are reductions and droppings. That's over half, and among the other traits are such things as multiple negatives ("Ain't nothin' nobody can do for no man no how") and good old *aks* and *graps* for *grasp*. Now, when consonants are reversed in cases like that, linguists call it "metathesis" and just think of it as something that happens to sounds sometimes. For example, the word for miracle in Latin was *miraculum*, but in Spanish the *r* and the *l* traded places and the result was *milagro*. But in the here and now, walking around listening to people speak English far, far away from Old Castile in both time and space, let's face it, *aks* just sounds like the wrong way to say *ask*.

The Wikipedia entry is an admirable job in itself. I have no idea who created it, and I single it out only because of its accessibility—it is typical of countless presentations elsewhere. My point is simply that if I weren't a linguist and I had read this entry or equivalent descriptions of Black English, I would be quietly baffled as to why it was not just bad English. Whether I said anything about it out loud would depend on my temperament, but as they used to say, they can't put you in jail for what you're thinking.

There is one feature of Black English that one may come across that does not seem like an abuse of Standard English. Here are some shades of meaning that you can express with a verb in Black English:

He *been* seen it! (He saw it a long time ago.)
He done seen it. (He saw it recently.)
He be seein' it. (He sees it regularly.)
He steady seein' it. (He is right now in the process
    of seeing it.)

It has often been claimed that Black English lets you express more nuances of this kind with verbs than Standard English does. However, despite my profound respect for and debt to pioneer scholars of the dialect who discovered these things, I must say that this area of the dialect cannot serve to convince people that it is legitimate, either, despite that the point in question is often considered the gold-standard demonstration that Black English is not bad English.

For one, it's not always clear that Standard English doesn't have equivalents to these things. If black people can say "He *been* had that!" and white people can say "He's had that *forever*!" does that really mean that Black English is richer somehow? If "He done seen it" refers to the recent past, isn't that just another way of saying "He has seen it?" Another example one could cite on a list of expressions is *finna* for *fixing to*, as in "She finna go, so tell her later." But I left it off, because *finna* is just *fixing to* said quickly. Some question whether the *steady* in "He steady seein' it" has ever really been part of Black English's grammar as such—that is, in its "DNA." To some, it seems as if it was more of a passing idiom decades ago that modern speakers don't use much.

I don't want to drag us too far into the weeds on this, but in the end, how you use verbs to situate things in time is just one item for our list. When told something as counter-intuitive as that the Black English he hears as a rappity, raggedy street mess is something worthy of the term *language,* the skeptic seeks more than one thing. One might allow that this one small list qualifies as system—albeit there's still that "unconjugated" *be* verb with "He be seein' it." But one might still feel that the mass of other elements in the dialect, all about *not* doing things, renders Black English overall exactly what you thought it was. In other words, expressions like "He steady seein' it" might seem like a few keys on that toy piano—but not part of anything we would consider a proper vehicle of intelligent expression.

Getting to a New Place:
Five Ways Black English Outdoes Standard English

THE WAY TO GET PAST THIS RETICENCE to accept Black English is to refashion how it is presented to the public. No more should Black English be presented largely as a dialect that leaves out this and reverses that, with specialists then wondering why the public continues to think of it as a cluster of errors and isn't impressed that the errors are systematic.

Rather, Black English must be introduced via a collection of ways in which it is *more complex than Standard*

English, not less. People respect complexity. People like simplicity in their music and in ways of preparing food, but in terms of grammar, not so much. Some people involved with presenting Black English to the public might wonder just what such a collection of complex features would consist of, other than the shadings of verb usage I just mentioned. The simple fact is that specialists in Black English have not been primed to seek out those features that outdo Standard English in complexity. Systematicity will intrigue and stimulate academic linguistic analysis, but the public isn't having it, so we must change the lens.

Below I will discuss five things in the dialect that demonstrate that anyone speaking Black English is doing something subtle and complex.

1. *Up* what?

I once had occasion to ask a black American with a solid command of Ebonics what *up* means in a sentence like "We was up in here havin' a good time." "Well, *up* is the opposite of *down*," she replied. That was a natural answer, since we all think of ourselves as using words according to their basic dictionary meanings. Yet quite often we don't use them that way. Imagine you peep into a room down the hall and see your little nephew in there playing with an Etch A Sketch when you thought he was outside in the yard with the other kids. "What are you doing in here?" you ask. And yet, it's quite clear what he's doing: playing with that Etch A Sketch. What you mean by that sentence, phrased just that way, is *why* he is in there, not what he's doing. You may not be conscious of it, but you are not using *what* in accordance with its basic meaning.

Up in Black English is like that. I said to the woman, "But if you think about it, you'd say 'We was up in here havin' a good time' even if you were in a basement." She said, "Yeah, I guess so!" "So," I continued, "what does *up* mean in that sentence?" Her response: "It's just slang." I stopped there— we were at an Outback Steakhouse; it wasn't the occasion for linguistic analysis. But in fact, *up* in Black English is not just slang in the sense of being a way of saying something that you'd say a different way in Standard English, such as "Whaddup?" for "How are you?" or even *finna* for *fixing to*. Rather, *up*, as random as it seems, has a meaning, just like *of*, *indeed*, and *Formica* do. But no one has any reason to think about the meaning of a word like *up*, so you have to smoke the meaning out by listening to how people use it.

Here are five sentences I have overheard:

We was sittin' up at Tony's.
Don't be sittin' up in my house askin' me where's the
    money.
It was buck naked people up in my house.
I was gettin' comfortable watchin' TV up in the bed.
I ain't got no food up in my house.

The first thing that should be clear is that the vertical meaning of *up* has nothing to do with these sentences. In fact, the first three sentences came from people who lived on the first floor of their buildings. The fourth one was from someone whose bed I had not had occasion to view, but the chances that her bed was oddly high were infinitesimal—who talks about climbing "up" into bed other than the princess in "The Princess and the Pea"? I heard the fifth one from a passing stranger, but it was similarly unlikely she was referring to her residence being "up" anything. Imagine how odd it would be if you lived on the ninth floor of a building and needed to do a supermarket trip and told someone, "I don't have any food up in my apartment." It would sound like you actually live somewhere on the ground but for some reason keep an extra apartment up high where you stashed your groceries like some squirrel.

Linguists have yet to discover a single instance in any human language or dialect where people randomly toss a word into their conversations all the time for no reason at all, just because it just feels good to say it or because everyone has mysteriously been possessed by some kind of tic. If people are using a word, it's there for a reason, just as the *ed* on *walked* is there to mark the past and we use *will* in *will walk* to mark the future. No matter how slangy, or even profane, something sounds to us, if people are saying it all the time, it's speech, and speech has rules.

So what is the function of this *up*? *Up* what? In this instance, *up* signifies that the place you're in is familiar and comfortable. Humans can choose to have a word that expresses all kinds of things, far beyond what Standard English conveys. Some languages make you mark whether you learned something by seeing it, hearing it, surmising it, or hearing it talked about. Some languages make you mark whether something happened in the morning or the afternoon. And there is one speech variety that makes you mark when the setting you are in is one you have a sense of intimacy with, and that is Black English. *Up* is a marker of intimacy, just as adding *ed* to a verb is a marker of past action.

"We was sittin' up at Tony's" means that Tony is a friend of yours. To say "We was waitin' up at the dentist's" would be incorrect Black English, because the dentist's office is a place you probably don't go to that much and experience little comfort in. "It was buck-naked people up in my house" is the statement of a man who was struck by the fact that in his place of residence, the intimate space he had carved for himself in this chaotic world, there were, unexpectedly, naked persons (it had been quite a party, apparently). Because bed is comfortable, naturally one will refer to being "up" in it, especially in the long term, as this woman was referring to. To refer to not having food "up" in one's house conveys the close, bodily aspect of having no food in one's home.

This intimacy marker *up*, then, is a grammatical element. Someone who had to learn Black English would find mastering it challenging. For example, it'd be easy to say something like "I'm up in the 7-Eleven and I can't find the Slim Jims," when, no, not quite—You don't know the cashier there and there's nowhere to sit; there's nothing "up," in the Black English sense, about a 7-Eleven. Black English *up* is complex—and it isn't about leaving something out or twisting it around. It's a nuance that Standard English cannot convey as easily and briefly. In terms of *up*, Black English has more going on.

2. Done

It has often been written that in a sentence like "I done seen it," *done* serves to mark the recent past as opposed to the more distant past. "I done drunk it" supposedly means you drank it this morning or yesterday, while you'd say "I drank it" if it was something like last month or last year.

However, this isn't the way people actually use *done*. It isn't just a random alternate way of indicating the past in general. You wouldn't say "Last summer after they done planted tomatoes, they planted some cucumbers." But it isn't because last summer was too far in the past, because you *would* say to someone "You done growed up!"—even though presumably the growing up happened years ago. "I done had a crush on you since you was twelve" is perfectly fine—and yet you could say this to somebody who was thirty (or seventy), referring to a crush that began eons ago.

Yet, there must be system to this *done,* since it is part of fluent human speech. A Black English speaker has a confident sense of whether *done* is being used properly or not, but figuring out just what determines what's right and what's wrong has thrown quite a few, myself included.

Elizabeth Dayton at the University of Puerto Rico did an interesting project where she apparently watched every black movie made from roughly *She's Gotta Have It* to *The Cookout* and tabulated uses of *done*. From this, she identified that the reason *done* has proven so elusive is that we have been trying to assign to it descriptions based on what we expect from English, or French or Spanish, where we think about things like the perfect (*have gone*) versus the simple past (*went*). But actually, the reason *done* can mark things in both the recent and the distant past, but only in *certain* sentences in either case, is that its function is more specific than it seems. It marks *counterexpectation*. That is, whether it's used in a sentence about 1973 or last week, a sentence with *done* is always about something the speaker finds somewhat surprising, contrary to what was expected.

"You done drunk it," then, does not mean "You drank it a little while ago." It could—but then you could also say "You done drunk it" about something that happened last summer. "You done drunk it" is something you would say if you left someone sitting outside with a can of soda that you expected to share with him, only to find when you got back that he had drunk the whole can. The *done* would convey that you hadn't expected him to do that. But that means that you could also say "You done drunk it" if you had stashed away one can of watermelon-flavored Jolly Rancher soda in the garage over the winter, looking forward to savoring it on the first hot day of the coming summer, only to find it missing on that day, and when you bring this up with your son, he turns out to have drunk it sometime last September. "You done drunk it?" you could ask—despite that it happened almost a year ago. "You done growed up!" conveys that a part of you always imagined the person as a tyke and it's a little odd to see the person now as an adult. "I done had a crush on you since you was twelve" is something you would impart to someone as news—presumably the woman you say this to hadn't been aware of it.

A counterexpectational marker—that may seem like bending over backwards a little. Is that really grammar? Do other languages have counterexpectational markers? Well, yes, they do! Take a tribe of people in the Amazon rain forest called the Jarawara. In their language, to say "The water is cold," you say "Faha siri!" But if you give someone a glass of water that strikes him as extremely cold—say, for example, you give a member of the Jarawara water from a refrigerator and he, as someone who lives in the rain forest, isn't used to water that cold—then he will say "Faha siri-**makoni**!" *Makoni* doesn't mean "very" or "Whew!"—there are other words for those. To a Jarawara, figuring out what *makoni* means is as odd and challenging as it is for black (or any) Americans to nail what *up* means in "We was sittin' up at Tony's." That's because, when you look at how it's used in lots of sentences, you glean that it marks the counterintuitive— a Jarawara can also use it to remark on how much bigger a Westerner's shoes turn out to be than his feet, or how an ant was walking in an odd way on a leaf.

That's one of endless examples worldwide. Like Jarawara, Black English has a clear and frequently used way of indicating the counterexpectational with a little marker: *makoni* in the Amazon, *done* in Atlanta. But *done* is not used that way in Standard English. Here, as with *up*, Black English has more going on.

3. Narrative *had*

Some languages have a verb tense that you use when you're telling stories. Swahili is one of them. The word *I* is *ni.* The word *eat* is *kula.* The present tense is *na.* So to say "I am eating," you say "*ni-na-kula.*" To say "I ate," you use the past tense marker, *li* – *ni-**li**-kula* means "I ate." But if you're telling a story about how you sat down and picked up a fork and you were eating when the wind blew out one of your windows, then you use a different marker, *ka.* You would say "*ni-**ka**-kula.*"

That's called a narrative tense, and it seems rather nice from a distance. But actually, Americans are surrounded by the same thing, because Black English has a narrative tense marker. Those speaking Black English use *had* in narratives. Here is a real-life example, from a ten-year-old boy describing a scuffle: "'Cause when he hit me like this, he had upper-cut me like that, and then he had hit me like that. He had kicked me, it was half-wrestling and then, one, I was tired, then he just beat me, and push me down, that's when he had push me down."

It can be strange to the uninitiated to hear this usage of *had.* My cousins used it quite fluently when I was a kid, and I remember that when I first noticed it, I felt as if they never quite got to the point when they recounted things at length. "Okay, so all that *had* happened, but what finally *did* happen?" (I recall the exact geographical point at which I encountered Black English's narrative *had*: at the bottom of the Marion Lane cul-de-sac in front of Carpenter's Woods on Mt. Pleasant Avenue in Philadelphia. Just thought that should be entered into the record.) But after a while I realized that the use of *had* did not signal a coming finale—it was telling the story itself. It's that way with the ten-year-old's narrative: "That's when he had push me down" is the conclusion, not a prelude to ". . . upon which my friend came and grabbed him . . . (etc.)."

The narrative *had* sounds like a flub, no doubt. In Standard English, *had* is used only for the pluperfect, or "past of the past": "She had already closed the door, and so the cat couldn't get in." However, *had* is used that way in Black English, as well; it's just that *had* has a double function. In this way, a person using Black English happens to arrange the "furniture" differently than someone would in Standard English. Nor is Black English slovenly in the use of *had* to convey two different meanings. That occurs in Standard English, too. Did you ever notice that putting an *s* on the end of something can mean either plural or possessive? *Dogs* or *dog's*—to the ear, they are the same; the apostrophe is just on paper. Yet we have no trouble keeping the two meanings apart. "Have you seen Peter?" we ask, but the *have* in that sentence has nothing to do with what *have* is supposed to mean, as in "I have a new book." We don't think twice about it. In Black English, *had* moonlights in the same way.

This means that, like Swahili, Black English has a narrative tense: The narrative *had* is grammar. For Black English speakers, the one phrase "Now, what had happened was . . ." is a running in-joke, associated with someone trying to worm their way out of some kind of jam, and is often thought of as a self-standing expression. Less obvious is that this phrase is an example of a general way of using *had* in reference to anything happening in the past, which is exactly the kind of thing that distinguishes Black English from

Standard English. More to the point, this use of *had* is one more way in which Black English has more going on than Standard English.

4. Keeping it *rill*

For all that Black English is dismissed as broken language, it is actually not the easiest to imitate. If a Standard English speaker had to master either an authentic British accent or an authentic black Pittsburgh accent, he'd likely do better with the British one.

This may not be obvious, given the tendency for sources on Black English to stress the ways that Black English sounds are simpler renditions of Standard English ones. For example, in Black English the vowel sound in *rice* comes out as *ah*, so that *rice* is "rahs," *my* is "mah" and *spider* is "spahder." The Standard English sound is two vowels, in a way: *ah* plus an *ee* gliding off, which is why this kind of sound is called a diphthong (*di* means "two" and the *phthong* means "sound"). Black English makes that *ah-ee* into one sound, *ah*. As such, you will see this described as monophthongization. Whatever it's called, it's an easier way of saying the sound than the way it's said in Standard English.

But Black English balances that monophthongization by outdoing Standard English sounds in some ways. We aren't trained to hear it and so it goes past our ears. Here's an example. In Standard English, the words *bee* and *meal* have the same vowel, the *ee* sound. In Black English, they don't. A speaker or hearer may not be aware of it, but in Black English, before an *l* and only then, the *ee* sound comes out more like *ih*. That means that in Black English, *meal* is more like *mill*, or, to be specific, it's a diphthong. First there is the *ih*, and then there's a little *uh* gliding off: "mih-ull." *Feel* is "fih-ull." *For real* is "for rih-ull."

In itself, that seems like a random bit of nothing much. But actually, it means that to know Black English, you don't just know the sound *ee*. You also have to know that before *l*, it takes on a different form and becomes "ih-uh." In an Ebonics 101 class, this would be an annoying aspect of accent that the teacher would lecture you about, just as the French class schoolmarm chides you about saying a word like *lune* for *moon,* where you don't just say "loon," but shape your mouth for *loon* and say *lean.* "You must improve your accent, my dear! Not 'loo-oon.' 'Leuwwwn.'" Next door in Ebonics 101, "Not 'fee-eeel.' 'Fih-ull'!"

And then, the *ih* here is not really *ih*—it's something in between *ee* and *ih*. It's a whole other sound that Black English has that Standard English doesn't have. It's an odd sound because it only comes up in very specific instances. Another one reveals itself thusly: say *bed* and then *pen.* Now, in Black English, those don't rhyme precisely, either. Before an *n* or an *m*—and only then!—an *eh* sound becomes more like *ih.* It's that same sound from "fih-ull." Many are familiar with southerners who pronounce *pen* and *pin* the same way; this is one of the many overlaps between Black and southern English. But that means that in Black English, *gem* and *pen* sound more like "jim" and "pin." Not exactly, but close—as in all human speech, distinctions between sounds in Black English can be very fine-grained.

So: in Black English there is a special sound, somewhere between *ee* and *ih*, that you turn *ee* into before *l*'s, and *eh* into before *m* and *n*. Any speaker of Black English is subconsciously doing that day in and day out. And it isn't about leaving anything out or off—this adds something, as if Standard English sounds weren't complicated enough already!

5. Pronouns

A language can be complicated in ways that we never think about; it takes an outsider to notice anything strange going on. Someone I once knew directed a play with a lead who was one of those enviably perfect bilinguals—in her case, between German and English. However, even though she had a perfect American accent and you'd ordinarily never think she was from anywhere but the United States, her Swiss upbringing had made her German ever so slightly better. This came out, for example, in how she read a line in rehearsals where her character asked, "So how do you like them apples?" She put the emphasis on the word *apples*, thinking the sentence was really about apples. "So how do you like them *apples*?" she would say.

But we natives know that this is a familiar expression where the proper rendition is "So how do you like *them* apples?" To be a native American English speaker is to know that you say it with the emphasis on *them*. None of us knows why we say that; apparently, there was once some situation contrasting certain new apples—*them* apples—from previous ones. We just say it. It's an exception, an oddity, something that doesn't follow the rules. It's a little challenge in the language, of the kind all languages have.

Now, think about the expression, "I'm going to fire his ass." Imagine how that Swiss actress would likely have said this. "I'm going to fire his *ass*," she'd have said, likely as baffled as to how buttocks can be cast from employment separately from their possessor as she must have been about the stray reference to apples in the middle of a play that was about kings and magic. But we native speakers know, black or not, that the way to say it is "I'm going to *fire* his ass." *His ass* is not emphasized. The sentence is basically a way of saying "I'm going to fire him," where you don't emphasize *him* anymore than you would *his ass*.

Here is a wider selection of examples from an article about the use of *ass* with pronuns:

> I'ma aggravate his ass.
>
> I pray to the Lord I ain' got no TBs from his ass.
>
> Ain' nobody told his ass that.
>
> He fell down with his stupid ass.

One laughs, but there's also system here. The Swiss actress would perkily enunciate "He fell *down* with his stupid *ass!*" But actually, Black English has an alternate pronoun to *him*, used to convey dismissal. Of course, this is true not only with *him* but with all of the pronouns: "I could sue they asses," "I got my ass out of there." To use this system, you have to know that the emphasis does not fall on *ass*, anymore than it does on *apples* in "How do you like them apples?" You also have to know that the meaning is idiomatic, that no actual ass is being discussed. This is, in other words, an irregularity, the kind of thing that makes a language complicated. Standard English requires that you know that the past tense of *drink* is *drank* but that of *think* is *thought*, and a hundred-plus other cases like that (which Black English speakers use just like everyone else). But in addition to those idiosyncrasies, Black English has pronouns that you have to store in the "irregularity" part of your brain, along with *thought* and *drank*.

And there's even more. "Why's she complaining about the low turnout? She didn't even come herself," someone might say. In that case, *herself* is an emphatic pronoun. However, Black English has a special set of those: In Black English, it could be "She didn't even come her damn self." But I don't just mean that a black person might curse, because anyone might, of course. There's an accent emphasis again. The correct enunciation is *her **damn** self*, not *her damn **self***. A savvy director of a black play might call someone out on this if it were in a line and they were reading it with the emphasis on the *self*. "You didn't even come your *damn* self," or, as I recall from an episode of the late, great black sitcom bonbon *Living Single*, Queen Latifah's Khadija telling Kim Fields's Régine "You grew up in the projects your *damn* self."

If we put together a Rosetta Stone kit to teach Ebonics, we'd have to get across a system of pronouns that looked like the list below, where you have to know that you use a different set of pronouns to convey dismissal, and that those pronouns are pronounced with unexpected emphasis patterns. To show that *his ass*, for example, is pronounced not "his *ass*" but as if you were just saying *him*, I am putting a grave accent over *ass*, as per linguists' practice when showing low pitch or tone. Note that this is all the kind of thing one would quietly dread having to master when paging ahead in a textbook to see what was coming up. This, ladies and gentlemen, is Ebonics!

object pronoun	emphatic	dismissive subject/object	emphatic dismissive
me	myself	my àss	my *damn* self
you	yourself	your àss	your *damn* self
him	himself	his àss	his *damn* self
her	herself	her àss	her *damn* selves
us	ourselves	our àsses	our *damn* selves
y'all	yourselves	y'all àsses	ya'll *damn* selves
them	themselves	they àsses	they *damn* selves

Black English has, of all things, a list of emphatic dismissive pronouns. Obviously, not all speakers use them, given that *ass* classifies as a bad word to many. However, profanity is still language: We use it according to rules just as complex and nuanced as those for the rest of the language's words.

And just in case it's hard to see that this type of usage makes Black English more rather than less, given that it's difficult to completely dissociate the profane from the trivial, I will add that I am giving a highly simplified portrait of this aspect of Black English. The *ass* here is quite complicated, almost intimidatingly so when one really digs in. To take just one example, you can also use the *ass* pronouns as subjects, at the start of a sentence. To say Frank is shy, you can say in Black English "Frank ass is shy," where the possessive has been elided from *Frank* but the sentence means "Frank's ass is shy." Or: "Carl's in trouble" can be "Carl ass in trouble." Now, what part of speech would you say *ass* is in "Frank ass is shy" or "Carl ass in trouble"? Is *ass* a noun, even when no posterior is actually being referred to? The sentence quite simply does not mean that Frank's butt is uncomfortable upon meeting new people, so how is *ass* a noun? But if it isn't, then what is it?

Only a linguist—and even there, only a certain sliver among them—could care. But the lesson is that Black English has a system, and in the case of these *ass* pronouns, it is more complex than Standard English. And while we're at it, note also that Black English is also more complex than Standard English in having a different *you* in the plural, *y'all*, instead of just having *you* for both one and more than one person.

But Black English Is Less Complex in So Many Ways. Why?

However, the fact that Black English "has it going on" as the expression goes, can't be the whole story. The skeptic—and I am assuming you, the reader, are one—will continue to notice that in so many other ways—and really, more—Black English is *less* complicated than Standard English. Skeptics, like everyone else, know how to count and are sensitive to issues of degree. Black English does have a narrative tense and a counterexpectational marker and other things, but this is also a dialect in which one expresses oneself in a sentence like this one: "Why she ain't call me when she know dis de best time?" There's "Why she ain't" instead of the more elaborate business of saying "Why didn't she." "She know" instead of "she knows." "Dis" instead of "this." "Dis de best," leaving out the "is." Knowing about the complexities doesn't render one suddenly deaf to these things, and the skeptic will still wonder, "Isn't there still something wrong with a way of speaking that leaves out so many things from Standard English, even if it does have some cool stuff of its own? To the skeptic, Black English may now be the equivalent of the person you call "sharp"—nominally a compliment, but actually a term used for people you don't really think are all that smart. "Sharp" really means "smarter than you'd expect for a dimwit."

There is a ready response to this, though. Here is a passage of Old English that is pretty easy for us to wrap our heads around, despite the fact that Old English was more like German than like the language we speak:

God gesceop us twa eagan and twa earan,	God made us two eyes and two ears,
twa nosðyrlu, twegen weleras,	two nostrils, two lips,
twa handa, and twegen fet	two hands, and two feet.

There are just two things to notice about the Old English.

First, there were lots more ways to make a noun plural than by adding an *s*. Today, there is a handful of words whose plurals are irregular: *men*, *women*, *children*, *geese*, *mice*, *oxen*, *feet,* and a few others. But in Old English, plurals like that were the norm. Thus, in our sentence, the only word that takes the *s* we're familiar with is the one for lips, *weleras*. Otherwise, the words for *eye* and *ear* take an *an*, the word for nostril takes a *u*, the word for hand takes an *a*, and then the plural *fet* is weird, just as forming the plural *feet* still is.

Then, second, notice that two hands and two feet is ***twa handa and twegen fet***. Why *twa* for some words and *twegen* for others? Because in Old English, as in any normal European language, things had genders for no real reason. *Twegen* was two when used with masculine nouns. *Twa* was for feminine and neuter ones.

Here's the point: Modern English has lost almost all of those plural forms, and it doesn't give gender to inanimate objects at all (except for quaint things like referring to ships as feminine, but, come on). That means that Modern English, for all the pride it has inspired in so many, is really crappy Old English! To someone who spoke English as it originally was, a person saying *ears* instead of *earan* and *hands* instead of *handa* would have sounded barbarian, and his using the word *two* with everything, instead of having different forms for different genders, would have sounded equally degraded. Plus—if we really want to get into it, the *y* in the nostril word—*nosðyrlu*—was pronounced like the cute and tricky *u* in French in words like *lune*. Old English had sounds like that; Modern English dumped them.

And of course, here in our time none of this matters a whit. Modern English chucked *most* of what made Old English complicated, in fact. It happened when the Vikings invaded England, learned Old English badly because as adults they picked it up imperfectly, and then passed their rendition on to the kids they conceived with English-speaking women. But here we are, quite unashamed, even if apprised of the reality. The English we speak certainly seems to do everything a language should, even if eons ago some people too old to completely learn a language tore off some of its tinsel.

The point is that later in the same way, English got another close shave when African adults were taken as slaves to the American South. They, too, were past the age when one can learn a language perfectly, and didn't pick up some of the bells and whistles that native speakers used, such as "Why *didn't she* call, she know*s*," and other things which, as familiar as they are to us, are not exactly necessary to communication. The *s* in the third-person-singular verb, for example, is no more necessary to expressing a point than silverware having genders was in Old English; life thrives without both features, and so very many others.

Black English subtracts from Standard English, then, for the very same reason Modern English subtracts from Old English. However, in the grand scheme of things, it bears mentioning that what Black English shaved away from Standard English is but a dribble compared to what Modern English dumped from Old. Roughly, Old English dumped a roasting pan's worth of grammar to become Modern English. To become Black English, Modern English dumped only about as much grammar as would fill the small glass one is typically served Bailey's liqueur in—you only ever get a generous smidgen, so little that if you spilled it on yourself, you'd barely bother to wipe it off.

So, unless we're going back to talking about our *eagan*, *earan*, *nosdyrlu*, and *handa*, what Black English lacks that Standard English has can't qualify it as the speech of dolts. When humans move, or are moved, in large numbers and have to pick up a language quickly, typically their version of the language is more streamlined than the original one. This is worldwide linguistic reality, not special pleading for the speech of black people in the United States. We know this from Modern English itself, as well as, if anyone asks, from Mandarin Chinese compared to other Chineses like Cantonese, Persian compared to languages related to it, like Pashto and Kurdish, Indonesian, Swahili, and many, many others.

A Worldwide Story

MY APPROACH APPLIES TO A GREAT MANY speech varieties beyond Black English. There are analogous misunderstandings between professors and the public about ways of speaking that linguists describe as a series of shirkings of standard language rules, supposing that the systematicity of the shirkings will earn the respect of the general public. This happens, for example, with Creole languages, created by slaves in the Caribbean and elsewhere, such as Jamaican patois, Guyanese "Creolese," Belizean Creole, and the "Pidgin" in Hawaii. At academic conferences today on Creole languages, one can attend presentations decrying Creole speakers' and their teachers' contempt for their own languages despite linguists' pointing to their systematicity for eons. Crucially, these presentations are unchanged from ones given in 1990, when I started out as a linguist, and surely even before that. New tactics are needed.

Some may still maintain that a shoe has yet to drop if we don't address the role that racism plays in people's evaluation of Black English and sociologically similar varieties. However, while that role is real, telling people that they are immoral if they consider a dialect broken does not do much of a job of convincing. Linguistic logic has a much better chance of doing so. It is reasonable to think that racism will make people resist the force of reason anyway. However, in my experience, this, luckily, is not the case—at least nothing close to always. I hope I have made at least some headway in convincing you that Black English is not broken English, but an alternate English.

CHAPTER TWO

What Do You Mean "Sounds Black"?

DON'T BLACK PEOPLE JUST HAVE SOUTHERN ACCENTS?

W HAT *does* SOMEBODY MEAN by "sounding black"? To be American is to find the very issue ticklish.

A Delicate Conversation

I WRITE ON RACE AS WELL AS LANGUAGE, and many of my opinions on race are termed *controversial*. Most people avoid controversy, and as such, many are under the impression that someone like me deliberately seeks out statements that he knows will make people angry, because he enjoys stirring up the pot. Actually, the root of all of my "controversial" ideas is that I initially assume that people have the same take on something that I do, only to discover, much to my surprise, that they do not.

I encountered this at a party in the early nineties when I made a casual reference to black people's having a dialect of their own. The guests were all black, with a range of educational levels, but all were cultured, intellectually omnivorous, opinionated people. Much to my surprise, no one in the room knew what I meant about there being a black way to talk. The very idea irritated most of them, and the conversation even got tense at times.

It was a learning experience for me, because these were all perfectly reasonable people. More to the point, almost any American would immediately have identified all of them as black on the phone, even if they were reciting from a phone book. That is, they all "sounded black." And yet, the closest they could come to an understanding of what I meant was that some of them acknowledged that there is uniquely black slang (to show how long ago this was, the prime example adduced was "MacDaddy").

These people were representative of a general relationship black people—and much of the rest of America—have to the idea that there is a black sound. During O. J. Simpson's first trial, his lawyer Johnnie Cochran rebutted a witness's claim to have heard a "black voice" when passing the fence of the house where Simpson's ex-wife was murdered. "What's a black voice?" Cochran indignantly asked, with the implication that the very idea was a stereotype founded in racism and minstrel caricature. The mostly black jury agreed.

We can't know whether Cochran genuinely thought there was no such thing as a black voice, and let's face it, he was doing his job. However, the very fact that doing it meant casting the "black voice" issue that way for the jury illustrated black America's take on the whole issue. It is reasonable to suppose that if Cochran and the jury had been at the dinner party I had been at, their response to the idea of a black dialect would have been similar to that of the people who were there.

Why does the very notion of sounding black get under people's skin? For black people, it's because Black English is so often associated with stupidity that one can't help wanting to disidentify from it. Especially when we are trained to avoid stereotyping, and because black people are often the object lessons, the idea of sounding black can bring minstrelsy and other caricatures to mind.

Yet what it all comes down to is something I noticed when I was a kid, something that countless other black people have mentioned noticing, too, as they grew up—with whites only occasionally doing so, because of a sense that the issue is somehow improper. When my mother was driving me to and from school, we used to listen to the local black radio stations (Philadelphia's WHAT and WDAS for those from there), and I noticed that during the commercials, even when the text was neutral, with no slang, and the man was speaking good old-fashioned announcerese, you could always tell that he or she was black. I asked Mom one day, "How come you can always tell the person talking is black?" She said, "It has something to do with the shape of the sinuses."

I don't know where Mom got that explanation, but it made sense to me at the time that there is clearly a black sound, and that it might seem as if black people have a differently shaped resonating chamber in their heads, a different ring or timbre. However, the black sound—and there is one—is not about biology.

Past the Distractions to the Heart of the Matter

I SUBMIT THAT ALMOST ANYBODY who grew up in the United States has a deep-seated sense that indeed there is a black way to sound. I do so on the basis not only of basic perception but of a great many studies that have proved it. Americans white and black are extremely accurate at determining white or black race when hearing only a voice. I doubt that surprises many, deep down. Let's face it: If Melissa McCarthy and Viola Davis both read the first five pages of *Green Eggs and Ham*, no one would be under the impression that McCarthy was black or Davis white. And that's despite the fact that neither of them have idiosyncratic voices that would identify them, in the way that Robin Williams or Joan Rivers did. (Once I heard a voice in a mainstream cartoon television show—*Sofia the First*—with my back turned, subconsciously processed a queen character's voice as black, and found on looking up the voice casting that the actress was, in fact, Viola Davis.) Moreover, one of the most paradoxical things I have ever come across as a linguist is that black Americans, despite often being so skeptical that there is such a thing as a black voice, at the same time readily observe it when a black person "doesn't sound black" or "sounds white."

All this shows that while resistance to the notion of a black voice is understandable, there is a lack of fit between that overt resistance and people's internal perceptions. Call it, along the lines taught us by Dr. Kahneman, the difference between thinking fast ("He doesn't sound black!") and thinking slow ("How can you sound black?"). The mind operates usefully on both levels.

However, the issue of black speech is so sensitive that various elisions, distractions, and misperceptions have accreted around it—it can be maddeningly difficult to see (or hear) it plain. As such, before analyzing our object of study, we must clarify just what we mean by this sound. We need to peel away some layers to get down to the case itself.

First, speech entails both sentence patterns and sound, and here we are concerned with sound, not the grammatical constructions of the kind discussed earlier. It's more obvious that some grammatical constructions are specific to black Americans (although of course, generally viewed as mistakes). The dropping of the verb *be* is an example: "She my sister" is not New England, Minnesota, or even uneducated white southern, but specifically Black English. However, black people don't say things like "She my sister" when speaking Standard English. The question is why you can hear that someone is black even when the person isn't saying anything of that kind.

Second, I don't mean slang. Again, I doubt anyone thinks there is no such thing as black slang, even if there are plenty of whites using it. Hip-hop slang alone makes the point rather clearly. The main thing is that even listening to a recording of an elderly black woman talking to a friend in church, most of us could hear that she was black even though she would be vastly unlikely to be using any street slang.

Third, it isn't simply that black men have deeper voices, à la Barry White and Isaac Hayes. Yes, some people do think this answers the question, including one of the people at the dinner party I described. And it wouldn't be impossible if *culturally* there was a tendency for black men to pitch their regular speaking voices at a lower point than other men do, subconsciously mimicking black men they grow up around who do this. I highly suspect there is such a *tendency*, although (1) there is no research on the issue and (2) the way such things generally pan out suggests that if one measured the default speaking pitch of hundreds of white men and hundreds of black men, then after averaging out the data we would find that the degree to which the American black male speaking voice is pitched statistically lower than the American white male's would turn out to be some uninterestingly small figure.

In any case, the whole issue is ultimately another layer of the onion we need to peel away. The black sound we think about can come from voices of any pitch. Does a black boy before his voice has cracked sound white? Of course not, which leads us back to the question: what makes a nine-year-old, or even a two-year-old, already sound black? In the same vein, one might suppose that more black women than white ones have what might be described as a certain huskiness in their vocal tone. That could prove to be true, but do black women without that husky tone sound white? Does the six-year-old black girl, sounding identifiably black already, have a husky vocal tone? No. There is a certain common element, a sound, beyond that.

Fourth, the black sound is not simply a southern one. The black sound and the white southern one overlap, but only that. The first time I heard a white person assume that black speech was simply southern, I was as struck as a person is when, say, they first learn that television shows are produced to sell the products advertised in the commercials, and thus are entertainment between commercials, rather than the commercials being interludes amid the entertainment. I had to change my lens, so to speak.

It had never occurred to me that there was no difference between the speech of my mother's Atlanta relatives and the speech of the white southerners around them. However, I understood where these whites were coming from. To have learned the dangers of stereotyping properly, one is aware that the sense that black people have their own way of talking may be an illusion. We might imagine, for example, that if we showed a video of a white person talking but dubbed in a black person's voice on the sound track, we would simply process the person as speaking with a Southern accent. But that's just it: We wouldn't. The raft of studies showing how accurate Americans are at telling race from voice alone cuts neatly through the idea that black people simply speak southern English, as does the fact that in describing southern white English versus Black English, linguists have identified a great many differences. Even if our hypothetical video included no slang at all, if someone filmed an interview with a white man, had Dave Chappelle record his words, and then dubbed them in and showed the interview, almost all observers would hear a black voice for some reason coming from a white man, not just a white southern accent.

It shouldn't be surprising that black people do not

sound exactly like white southerners. Given the rather hideous relationship between white and black southerners throughout most of American history, wouldn't it seem counterintuitive that whites and blacks there ended up talking exactly the same way? Given that whites and blacks have coexisted in the South for so long, we would expect that their speech varieties would overlap partially, of course, and they do. But in newsreels of Montgomery, Selma, and Birmingham in the 1950s and 1960s, the black people most certainly did not speak with the same sound as the whites, and we would be shocked if they had.

Fifth—and this is probably the most important caveat here—I don't mean that every black person in the United States has this sound.

Of course, just as it is often said that Barack Obama isn't a Muslim, *although there wouldn't be anything wrong with it if he were*, if every black person for some reason sounded black there wouldn't be anything wrong with that, either, because the "blaccent," as I like to call it, is not wrong in any way. I am unaware of any sentiment that what makes someone sound black is erroneous per se, in contrast to how people feel about Black English grammatical constructions. However, as it happens, all black people do not have a blaccent. Black people who don't happen to grow up around many other blacks, or whose black families for one reason or another don't use the dialect themselves and don't have the sound, may lack it entirely. There are no official numbers on this, but I would venture, based on my experience since 1965, that while a great many black people don't use Black English grammar or slang or use it very little, about forty-nine out of fifty black people do, to some degree, sound identifiably black when they speak.

Thus, to assert that there is a black sound is not to assert something as kooky as that anyone who is a black American has, for some genetic reason, a particular way of configuring his mouth and vocal cords when speaking. It is to say that black culture, like most cultures, includes a way of speaking, and that this way of speaking includes not only consciously wielded things such as slang and expressions but also something less consciously wielded, the blaccent.

This sheds light on, for example, an episode in a chat group where someone once asked, "What makes a white person's voice and a black person's voice sound different? Usually you can tell if a person is white or black by the sound of their voice, though there are exceptions." One respondent said it was that black men have deeper voices. More interesting, though, was a later response:

> Do you realize how utterly nonsensical this query is? Can you tell the difference between a black Estonian's voice and a White South African's? Or, the difference between a White Brazilian and Black Swede's voice? Or, what about that of a White Nigerian and a Black uruguayan[*sic*]? You are aware that such people can and do exist, correct? It would only take one test of any of the pairs above to falsify your claim. Perhaps you should get out more. . . .

Shortly after this, one of the administrators declared, "This thread is nonsense, therefore it is closed." But no, let's reopen it, because there is no claim about all black people in the world, or, therefore, genes.

We are now prepared to address the actual issue before us. Why is it here in the United States we all sense—or maybe *almost* all of us sense—that a voice can sound black? I will first present what the difference consists of, and then why it exists.

Blaccent, Level One

ALTHOUGH WE DON'T PUT IT THIS WAY, in relation to white American English, black people tend to have an accent. It isn't that either way of speaking is better in any way; one could also declare that white people have an accent, or that we all have accents. But given that the majority defines the norm, and there are fewer black people than white people in America, the common intuition will be that black people have an accent, just like Minnesotans, southern whites, and South Bostonians.

This issue can be viewed as having two levels. The surface level, more easily perceptible, has been mined by linguists for decades and constitutes the "classic," obvious differences in sound between black and white American speech. The deeper level is the aspect of the sound that leads one to wonder why even if a person doesn't sound black in an immediately obvious way—for example, like the typical rapper—we can still somehow detect "blackness" in their voice. There is a correlation here, imperfect but robust, with class and education: Those black Americans I refer to when describing the deeper level tend to have more access to education and more contact with whites.

On the surface level are such things as *ing* and *ang*. One shakes that *thang* more than that *thing*; one might hear someone *sang* rather than sing, and one hears the occasional joke about someone ordering chicken *wangs*. Such speech paterns are also used by some white southerners, demonstrating the overlap between Black English and southern English.

However, other things are local to Black English. One is that wrinkle I mentioned earlier, that a word like *eel* sounds more like *ill*—or, "ih-uhl"—and therefore *meal* as *mill*, *wheel* as *will*, and so on. I first noticed this while watching, of all things, a Burger King commercial in the early nineties and became aware that I spontaneously knew that the boy doing the voiceover was black, since he pronounced *meal* as "mih-ull" (I soon found out that specialists had identified this long before). Another subtle feature like that one is that *ar* sounds more like *or*—though not exactly like it, but in between, such that "Get in the car" sounds rather like "Get in the cawr"—or, *hard* is more like *hawrd*. I recall hearing one person doing this around 1980 as she became close to a circle of black girls, though she hadn't grown up in the dialect. One of the girls' names was Warri, and I noticed that the girl who was taking up Black English started pronouncing her name more like "Wore-y," which was the way the other girls pronounced it. This young lady was subconsciously internalizing the Black English sound system.

As for the consonants, in Black English *r* is eliminated after vowels, and hence *mo'* for *more*, *flo'* for *floor*, and the famous *ho'* for *whore*. And then there is Tyler Perry's character's name Madea, which is a traditional black American shortening of *my dear.* In other American dialects, *r* ia dropped like this, too, but is replaced with a little *uh* sound: The New Yawkese speaker says *staw-uh* for *store.* Black English takes it all the way to *sto'.*

Black English also treats *th* differently depending on where it sits in the word. We should zero in for a second on something about *th*: There are two ways to say it. The *th* sound in *thin* is different from the *th* sound in *this*—we might say that the one in *this* is softer. At the front of a word, for the softer *th,* Black English has *d*: *dis, dat, doze.* This, of course, is typical of colloquial white English in a great many places, too. But then if the *th* at the beginning of the word is the harder sound, as in *thin*, Black English isn't different at all: *Thin* in Black English is just *thin.*

But, when *th* is at the end of a word, it changes in a different way in Black English. One of the most gracious things I have ever seen a person do was after a wedding. I was standing with a group in the lobby and someone's father went around passing out Clorets mints, saying "Bad breath . . . , Bad breath . . ." This is one of those cases where print just can't convey the intonation. Imagine the way someone says, when there's no danger afoot but he's just letting you know you should be wary of something, "Watch out—you never know." "Watch out" is said with "out" higher than "watch" and then falling down a touch, as in "WATCH ᴼᵁᵁᵀ. . ." That's how this man said, gently as he passed each clump of people, "ʙᴀᴅ ᴮᴿᴱᴬᵀᴴ. . .," as in "You might have gotten bad breath while sitting with your mouth closed for so long—here's relief." A very apt, useful, and generous thing to do. But, I'm leaving something out. He was black, most of the crowd was as well, and so he was naturally dwelling in the dialect, and what he actually was saying was "BAD ^BREF. . . , BAD ^BREF. . ."

That was because the harder *th* of *thin*, when at the end of a word, becomes *f*. Meanwhile, if it's the softer *th*, as in *smooth*, then you get *v*. That's where someone like black comedian J. B. Smoove (best known for his character on *Curb Your Enthusiasm*) gets his name: *Smoove* is good Black English for *smooth*.

Blaccent, Level Two

I have by no means given a complete list of the ways that the sounds in full-blown Black English differ from their equivalents in Standard English. I needed only sketch in a few of the details. However, some black people don't use these sounds at all. Most do, but more as seasoning rather than as default speech. A person who might say *bref* in a certain situation might well say *breath* in a different one. This is termed *code switching*, which people do worldwide across separate languages as well as separate dialects, with one code used for formality and another for intimacy. In Black English, *bref* and *aks* are for the informal, the humorous, for striking a note of honesty, etc., and are most likely used with other black people, or nonblack people one is especially comfortable with. Otherwise, one says *breath* and *ask* and thinks nothing of it. It's a cookout versus a staff meeting. The practice is largely subconscious; most rarely think of themselves as talking in two ways until it's brought up. Code switching is often presented as complicated or exotic, but it is a perfectly normal way of using language, as I will discuss later.

However, the kind of blaccent I am interested in is the kind that is *not* subject to code switching, but is instead a background factor, leading to the question people ask as to how it is that you can always hear a person's race even when that person doesn't sound especially black in the classic, surface ways I just described. Even black people saying *breath* and *ask* rather than *bref* and *aks* are usually still perceptible as black in this subtler but unmistakable way. It is natural to wonder why.

It's mostly about vowels. Obscure sonic flutters though they seem to be, they are part of the black American cultural tool kit. Five little frills, one could call them, that immediately say black to an American listener even when someone is speaking Standard English. It's a random collection of things, nevertheless, each frill does much to define black American speech. (My students Samuel Heavenrich and Cole Hickman have shed beautiful light on this—thank you gentlemen!)

Basically, much of what sounds black even when someone is speaking Standard English comes from the middle of the mouth. It can feel as if our speech just comes from the throat, and it does at first. But before it comes out, it gets channeled through different levels of the space inside of our mouths—namely, the top, the middle, and the bottom. It doesn't feel that way all the time, because we're not dealing with anything as topward as the nasal cavity or downward as under the tongue. But here's how to get a feel for it, literally: Say *cat, cot.* Did you do it? Okay, now say *bet, boat,* and then say *beet, boot.* Now say those pairs in sequence: *cat, cot; bet, boat; beet, boot.* then do it again. Notice that the pairs sit in different places, and that more specifically the pairs sit on different levels in the mouth. Namely, they feel like this:

beet, boot
bet, boat
cat, cot

Cat, cot is down on the bottom, *bet, boat* is in the middle, and *beet, boat* is up top.

Here is Frill One. One of the middle vowels is *e,* and when it comes before *m* or *n,* it sounds more like *i*: this is the famous southern trait where *pen* sounds more like *pin.* But it must be understood that this is not a matter of just the one word *pen,* but any word where *e* comes before *m* or *n.* This trait holds fast among black speakers, even when *bref* for *breath* doesn't, partly because it's subtle, something almost no one would notice (except with *pen,* which has by chance attracted a lot of attention). Even among highly Standard-sounding black announcers and newscasters, for example, *extent* sounds a bit like *extint, sense* will sound a bit like *since,* and *attention* will sound rather like *attintion.*

Frill Two is also in this middle zone. Say *bet, Bert,* and *boat* and notice that all the words sit on one level in your mouth—you didn't have to shift up or down. Try *bet,* **bat** and *boat* to get a sense of how it would feel to shift levels in the middle, and then do *bet, Bert, boat* again and sense how it feels like driving a smooth old-fashioned *boat* of a car, such as the Caprice Classic my parents bought around the time I asked Mom that question (you rolled the windows up by *pressing a button*!!!!!). Often there's something going on with the *er* sound in black Standard English: It is more like "uh-r" than "er." The word *work*, instead of the Standard English pronunciation "werk," is more like "wuh-rk." *Curb* is "cuh-rb," rather than "cerb," and so on. Not in a drawly, obvious way—but just enough that these words, quietly, different from the way in which whites say them.

Frill Three is one more thing on the middle plain, the sound *uh*. Nothing seems outwardly middle about that sound, but again, you can feel it with a quick trick. This time say *bet*, **but**, and *boat*, and notice that just as with *bet*, *Bert*, and *boat*, there's no bump on the path from *bet* to *boat*. The vowels are all on the same level, the middle.

One of the things that makes a person sound black is that the *uh* sound is pronounced a little higher up in the mouth. This difference is utterly impossible to indicate via spelling. However, the way a person might spontaneously try to imitate either a white southerner or a black person saying the sound *uh* will capture, in exaggerated fashion, what this difference is. Venture a "redneck" pronunciation of *love*—you are pronouncing *uh* further up in the mouth than you would normally. That, done to a much lesser, but perceptible, extent, is part of the black sound. *But*, *cut*, *love*, *up*, *must*, *tub*, *button*, *come*, *does*—any word with the *uh* sound will have that slight difference.

The last two Frills are down on the bottom. To force

a metaphor, Black Standard English is just like mainstream Standard English on the top—you have to peel away the surface and look at the middle and then the bottom to see the differences. On the bottom, remember our shop-window words are *cat, cot*. This is where Frill Four happens. It's a quiet little chain reaction between those two sounds.

First, many black speakers pronounce the *ah* sound (as in *cot*) a little further to the front than most whites, in the direction where the *cat* vowel is pronounced. That is, a light blaccent often means that, say, *cot* is pronounced with a shade of *cat* in it.

Then, because this puts a little pressure on the *cat* vowel, this vowel moves up a litle bit and sounds a tiny it like "ket." Just a bit. What happens to the *cot* and *cat* vowels is almost impossible to indicate in ordinary writing, but imagine how Chris Rock would say "Got that?" The difference between how he would say that and Rachel Maddow would nails the nature of these vowels in a light blaccent: as subtle as it is, it is part of what reads "black" in the back of an American mind.

Finally, Frill Five is also on the bottom. It involves a little more about the sound *ah*, this time when it is part of the diphthong *ah-ee*, as in *rice, high*, or *tidy*. I've mentioned the monophthongization of this sound into "ah" alone: *Nice* becoming "nahs." This isn't only a trait of full-blown Black English; a shade of it seasons the speech of many black speakers even in Standard English, though not so much that it sounds rural or cartoonish, as if someone were doing a news report and saying "watt rahs" for *white rice*. However, for such speakers *white rice* sounds *a little more like* "watt rahs" than if a white person said it—just enough more that one hears the voice as not coming from a white person.

And that, ladies and gentlemen, is quite a bit of why you can tell someone is black even when they are speaking Standard English. To wit, a simple sentence like "But, what's worse is, the event isn't even happening" can sound black, simply in that *But* would have the slightly higher *uh* sound, *worse* would sound somewhat like "wuh-rs," *event* would sound a little like "evint," and the *a* sound in *happening* would be pronounced a touch further to the front than if a white person was saying it. It's just tiny things like that, hardly things anyone would consider mispronunciations, or often even consider at all. They just are.

Diversities Amidst the Unity

MY APPROACH HERE IS DEFINITELY more macro than micro. The full picture is busier. Without a doubt, Black English manifests itself in different subdialects nationwide—black people in New York sound different from black people in Atlanta, who sound different from black people in Los Angeles and Texas and Detroit and so on. Competing schools of hip-hop have revealed this more vibrantly than ever, a memorable example being the *thurr* for *there* in St. Louis, broadcast nationwide by the hit song "Right Thurr" in 2003. (As always, it's not just about words but sounds in general; as, for example, in St. Louis, that *ere/air* sound—at the St. Louis airport I once heard a black woman tell a coworker to get a passenger a "wheelchurr").

But: the diversity of Black English dialects must not be taken as evidence that it is a distortion to think of a single Black English at all, because the basic traits I have described are found in all these dialects. The New York black person may well pronounce a word like *call* more like "coo-ull" and *boy* like "boo-ee," but she also has the "watt rahs" hint, the tight *cat/cot* sound, and everything else. Southern black people have various features of speech known only in their region, but also the core ones of everywhere else. A neat example: The St. Louis woman actually said not "wheel-churr" but "willchurr," with the general Black English pronunciation of the *ee* sound more like *ih* before *l*. The woman's pronunciation of *chair* was local; the *wheel* was national. To speak of one Black English is no less reductive than to speak of cats rather than of specific types of cats, such as Angora, Burmese, and Siamese.

Gender can also condition the extent to which one sounds black and when. Studies of Black English have often found that black men tend to sample the dialect in their speech to a higher degree than black women. This correlates with my intuition from my own experience, and, I highly suspect, that of others, which is that black women are more likely to be completely, or all but, undetectable as black when speaking Standard English than black men. This difference is hardly a quirk about black Americans, but conforms to a worldwide pattern linguists have discovered, according to which women are more proper in their speech in more contexts than men are. While American men and women may both say *in'* instead of *ing* depending on where they are and whom they are talking to, typically men will say *in'* more than women, and it will be women who in formal situations are more likely to let *in'* go completely. Given that Black English is processed as informal (and even as wrong), it is natural that black women speaking Standard English would leave the "seasoning" of the frills behind more than men do.

Why Do Black People Have Vowels That Are Slightly Different From Those of Other Americans?

THE EXPLANATION BEGINS WITH the kind of thing that makes French different from Spanish, believe it or not. In Latin, the word for *new* was *novum*. The Romance languages developed from Latin. In French, *new* is *neuf*. In Spanish, it is *nuevo*. In Italian, it is *nuovo*; in Romanian, *nou*. The vowel *o* in Latin's *novum* has changed from language to language because it is natural for vowels to change. In fact, we know they always will. The only question is which new vowel they will change into; there are always many possibilities, the choice of which is often determined by chance. An *o* sound like the one in Latin's *novum*, for example, could become an *oo*, or an *aw*, or even become pronounced as "way"—as it did in Spanish's *nuevo* (pronounced "nw**ay**-vo"). In one place, a vowel will become one thing; somewhere else it will go in a different direction.

This means that the way a language is spoken from place to place will differ in terms of sounds overall. If the differences are allowed to progress for long enough, the two ways of speaking will vary so much that they become separate languages. That's the case with French and Spanish. But if the process has only gone so far, then all you have is different dialects. That's *cat* pronounced a touch more like "ket," "extint" versus *extent*, and the other linguistic differences between black and white Americans even when speaking Standard English.

In other words, different communities have different dialects, and this affects vowels. We are not surprised that whites in Brooklyn, New York, speak differently than the ones in Connecticut, or that ones in Minnesota speak differently than the ones in Arizona. One could wonder, then, why black Americans have their own way of speaking despite living so often among whites and hearing Standard English as spoken by whites in the media so much (I have encountered that question now and then). Crucially, however, a community need not be a geographic entity: Communities of people can occupy the same physical space and remain distinct in various ways. The status of community is determined as much by social identification as by location—your community is whom you are closest to socially and emotionally. Also, the way one speaks is primarily shaped by one's peers in live interaction, not by language as heard on television nor by the speech of people you interact with often but do not consider intimates.

For example, when I refer to the speech of whites in Brooklyn, most will intuit that I mean not the speech of the educated, upwardly mobile characters on *Girls*, but the working-class Brooklyn "New Yawkese." Note: One is not surprised that working-class Brooklyn whites do not sound like affluent Brooklyn whites, even though they work among them and are bathed in mainstream Standard English in the media throughout their lives. Working-class white Brooklyn is a community within the larger New York community, and as such, it has its own accent. Naturally, we think "They talk like one another." In the same way, in the black community, whether or not the community is geographically separate, you learn your vowels not from the people on TV, nor from your white teachers at school or white neighbors, but from your family and especially your friends. Within a community in this sense, black Americans, whether they live in segregated communities or not, have their own vowels, just as Spanish people have their own vowels, which are different from French people's.

In the 1970s, I lived for the first half of my childhood in the Philadelphia neighborhood of Mount Airy, one of America's first officially integrated neighborhoods. Black and white people lived there in roughly equal numbers, often with black households alternating with white ones. Black kids growing up there had many white teachers, as well as white neighbors often right next door. Plus, in the seventies, especially, these black kids grew up watching television shows that were still mostly white. Yet, all of them whom I knew grew up identifiable as black on the phone. This is what we would expect: They spoke like the people they were closest to emotionally, not residentially.

The fact that highly educated black American people usually speak with the Five Frills even in the most formal of situations can be taken as an indication that on a profound level, however comfortably they have navigated the mainstream world, their ultimate comfort zone is with other black people. In Mount Airy in the seventies, although there were no overt interethnic tensions, by and large black kids played with black kids and white kids played with white kids. The normal result of black kids spending more time with one another was the preservation of their particular sound colorings, in contrast to the sound colorings of the white kids playing down the street.

One could see the Five Frills as linguistic evidence of the persistence of a color line in America. People truly comfortable with one another talk alike, especially after a while, and certainly after generations. We're not there yet.

Expressing an Identity?

THERE IS A STRAIN OF THOUGHT that would distort my meaning here—namely, that black people purposely change their speech as a matter of ethnic self-presentation. This approach fits into a larger way of thinking, common in the social sciences, that describes people shaping their language in order to express their identities. They do in some ways, but the reader would be misled in taking that from what I have described. A great deal of language use and the way it changes is subconscious. The Black English sounds evolved because black people have existed separately from whites geographically and spiritually. That means there is no way black people could *not* have developed a different sound system from whites under these conditions, any more than that people could still be speaking Latin now in France and Spain.

The Five Frills, then, are not intentional, either. They are the last things remaining from Level One, when a black person has had richer contact with the mainstream than all but a sliver of black people did in the past. Operating below the level of consciousness, the Five Frills are not "expressions," but echoes. In terms of how language and linguistics work, it is predictable that for the most educated black speakers, blaccent would be the one aspect of Black English that they display. When people learn new languages, their native accent is the hardest thing to let go of—we are all familiar with people whose English is perfect except for a slight accent; your sound holds on tight deep within you. For exactly that reason, when black Americans have had enough contact with white Americans to talk very much like them, if a whisper of difference remains, it is in the accent that we would expect to find it. Because accent operates below the level of consciousness, black people may find it genuinely confusing to be told that they sound black when speaking perfect Standard English, just as white Americans might be surprised when told that they pronounce the *t*'s in *butter* more like *d*'s, unlike most Brits, who do not.

Language is hardly the only part of human culture that operates below the level of consciousness. A person often doesn't realize they exhibit a cultural trait until they come in contact with people of other cultures, as per the common observation that you can't truly know what it is to be an American until you've spent time in a different country.

For example, it is often noted that many black American men have a certain way of walking (sometimes termed the *short drop*). This highly particular sequence of muscular movements is not taught, but subconsciously internalized by boys watching men. Another example: I once watched four black girls doing a dance routine they had informally worked up to a pop song. All four were doing the very same moves. However, one of them had grown up in a mostly white neighborhood and gone to a mostly white school. She was executing every step the other girls were, but there was a certain Element X missing, a very particular kind of connection with the rhythm of the song, a brand of attitude in the motions, that she could not pull off spontaneously the way the other girls did. One of the girls was only six, and yet "had it" just as two of the others did. The three girls had learned a way of moving to music from watching, feeling, and doing it since toddlerhood that the other one simply had not. Unsurprisingly, the fourth girl also did not have a blaccent.

The particular sound of most black Americans' Standard English is formed in this way. Black toddlers already use the sounds of Black English if they are growing up around those speaking the dialect, and obviously they aren't working at "expressing" anything. Rather, to be a black American is usually to subconsciously acquire certain positionings of the tongue and lips, slightly different from the ones whites use, when producing certain sounds. Because in our times even that statement lends itself to misinterpretation, note the following: *To be a white*

American is usually to subconsciously acquire certain posi-
tionings of the tongue and lips, slightly different from the
ones black people use. This is purely observational. I cannot
stress more that there is no value judgment here. Different
groups of people speaking the same language—whether
geographically separate or not—differ in terms of their
vowels all over the world. Black people shape their mouths
to speak in a certain way because the positionings happen
to be the ones that the people closest to them are using
when they are learning the subtle and complex thing that
language is. As dry as that sounds, it's what makes it so that
you know what color someone is when they say "But what's
worse is, the event isn't even happening."

Most important, the blaccent is normal. *What would*
be strange is if it didn't exist.

Beyond Vowels

It bears mentioning that vowels are not all of the story
when it comes to how to sound black. There are aspects of
intonation, for one—Black English has different melodies,
we might say, from those of Standard English.

Research has revealed, for example, that my mother's
hypothesis about sinuses wasn't completely off the mark,
if recast as grounded in cultural conditioning rather than
anatomy. There is evidence that black people tend to produce the basic sound of speech—that is, the vocal airstream
independently of how the specific vowels are shaped—in
a particular way that reads subconsciously to others as
black. That is the kind of thing many sense as awkward or

risky to state, but this kind of difference in vocal quality or timbre is by no means a black issue. Aspects of voice quality distinguish different languages and dialects worldwide. For example, formal British English is produced more forward in the mouth than American, for nothing a linguist or anyone else would call a reason; that's just the way it is. Another example is the "vocal fry" that the media has explored widely in American whites below a certain age (the trait may have begun with women but has rapidly spread to men, as well). This so-called fry is a slightly creaky tone that people frequently use, often to single out a point as significant, toward the end of sentences. This is something almost no one would think about consciously— no one executes it on purpose. It certainly has nothing to do with anyone "expressing an identity," and most people have to listen closely to recordings even to understand what linguists mean by it. However, this quality of voice has settled in among young people over the past twenty years. An invaluable demonstration is a report by linguistics blog Language Log contrasting the voice of National Public Radio reporter Sarah Koenig in 2000 and 2014, at which time she exemplifies a solid—although, as always, subtle—vocal fry she did not use fourteen years before.

What's key about vocal fry in our discussion is that it is an utterly subconscious feature of vocal production that has emerged among a certain subpopulation of Americans that has nothing to do with personhood and developed for no more reason than does a particular fingerprint or snowflake pattern. Language is, to an extent it can be ever so hard to wrap our heads around, serendipitous in that way. In Black English, the particular random type of timbre in question is what creates the husky impression, although the study that identified this difference in black vocal quality found it in men as well as women. Specialists in acoustic phonetics have precise characterizations for factors like these, and it will be interesting to see them further applied to this question.

This difference in vocal quality is the last whisper of Black English a person might have. A person speaks a dialect to varying extents—you can do it strong or take it light, with every step in between. However, the steps occur in a certain order, from sentence structure, to sound, to more elusive aspects of melody and vocal quality. To speak full-blown Black English is to have the grammar, the sound, and the quality. However, a person might also not use the grammar but still have a solid, readily perceptible black sound—that is, only the blaccent, specifically the obvious surface-level kind. Or, a person might have only the less immediately identifiable, yet present, deep-level kind of blaccent—that's taking it even lighter. Finally, a person may not use Black English's sentence structures or even the vowels but will still have the quality. Then, individuals may slide left and right on this scale from moment to moment, depending on whom they are talking to and what they are talking about. Plus, some black people have more range in this ability than others, depending on life experience.

The order that these components stack in is very important to realize. This schema is a handy way to think of the matter:

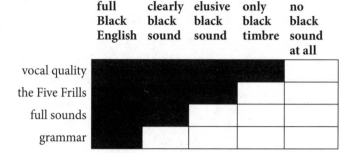

This means that there are some aspects of sounding black that you can have only if you have others as well, and only one aspect that you can have only by itself. No one uses Black English grammar without having the sound as well, even though you can indeed have the sound without using the grammar. Why? Because sound sits deep in the brain. The analogy is to someone who speaks your language with full idiomatic command but with an accent. Note: There is no such thing as someone who speaks your language with a perfect accent but whose sentences are full of grammatical mistakes. If the person has mastered the sounds, then it follows that before that, he had the sentence structures down. People learn a language's parts in order of difficulty. Grammar comes more easily than changing your sound. Crucially, when a group of people start losing their dialect in favor of a dominant dialect, what's lost goes in the opposite order. It's easier to pick up the dominant dialect's grammar than its sound. Your own sound in your own dialect will hold on longer. Only with truly intimate and long-term contact will you lose your sound completely.

This explains our table about degrees of black English and why the features stack in the way that they do. This order explains why there is such a thing as sounding black even when someone isn't saying anything black in terms of vocabulary or sentence patterns. It also explains why to utter a phrase of Black English with Standard English vowels and intonation sounds ridiculous: "What up, yo? This where the place at?" intoned in the voice of Steve Martin doesn't work at all. A table like the one above, then, is not just about Black English or black people but about how humans use language in general.

It is possible the vocal quality of Black English will turn out to have links with African speech. I don't mean African anatomy, but aspects of African languages that black Americans' ancestors spoke. Despite some claims (usually from outside of linguistics itself) that Black English consists of English words with African grammar, the search for actual inheritances from African languages in Black English has yielded very little. However, I think of a bizarre experience I once had in Senegal. The European language of Senegal is French. A TV show was playing in the next room; I was occupied with something and only passively listening to it. What was being said was pretty mundane—there was nothing "cultural" about it. And yet, after a while I realized that I was hearing these voices as black somehow. It wasn't because I was in a black country, since during my stay I had already seen a good deal of television, almost all of which had been with white people speaking French (movies and dubbed sitcoms, mostly). My default sense of television language there was, thus, white French. Rather, I had subconsciously processed a black sound in the French of this television show, despite not having directed my attention to the dialogue, and not having enough experience living in a Francophone context to have even ever considered the question as to whether there was a black-sounding French, much less listened for it.

Yet indeed, when I went into the next room to see if by some off chance I might be right, the show turned out to be a cartoon about black people, and when I checked the end credits, the voices were indeed done by people with African-language names. The quality that tipped me off was the same husky quality that people often mention black American women have. Just maybe, this vocal trait is, of all things, part of the African diaspora. Researchers: Go!

Onward

OBVIOUSLY, HOW ONE SOUNDS BLACK is a rich issue. A note to academic specialists on Black English: This topic requires further exploration, and should also be presented in ways that nonlinguists can engage with. We can't blame the public for not understanding that black American speech is okay if the discussion (1) focuses mainly on what cannot help but look like broken English and (2) is largely only about tiny little crumbs buried in academic articles and books the general public never sees and couldn't learn from.

In any case, I hope to have shown that there should be no guilt in squarely attesting to the fact that there is a such thing as a black-sounding voice. Whites need not wonder whether they are being racist in discussing it, and black people need not feel like the topic is a coded stamp of approval for minstrel shows. All of us, as long as the facts have been shown, can rest assured that this is one case where what our senses are telling us is utterly harmless fact.

When a child asks, for example, "Why do black people sound different even when they aren't using slang?" should we tense up and worry that our child might be internalizing racist ideas in their assumption that black people all talk one way? No. We might tell the child that not all black people have that sound. But alone, that doesn't answer the child's question, because she can hear just what the rest of us do. *Most* black people do sound a way that *most* whites don't. What's the answer to her actual question?

"When people spend more time with one another than with other people, they start talking in their own way, just like people do their hair in different ways and listen to different music. Black people spend more time with black people than with white people, and so their sounds are a little different from white people's sounds, just like Spanish-speaking people's sounds are even more different from everybody else's."

A Lesson for All of Us

SOMETHING ELSE WORTH JUST TOSSING IN, however: There is a quick joke in the French film version of what Americans later came to know as the stage musical *La Cage aux Folles*, where a black character makes a joke about an expectation that a black man have a deep voice. This idea apparently reigns even beyond the United States, apparently—clearly a study is needed of this business of black men and deep voices. Whether it is proven, disproven, or both, some empirical conclusions would be both interesting and useful.

CHAPTER THREE

But They Can't Talk That Way at a Job Interview!

WHY AMERICANS THINK YOU CAN TALK ONLY ONE WAY

"BUT THEY CAN'T TALK THAT WAY at a job interview!"

You can almost count on someone saying that during any discussion about the fact that Black English is not bad English. The idea is that even if Black English is complex, even if the ways it differs from Standard English is in the use of alternates rather than bastardizations, real-world factors must guide choices. In that light, Black English will never sound appropriate in a formal setting, and therefore people must be trained out of it. Under this analysis, protestations to the contrary are mere advocacy, a product of the leftward tilt of the academy and schools of education, identity politics, et cetera. There comes a time, people of this mind feel, when we must drop the special pleading and get real.

The objection about the job interview, however, is a gunshot that misses its target. A linguist has to adjust to the very notion that "They can't talk that way at a job interview!" constitutes a response to the arguments typically made in favor of Black English. It's because, quite simply, no one thinks people should speak Black English when interviewing for a job.

Perhaps a fringe few call for a world where one could indeed talk however one wanted wherever one wanted. However, this is a fringe indeed, the true left, and even their focus is on the future. None of them would condemn to unemployment a present-day human being by hoping the person will stride into an interviewer's office saying "Whaddup!?" and "Dis da place I wanna work at." Even the most vernacular of persons finds the very notion of such a thing funny, because of its sheer absurdity. As such, no Black English advocate is calling for Black English to be allowed in interviews. Frankly, interviews are the last thing on that person's mind.

Since when is all of life a job interview?

Real Life: Working Hard for the Money versus Thank God It's Friday

IF "THEY CAN'T TALK THAT WAY on a job interview!" negates any support of Black English as legitimate speech, then presumably people live in a world where they are always in suits, conversing in feigned comfort with strangers. But I, for one, have never encountered such a human being.

Any black person knows there is a way you talk with friends and a way you talk when things are more serious. The scenario of someone jiving around with a perplexed white manager is a hypothetical that some feel especially alarmed about even if it is not an actual problem. Yet this objection about the job interview lives ever on, processed as a smackdown comment, as if it somehow cuts through all the nonsense and zeroes in on common sense. But anyone knows that most of black people's lives, like the majority of most people's lives, is lived *in*formally. So what's the problem with using Black English *in*formally?

The concern about job interviews follows logically from an impression that *if black people speak Black English even informally, then they won't be able to speak Standard English when they need to*. The universality of the interview comment, and the confidence with which it is hurled, makes sense only when the assumption is that using Black English somehow *cancels Standard English out*.

It's hardly a crazy notion. This person speaks Italian. That one speaks Hebrew. She speaks Spanish. He speaks English. She speaks Black English. But we need to teach her to speak Standard English instead, because Black English— that other thing—sounds low-down.

To be sure, the fact that the person speaking Black English is black affects the evaluation. Race is certainly the reason Black English occasions so much more comment than rural southern English—it makes Black English seem more different, and more wrong. However, I submit that to stop this conversation at pointing out the role of racism is a disengagement. It tacitly classifies the problem as unsolvable, at least within a human lifetime.

People can speak both Black English *and* Standard English. The two ways of speaking can occupy the same mind and mouth. A person can quite plausibly speak Black English with friends and Standard English at that job interview.

Rather than saying "We need her to speak Black English instead," we should say, "We need her to speak Standard English, *too*." In fact, she probably already does.

The American Sense of Language

FISH DON'T KNOW THEY'RE WET. And Americans, in that sense, don't know that their typical native linguistic repertoire is narrow and dull compared to that of a great many of the world's people.

I mean no insult, as I am referring to myself, as well. My native dialect is a bland middle-class Mid-Atlantic (as linguists term it) Standard. I am the kind of American English speaker often described as exhibiting "no dialect" (although technically, everyone speaks a dialect, and what people really mean about speech like mine is that it is not nonstandard). I also had the misfortune of not being raised around Black English enough for it to have become part of my own natural speech patterns (I have a thoroughly robust "passive competence," as linguists call it). When I open my mouth, what comes out is the voice of a Disney announcer circa 1946, and if you woke me up out of a sound sleep, I'd talk the same way. After glasses of wine, I sound the same way. When I feel comfortable with someone, I sound the same way. I have no real range.

In that, as an American I'm unusual only as a black one. Standard American English, as speech varieties go worldwide, is rather uniform. Yes, if you listen closely, there are all manner of pronunciation differences across this great nation, as the wonderful map by Rick Aschmann that appears online shows (aschmann.net/AmEng). However, the very fact that these differences come as a surprise to us is key. In a great many places in the world, a map like that would occasion no surprise, and would document not just fine differences in pronunciation, plus a few expressions like "needs washed" for "needs to be washed," but vastly distinct dialects that border on being different languages.

Take, for example, how the difference between the old rural dialects of Cornwall and Dorset, the northern dialects like Yorkshire, the West Country dialects, and then Scots—if one is even to classify it as English, as some would prefer not to—dwarf any differences between southern and California speech in the United States. Those differences are the result of the kind of drifting language change that I described as creating French, Spanish, and Italian from Latin. English has occupied England now for sixteen hundred years, allowing lots of time for divergence. English came to America only four hundred years ago, at which time various dialects from across the Atlantic mixed together into something new and set things at the starting point again. Four hundred years is a relatively short time for major regional differences to evolve. Moreover, increasing literacy and then modern media have made it harder for that kind of thing to happen in America's life span anyway. Since, especially, commercial radio and sound films in the 1930s—plus the explosion in college degrees after the GI Bill of the 1940s—Americans have come to speak more like one another than they used to. Warnings that dialects are disappearing in the United States entirely are overblown, but dialects are less diverse from one another than before.

As a result, to be, especially, a middle-class educated American is to have a default sense of talking as involving one way of doing it. You open your mouth, and out comes standard American English or something close. You may talk somewhat differently over a beer than at a board meeting, but not differently enough that you'd consider it a topic worthy of discussion. "Dude," "whatcha" instead of "what do you," a little "ain't" here and there, but not much else.

Does this mean that a black person speaking Black English is handicapped? Such an impression reveals us as fish unaware of the legions of creatures up on land living meaningful lives nice and dry. Worldwide, people speak their respective languages in vastly different forms depending on social contexts—one way in that interview, another *very different* way when talking to a friend about it later.

The Normal Sense of Language: To Talk Differently Than You Speak

AND I REALLY MEAN VASTLY DIFFERENT, not just a little slangier or enunciating a little less crisply. To truly get this, we must look to other countries.

One thing you should know about almost any Arabic speaker you talk to is that the person is not just bilingual, but trilingual. This person speaks English, uses Standard Arabic in school, worship, and ceremonies, but in casual conversation, he or she uses a different language, although it, too, is called Arabic. In actuality, that person's casual Arabic has the relationship to Standard Arabic that Spanish does to Latin. Standard Arabic is essentially frozen in time, based on the language of the Qur'an. The casual language is what has happened to Arabic when allowed to move on and become, as it were, analagous to Spanish.

While Standard Arabic is the same across the Arabophone world, casual Arabic is a different language in each region. Let's zero in on what an Egyptian, for example, actually speaks. In Standard Arabic, *these* is *haḏān*, but in Egyptian *these* is *dōl*. In Standard Arabic, *the* is *al*, but in Egyptian, *il*. So, in Standard Arabic, "these professors" is:

Haḏān   al-'ustāḏān
   these   the professors

But Egyptian Arabic has other words for *these* and *the*, the word for *professor* is also somewhat different from the standard one, and even the grammar is different: You put the word for *these* after *professors* instead of before it:

   il-'ustazēn   dōl
the professors   these

In Standard Arabic, *they walk* is *yamšiyan*. In Egyptian, it is *biyimšu*. The Standard Arabic word for *nose* is *'anf*. The Egyptian word is *manaxir*.

As you can see, Standard Arabic and Egyptian Arabic are two different languages. One learns Egyptian as a child, and then picks up Standard Arabic in school and from religious worship. And yet, Egyptians move casually between these two languages day in and day out. An adult Egyptian speaks Egyptian most of the time but uses Standard Arabic in, say, a job interview, if the job is one that would require him to "represent" as a formal, public person.

Not that an Egyptian usually thinks of herself as speaking two languages. To her, the switching is something that just is, in the way that an American knows that for a cookout one puts out chips and salsa and grills hot dogs and burgers but for a more formal dinner puts out Brie and olives and ventures rack of lamb. We assume no one would need to be taught those customs, and wouldn't even think of them as customs. In the same way, an Egyptian does not think of the difference between the Standard Arabic and Egyptian as exotic. To her, the very idea that she speaks two separate languages seems somewhat counterintuitive, in the same way that it would seem to us if we were told that we had mastered two distinct food cultures.

After all, an Egyptian can use some Standard Arabic words while speaking Egyptian, and may even speak on a kind of intermediate level between Standard Arabic and Egyptian—just as one could serve, if not hot dogs, sausages from Whole Foods to guests at a dinner party. An Egyptian tends to think of Standard Arabic and Egyptian as Arabic, just as an American thinks of Brie, olives, the lamb, chips, and hot dogs as food, and would be bemused to see those things separated on a formality hierarchy. If anything, there is a sense that Egyptian is slang Arabic. But is a whole alternate vocabulary and different grammatical system just slang? Likely there were people speaking early Spanish who called it "Latin slang," but we'd hear them as speaking a different language from Latin, and it is reasonable to view Egyptian Arabic the same way.

All of which is to say that Arabs continually toggle between two ways of speaking as different as that and yet barely even think about it. People can speak two ways, a standard way and a casual way. No one worries that Egyptian Arabic threatens Standard Arabic, or supposes that someone speaking Egyptian is somehow compromised in their ability to learn Standard Arabic. This is linguistic reality in Egypt, Syria, Palestine, Iraq, Libya, Algeria, Morocco, Tunisia, Saudi Arabia, Sudan, and elsewhere.

This is a way of living in a language that Americans are poorly positioned to even be able to imagine. We can get a sense of it in differences that we rarely consider explicitly but internalize as matters of formality. Ordinarily, we *get* things, but in writing about that, we might use *receive* instead of *get*. It's the same with *place* versus *put*, *child* versus *kid*, and *possessions* versus *stuff*. Imagine if there were pairs like this for almost any word—maybe as if we were expected to say *house* at home but when writing to use *domicile* instead. Or suppose there were pairs of ways of conjugating verbs, such that we said *walks* at home but *walketh* in school. That is roughly what it is to speak Arabic.

For many Canadians, this is true of French. I once had a rather eccentric French literature teacher who casually assigned us a novel written in the French of Quebec, with liberal doses of dialogue in the colloquial French of working-class Montrealers. This was a little inconsiderate, because the French these people speak is so different from the Parisian

French taught in American classrooms that it was hard to understand much of anything the characters were saying to one another, even when laid out in cold print. (The book was *The Fat Lady Next Door Is Pregnant,* by Michel Tremblay, which, for those interested, turned out to be a fantastic book when I went back to it better equipped fifteen years later.)

To give a sense of how different this speech is from textbook Parisian French, the dialect is colloquially called joual, pronounced "jwal." That word, believe it or not, is the Standard French word for *horse, cheval,* as pronounced in this dialect. *Cheval* is pronounced "shuh-VOLL." Now imagine if the *v* in that word became a *w*, which it might, since *w* is basically what happens if you let your top teeth come away from your bottom lip while saying *v*, giving you "shuh-WOLL." Now say that fast a few times, and you get from "shWOLL" to "jWOLL"—that is, joual!

Joual speakers in Canada are hardly unfamiliar with Standard French, which is the language of schooling, print, and the media. For them, casual speech simply differs more from Standard speech than anything most Americans are used to. "*Toi, qu'est-ce que tu fais?*"—"You, what are you doing?"—someone might ask in Standard French. But in joual, that's "*Twe, que c'est que tu fas?*" For those of you who know French, the *fas* in that last sentence is not a typo. That's how the "to do" verb *faire* is conjugated in joual. Overall, look at the difference:

Standard French: "Twa, KES-kuh tu FAY?"
          Joual: "Tway, kuh SAY-kuh tu FAH?"

The distance from Standard French is quite similar to that of Black English from Standard English, and, in fact, more. Yet no one is writing about how joual needs to be stamped out in favor of Standard French, or insisting that you can't use it in a job interview—because no one does, unless by chance the interviewer is a fellow joual speaker and wants to bond. A joual speaker has two ways they can talk, and *c'est la vie*.

There are cases like this all over the world. In Finland, *nobody* speaks the standard language casually. There is a different kind of Finnish, a kind of universal colloquial alternate, that real Finnish life is lived in, and that someone learning the language has to master alongside the standard forms. The differences between standard and colloquial are similar to these between Standard English and Black English. A Finnish textbook simply lists the colloquial forms along with the standard ones and calmly, in true Finn style, explains that you have to know them, too. No one in Helsinki thinks of colloquial Finnish as something to worry about.

Many Italians call cappicola ham *gabagul*. That's because that is the word for cappicola in the Sicilian dialect of Italian: *Gabagul* is basically cappicola after being said a billion times. The standard's word *cappicola* preserves a past state, as standard languages tend to. *Gabagul* is how the word has come out when left to its own devices. In Sicily, casually people speak Sicilian rather than the Tuscan standard. Really, Sicilian is so different from Italian that in an objective sense, it is a different language—it's almost as different from Italian as Portuguese is from Spanish, and if Sicily were a separate country, Sicilian would strike no one as a kind of Italian. This is why media depictions of Sicilians talking among themselves, such as in *The Godfather*, *The Sopranos*, and *Boardwalk Empire*, are scrupulous about having the characters speak actual Sicilian rather than Tuscan Italian, which would seem not just imprecise but absurd to any Italian watching. But to Sicilians, as different from schoolroom Italian as their daily speech is, a discussion assuming that to master Standard Italian requires letting Sicilian go would sound absurd—they don't doubt that people can speak both.

There is a term for people whose casual and formal speech differs to this degree: *diglossia*, from the Greek for "two tongues." However, I have held off on introducing that term, because giving this bidialectal linguistic existence a label implies that it is exotic, when in fact it is extremely common and even a norm. Around the world, if a language has a strong written tradition and is also spoken widely, then often its spoken versions have drifted from the conservative written standard to varying degrees. As often as not, this means that there is a gulf between the way people *chat* and the way they speak. They *speak* the written version; they *talk* the other version. As such, there is ample diglossia in many languages of South Asia, across Indonesia, and in Tibetan, Swahili, German, Italian itself, as well as in Greece, China, parts of Sweden, Norway, and Denmark, and elsewhere. If anything, what merits a special term is *monoglossia*—speaking always basically one thing.

Back to America: How Diglossia Changes Your Lens

BLACK AMERICANS ARE DIGLOSSIC—perfectly normally diglossic. Whether they would be allowed to use Black English in a job interview is as loopy an issue to focus on as whether a Moroccan would defend his master's thesis in Moroccan Arabic—almost as different from Standard Arabic as French is from Latin—or whether a Finn who gets a job as a newscaster would talk on the air the same way as she does to her mom.

The most perfect expression of this perspective I have ever known is a passage by Maya Angelou in *I Know Why the Caged Bird Sings*:

> In the classroom we all learned past participles, but in the streets and in our homes the Blacks learned to drop s's from plurals and suffixes from past-tense verbs. We were alert to the gap separating the written word from the colloquial. We learned to slide out of one language and into another without being conscious of the effort. At school, in a given situation, we might respond with "That's not unusual." But in the street, meeting the same situation, we easily said "It be's like that sometimes."

Here is an example of what this perspective can help us with as American English speakers. Just as some are under the impression that someone who speaks Black English cannot speak Standard English, too, others might think that a black person who speaks Standard English cannot also be fluent in Black English. More to the point, they assume that when such a person speaks Black English, they're a fake.

That impression reveals itself in complaints about Barack Obama's adoption of black cadences and occasional black slang in public addresses, especially when he speaks to black audiences. Just as it has genuinely surprised me that people consider Black English's lack of fit in an interview to be a case against Black English as a whole, it truly threw me that some people have heard Obama's black speech stylings as phony, and even cynical.

The idea seems to be that since Obama can speak Standard English, when he uses Black English he is "putting it on," fashioning a stunt in order to mesmerize black audiences. The argument is similar to suspicions that George W. Bush's twangish elocution and moments of stark inarticulateness were designed to make him seem folksy.

But the idea that Obama "knows better" than to speak that way reveals a belief that Black English is fundamentally wrong, rather than being an alternate form of English. One does not switch to Black English randomly, however; the dialect is an expression of cultural fellowship among black people. Obama's use of aspects of Black English with black audiences is, therefore, natural and not surprising.

The black person who speaks Black English can most likely speak Standard English, too. In the same way, so can the black person who speaks Standard English often speak Black English. The two things do not cancel each other out: They coexist.

Always the Twain Shall Meet

SOME MAY SUSPECT ME OF IDEALIZING when describing black Americans as people who speak two ways. I am. We might ask whether it jibes with reality that all black Americans are, as Maya Angelou had it, readily using their "past participles" and saying things like "That's not unusual" in formal contexts and then switching into a vernacular mode only when it's time to chat. That is, do most black people actually talk "white" in public and "black" in private?

That is indeed a highly oversimplified depiction of something subtler—more "dynamic," as the scholars on the subject put it. The academic literature on Black English richly explores how even in nonformal situations, black Americans do not use Black English forms each and every time they could, while in formal situations, they use some Black English forms according to interlocutor, nuance, and other factors. Often Black English features correlate with the subject as it evolves throughout a dialogue: One is more likely to use a Black English word or construction in reference to something closer to the heart, funnier, or more central in importance while speaking largely in Standard English. This is in line with what linguists who study this kind of variation between formality and informality in speech (the subfield is called "variationist sociolinguistics") have discovered in many languages and dialects.

This kind of alternation is rapid, fluid, and subtle—it is an art to capture it in written dialogue. In the seventies sitcom *The Jeffersons*, depicting a black couple of working-class origins having risen to affluence, Louise Jefferson was portrayed as speaking a very Standard English in contrast to her husband. Whether this was a conscious decision or not, it corresponded with the reality that women tend to embrace the standard dialect more than men, regardless of race. In an early episode, however, the writers had the usually almost grandiloquent Louise muse during a speech ". . . but it ain't." The writers clearly wanted Louise to indicate her roots in a search for authenticity, but for her to pop off with this "ain't" just that one time, especially in actress Isabel Sanford's rather plummy stage diction, was a flub. On the other hand, the variable usage of Black English is depicted magnificently in the campy drama series *Empire*. The curious could do much worse than to listen to the show's dialogue to get a sense of how real people use the dialect.

The point is that black Americans do not keep Standard and Black English as separate as Egyptians keep Standard Arabic and Egyptian Arabic. However, it bears mentioning that before the 1970s the two cases were more parallel for many black speakers, for whom one could call my description of things less inaccurate than a little old-fashioned. Angelou, raised in the thirties and forties, grew up during a time when black people tended to speak more formally in public contexts than they do today. This was in line with the more formal atmosphere of public events in America as a whole at the time, an era when one made a speech rather than giving a talk, elocution training and oratory competitions were a standard part of school curricula, and the writer was expected to master layered sentence construction and embrace language arts–style vocabulary. This aspect of American linguistic culture felt no less natural to black people than to anyone else who sought to make a name for themselves in the wider world.

The extent to which many famous black people of the old days sounded white would throw many listeners were they able to travel back in time and hear these people give a talk—or, no, make a speech, as they would have thought of it. Educator and political adviser Mary McLeod Bethune, born poor in South Carolina, sounded like any white society matron when she gave a speech. In her time, it was natural for her to master that way of speaking in order to be taken seriously by the public. Booker T. Washington, born in slavery, also spoke in a way that gave no indication of his childhood environment when giving a public address. I doubt it would occur to anyone today hearing the recording of his Atlanta Compromise speech that a black man was talking, despite the fact that Washington surely spoke the southern Black English of Virginia as a child. Civil Rights pioneer A. Philip Randolph, raised in Florida, also sounded basically white when speaking to the public. Voting rights activist Fannie Lou Hamer was well known for freely speaking in her Mississippian Black English to audiences in the fifties and sixties, but in her time this was considered pushing the envelope, and even made some Civil Rights leaders uncomfortable.

Maya Angelou is a useful example, as well, for the famously grandiloquent air of her speaking style. There was a similar tone in much of her writing. Had she been an

Egyptian, she would have had a certain preference for the Standard Arabic words over the Egyptian ones—*motoring* rather than *driving*, *commodious* rather than *comfortable*, et cetera. One senses that Angelou, like many black writers of her generation and before, was not only conforming to the norms of the era's language culture but also making a point: that black people, too, can speak as high as anyone else. That was a point more urgent in the era when minstrel speech was either common coin in entertainment or remained within recent memory. The Angelou speaking style was less idiosyncratic than many suppose—black actresses of her time often spoke in that elegantly studied fashion. An example is the orotund diction of Marlene Warfield (born in 1940) when playing the black activist in the film *Network*. Diana Sands's diction was often similar (most accessibly as Beneatha in the film *Raisin in the Sun*).

I am aware of no record of any of these people being thought peculiar in not sounding black in what they were saying. In their time, it would have seemed more intuitive than it may today that black people are bidialectal. Today, however, in addition to the informality of our times—America's sense of language took it easy along with taking off the hats, coats, gowns, and girdles—grammar is not taught formally in schools as frequently, or as rigorously, as it used to be. As a result, black people are often less stringent about the boundary between public and private language, just as the rest of the nation is. At an open house, I recall a black school principal once addressing the student body's parents, listing "Mr. Rivers, which is the athletic instructor, and Mrs. Jenkins, which is the librarian" (upon which someone in the audience whispered, "And after this will be the reception, who is in the auditorium!").

This person was trying her best, and her grammatical slipup had nothing to do with her adminstrative competence. Yet I suspect she wouldn't have confused *which* and *who* that way in a public address in, say, 1940. And the truth is that these days, there are young black Americans who could benefit from some good old-fashioned tutelage in speaking Standard English consistently. The fashion for informality has a way of penalizing black speakers. The white person who "just talks" in a formal setting is classified as approachable, real, sexy. Whether we like it or not, the black person who "just talks" in a formal setting (as opposed to in music, in the movies, or on TV) is more susceptible to being classified as dim.

Yet even today there are plenty of black Americans who are indeed as fluently, effortlessly bidialectal as Egyptians. An especially prominent contemporary example would be the comedians Keegan-Michael Key and Jordan Peele, who can sound like prep school scions on National Public Radio and then use Black English fluently not only in their sketches but also in their casual speech. In happily describing "ax" for *ask* as something that will "come out" when things get going, they are perfect examples of the fact that to be a bidialectal black American is to speak *more* English than many Americans, very much *a larger English* (as I wanted to title an early book of mine and therefore feel the need to squeeze in here). Just as someone who speaks both Standard Arabic and Egyptian Arabic is enviably bilingual, someone who is truly comfortable in Standard English and in Black English has something on the monodialectal American. They are articulate, although we don't usually apply the term that way.

I once heard a public school chancellor speak about her work; she was one of those people who commanded a goodly range between official Standard English speech and solid Black English. Among the assorted (and mostly white) talking-head sorts at the event, she was definitely, in my mind, the most articulate one there. And yet, just as with most Arabic speakers, it was the last thing on her mind that her ability to speak two ways was of note at all—which made it all that much more impressive.

If Someone *Can* Speak Standard English, Though, Why Don't They?

WE MAY NOT BE THERE YET. An Egyptian speaks something different from Standard Arabic, a Sicilian speaks an alternate language from Tuscan Italian, but is the analogy with Black English really apt? One might not be surprised that adult African slaves did not master English perfectly. One might affirm that the imperfect English they created can't be dismissed as "bad" anymore than Modern English can be dismissed as "bad" because Vikings created it by massacring Old English.

Yet Modern English was accepted in a largely nonliterate context, where almost no one was privy to documents written in the language as it once had been. Even if we might understand why the first generation, or even generations, of slaves' kids held on to so-called broken English—they were so segregated from whites that it was no surprise they didn't adopt Standard English as their home language—what about later? Especially after the Civil War, and especially *now*? As all of us can hear plenty of black people who are speaking Standard English with and around one another day in and day out. So why haven't black people just adopted Standard English, given its prestige, instead of fashioning a linguistically bifurcated existence in which they speak Standard English and talk Black English? A light blaccent is one thing, but why does any black person today still say things like "Dis da way in?"

This is a legitimate question, and its answer requires understanding that prestige itself is a bifurcated thing. There is overt prestige, connected to a way of speaking considered crucial in formal, public settings. But human beings also place a value on in-group contacts, a sense of belonging to a group within the larger society. Within that in group, too, there will often be nonstandard ways of speaking that are valued, thought of as "what we do." This, too, is a kind of prestige, although we don't conventionally associate the word *prestige* with the vernacular and the informal. More often we circle around the concept with *cool*, down with, *street cred*, and so on, but anthropologically speaking, all of these concepts are as much about prestige, in its general meaning, as salad forks and boutonnieres.

Just as an ordinary person might cherish both his tuxedo and his most comfortable jeans, a person can feel as warmly about his informal speech as his formal. This means that ways of speaking that go against the rules of the Standard variety are not always simply rejected as foul. Rather, humans often adopt such varieties as expressions of in-group identity. The fact that the informal variety doesn't conform to the standard rules is often part of why it feels so appropriate as the in-group way of speaking—there is an aspect of local pride in it.

Of course, feelings about the informal variety will be complex. People may simultaneously embrace it as "us" while also maintaining an analytic sense that it is fundamentally deficient, mistaken, "just slang," and so on. Some will claim not to speak it, only to reveal themselves as readily using it when the occasion demands it. Most will think more of the words than the grammatical structure, often embracing the words as "ours" while dismissing the grammatical structure as "wrong." All that is amply documented among diglossic speakers worldwide. And yet, in terms of the survival status of the informal variety, all of it is mere static. Whatever the attitudes, the variety lives, thrives, transforms, and, after a while, even infuses the standard.

This, of course, describes Black English, but as part of a general phenomenon. To wit, second-generation immigrant youth can adopt elements of their parents' generation's incomplete rendition of the dominant language as a permanent marker of in-group identity. There is no one term for this process as of now, but it often happens when people speaking different languages settle in a city and fashion their own version of the language as they learn it.

Children of immigrants don't speak exactly like their parents, any more than a black person born in the United

States talked like an African who never truly spoke fluent English. However, the new youth speaking lingua francas do not observe all the rules of the standard language; they shave away a lot of the unnecessarily harder stuff. These varieties seem, at a glance, like Black English versions of whichever language is in question.

For example, in Germany, urban children of immigrants speak what is called "Kiezdeutsch," with a relationship to Standard German quite similar to the one between Black English and Standard English. Standard German for "Tomorrow I'm going to the movies" is: "*Morgen gehe ich ins Kino.*"—that is, "Tomorrow go I to movies." The Kiezdeutsch version is: "*Morgen ich geh Kino.*"— that is, "Tomorrow I go movies." Kiezdeutsch leaves off the *e* ending of the *go* verb— *geh* instead of *gehe*—the word order is more straightforward ("I go" instead of "go I"), and you just "go movies," not "go to the movies." This is much like "Why she like me anyway?" in Black English instead of "Why does she like me anyway? Many Germans have the same feelings about Kiezdeutsch that people have about Black English in America, including a fear that Kiezdeutsch somehow cancels out Standard German. However, Kiezdeutsch speakers are quite capable of speaking Standard German when they have to. They just have two ways of communicating—one for the public, one for the realm that in Black English would be referred to as "up in here," the intimate sphere.

There are versions of this documented in Denmark, Sweden, Norway, and the Netherlands, as well. It is certain that increasing emigration to other European countries will produce similar varieties elsewhere on that continent. In Africa, the way dominant African languages like Swahili and Fula are spoken in cities, where speakers of many less dominant languages have long gathered and settled for good, is equivalent to these European varieties. Popularly, these ways of speaking go under any number of names, often misleadingly as "pidgin" versions, as if speakers were merely stringing words together with barely any structure. The reality is that these ways of speaking are complex language, just as Black English is.

In Senegal, for example, Wolof divides things into about ten genders. Unsurprisingly, one of the most obvious traits of the Wolof spoken by Senegalese immigrants and children of these immigrants in cities like St. Louis and Dakar is that often just one gender marker is used instead of a variety of the ten available. That's what we would likely find ourselves doing if we had to learn Wolof, and yet we would still find learning this "urban Wolof" version of the language a challenge indeed.

Black English, then, is America's manifestation of something that happens all over the world. Few of us would be prepared to say that languages are falling apart all over the world. Or, if we are, then we have to be ready to say that in earlier times, English, Persian, Mandarin, and Indonesian all fell apart—all those languages developed from more elaborate versions of their past selves, streamlined by grown-ups and passed along in their less encumbered state. I'm assuming no one would go that far, which means that we acknowledge that Black English is a development, not a disaster, and a development that happens *alongside* the standard variety, not in opposition to it.

Now We Can Aks

AT THIS POINT, WE ARE IN A POSITION to tackle the *aks* for *ask* business for real. It's all well and good to dwell on these things from a distance—language of identity, Old English, but this serves little purpose until we fully understand that it applies to that which really sticks out. And few things stick out more in black American speech than *aks* for *ask*.

It's often the first thing people bring up as an example of why Black English is bad grammar—and in my experience, at least, black people are as eager to discuss it as others. Garrard McClendon, black professor and talk-show host, has titled a book *Ax or Ask: The African American Guide to Better English*. "What's with *aks*?" someone regularly asks after a talk I give on language, with the audience dependably nodding and tittering. So, what *is* with it?

The answer a linguist is supposed to give is that way back in Old English, the word for *ask* swung randomly between *ascian* and *acsian*. And this is true—black people didn't simply take *ask* and change it. They received *aks*, which was a perfectly normal thing to happen to a word like *ask*.

Fish was, believe it or not, a similar case. It started as *fisk*, ending in *sk* just as *ask* does. Some people started saying *fiks* rather than *fisk*. Others said fish instead. After a while, *fish* won out over *fiks*—and so we say *fish* and wonder that anyone ever said anything different. *Mash* was similar. It started as *mask*. Some people said *maks*, while others said *mash*. *Mash* won, and now the idea of anyone "masking" potatoes sounds absurd.

But the fates happened to treat *ask* differently. Some people said *aks*, some said *ash*. But it was *aks* that won out over *ash*, for no more explainable reason than why this snowflake differs from that snowflake. Language change is, as we have seen, partly a matter of serendipity. Chaucer used *aks* quite freely: "Men aksed him, what sholde bifalle" and "Yow loveres axe I now this questioun." But the original *ask* hung around on the margins, and the people whose English ended up being anointed as the standard dialect—if you had rolled the dice again, it could have been any number of dialects—happened to be *ask* people rather than *aks* people.

This, and only this, is why we hear *aks* for *ask* as tacky and *ask* as correct. *Aks* was now quaint, typical of indentured servants—whom black slaves in America worked alongside and learned English from. *Aks* has a long and innocent history, and the way we hear it makes no more logical sense than the fact that one person's favorite color is green, while another person's isn't.

But that answer never truly convinces anyone. Whatever the linguistic tendencies of Iron Age villagers speaking Old English happened to be, we figure that here and now, *aks* sounds ignorant, and that beyond a certain point there's no more discussing the whys and wherefores of that than there is of proposing that slush, in all of its ugliness and inconvenience, could be considered good for soil. "Language always changes." "People talk in different ways." "Yeah, okay, but why can't some people stick to the way it's now being used by most people? After all, when you get a pimple, you don't say 'Skin changes.' Why can't these others 'identify' with the proper language?" *Aks* is part of the informal wing of black people's speech repertoire, that alternate track to Standard English. Specifically, *aks* is part of how a black person, in a fashion both effortless and yet deeply felt, *is* or "be's" him or herself.

Aks has a vernacular *prestige* for black Americans. It is drunk in from childhood and has indelible associations, just as we link gingerbread with childhood and Christmas. That sentiment is powerful enough to cut across conscious feelings as to what is standard or proper. This is why black people can both make fun of and also regularly use *aks*, even as college graduates.

I'd be dishonest to pretend that this is the end of the story on *aks*. Reality intrudes. *Aks* has a way of getting under people's skin like almost no other aspect of Black English, and nothing will change that. Part of the reason is that the word *ask* is so commonly used; another part is that the very subject of asking—that is, requesting—refers to courtesy and politeness, an inherently formal topic, in which an alternate pronunciation of *ask* can't help but sound especially incongruous.

Given today's looser sense of formality, because black Americans may sense less of a bright line between Black English and Standard English than they once did, they might use *aks* sometimes in a work setting or public statement. In other words, when a black speaker gets in a groove, being most articulate, the most *themselves*, is exactly when he may slide in an *aks* for *ask*—and whatever Old English was like, he immediately sounds ignorant to any nonblack person who hears him, not to mention to quite a few black ones. Unpleasant though it may be, that's the truth, and I fear that the *aks* issue is largely unreachable by logic.

As such, just as I think all young people should be taught to abstain from using *like* when seeking to sound authoritative, given that logic simply cannot prevent Americans from hearing "It was, like," as unauthoritative, I am hardly against black people being taught that one Black English feature that must be kept in the cabinet for private occasions only is *aks*. On that little item, the stringent requirements of old-time elocution and oratory lessons have modern application.

Yet we can suggest this without thinking of *aks* as a willful or lazy flouting of Standard English. What's up with *aks*? The same thing that's up with the fact that *who* in Standard Arabic is *man*, but in casual speech, an Egyptian says *min*.

Standard English, Too—Not Standard English Instead

The main lesson here is that Black English is not Standard English spoken badly. It is something else entirely, spoken with, not in substitution for, Standard English. A black person has no intention of speaking Ebonics during a job interview. An educated black person using Black English when talking to black people is not being affected. Black people don't say *aks* because they can't pronounce an *s* and a *k* in the right order—just listen to them saying *mask, task,* and *risk* as effortlessly as anyone else.

People can talk two ways, is all. We lack a ready terminology to discuss this, and our judgments of people can be clouded by discrimination. Our sense of our own speech can correspond incompletely to how we actually talk. All this makes Black English hard to discuss. The best place to start is to understand that Black English is not *instead of* Standard English, but *in addition to* it.

CHAPTER FOUR

Speaking Black or Speaking Minstrel?

AND HOW MUCH OF IT DID WHITE PEOPLE MAKE UP?

NO LONGER IS INFORMATION about minstrel shows available only in old static photos and scholarly monographs. You can actually hear minstrel performers these days without going to an archive, thanks to the Internet as well as to commercially released recordings. White minstrels Leonard Spencer and Billy Williams, celebrated in their day, are now extremely dead and just as obscure. But we can get a listen to what they did way back in 1894, when the president was Grover Cleveland and the Spanish-American War had yet to happen.

High comedy, apparently, included exchanges such as these:

BILLY: Hey, Leonard.

LEN: What?

BILLY: You'se a man with a heap of intellectualities, am you not?

LEN: Oh, I dunno.

BILLY: Well I'm not goin' to ask you a hard one
        this time.

LEN: Let 'er go.

BILLY: What makes a coon dog spotted?

LEN: Uh-huh, uh-huh, you got me now, boy.
        I don't know, Billy, what do make a coon
        dog spotted?

BILLY: Why, the spots what am on him, of course!

This kind of dialogue is how black Americans were depicted as speaking in the popular culture of the mid-nineteenth century into the twentieth, when minstrel shows were in flower. Note the use of *am* instead of *is*, the *you'se* for *you are*, and the made-up Latinate *intellectualities*. Those were staple elements of minstrelese, and this lingo has modern-day repercussions.

Hovering over discussions of Black English is an idea that a black way to talk has something to do with white racist caricature, if only as something to keep in mind. This is especially when the dialect is written by whites, and more especially when that dialogue was written before 1965. But even when the topic of how black people speak in our time comes up, people sometimes mock the idea by launching into a rendition of minstrelese, with a theatrical pitch, an exaggerated southern twang, sprinkled with the likes of *I'se* and *you'se*.

The Way We Talk or The Way They Say We Talk?

IT ISN'T HARD TO SEE WHERE THIS SUSPICION about Black English comes from, especially since black people were portrayed as speaking in minstrelese long after minstrel shows themselves were ancient history. One of the latest examples I know of is a theatrical cartoon series that continued into the 1950s featuring Buzzy the Crow, an obvious retread of the black crows in the Disney film *Dumbo*. Buzzy is supposed to be black, and in, for example, *No Ifs, Ands or Butts* (1954) remarks, "Dat cat am a tobacco smokin' fiend!" The Buzzy cartoons were created by the same studio that otherwise produced fare as bland as Casper the Friendly Ghost and Baby Huey, to give an idea of how much of a mainstream norm this minstrelese was at the time.

Here was what was supposed to be a modern black "person," speaking in the lingo associated with corked-up white men. In the wake of depictions like this, we are left with a range of suspicions regarding the relationship between minstrelese and reality. Some people suppose that Black English traces back to minstrelese as created by whites, period, with the oppressed having unwittingly internalized the oppressors' take on them. One black thinker, for example, understands that black Americans developed a way of speaking in the deep past, but he thinks that today's Black English sprang from a different source: "The Negro dialect as we know it today was formed by White song-writers for minstrel shows around the time of the Civil War."

That theory is more often shared in conversation than

written down, but it is hardly uncommon. Amid the controversy over using Black English in the classroom in Oakland in 1997, Jack White, a black writer, wrote a piece in *Time* implying that Black English was merely a continuation of the ancient radio show *Amos 'n' Andy*, in which white actors played comic characters in minstrel dialect: "I put in a call to the Home of Retired Racial Stereotypes in a black section of Hollywood. The Kingfish answered. 'Holy mack'rul dere, Andy, somebody wants to talk 'bout dis 'ere Ebonics. Could you or Tonto tell Buckwheat come to da phone? He de resident expert.'" White's precise belief in the relationship between the speech of *Our Gang*'s Buckwheat and today's Black English is unknown. Yet his implications here are that no actual person ever spoke like Buckwheat and that his lines were caricatures.

Some writers have accused journalist H. L. Mencken of supporting this idea, with a comment in his *The American Language* opus that "The Negro dialect, as we know it today, seems to have been formulated by the song-writers for minstrel shows." However, Mencken has been misinterpreted. Too seldom consulted is what he wrote after that endlessly quoted sentence, where it is clear that he was referring to Black English in writing, not Black English as spoken. He wrote that Black English "did not appear in literature until the time of the Civil War; before that, as George Phillip Krapp shows in 'The English Language in America,' it was a vague and artificial lingo which had little relation to the actual speech of the Southern blacks." In referring to "the actual speech of Southern blacks," it is highly unlikely that Mencken thought they spoke the same way as southern whites. An American of his time would neither have assumed such a thing nor felt a compunction to pretend to, as many whites do today in surmising that black people simply speak southern English. Rather, Mencken was aware of an indigenously born black dialect, and considered it different from minstrelese. The black speech "as we know it today" that he referred to was this minstrelese, which would have indeed been the closest most American whites at the time got to any substantive amount of black speech.

Thus, to the extent to which tracing Black English to minstrelese has been influenced by Mencken's sentence, he didn't intend this. Nevertheless, given how often Black English is ridiculed, it is hardly a leap to suppose that its very roots are in the same kind of ridicule, which is what minstrel shows were all about.

In fact, many black people agree with Mencken and readily allow that there is a legitimate black speech variety, while perceiving a minstrel distortion ever looming elsewhere. For example, recall Maya Angelou's passage: "At school, in a given situation, we might respond with 'That's not unusual.' But in the street, meeting the same situation, we easily said 'It be's like that sometimes.'"

Yet people who would agree with that passage feel that what Angelou was referring to is different from the lyric to Irving Berlin's "Alexander's Ragtime Band," which is actually intended as a black statement, with lines such as "That's just the bestest band what am!" Or different from

Andy on *Amos 'n' Andy*, one of whose catchphrases was "I'se regusted" for "I'm disgusted." That, one senses, is a language no one ever spoke.

Especially clear on this point was Zora Neale Hurston, who laid down a skeptical analysis of minstrelese in 1934. She was fully aware that there was such a thing as Black English, and lovingly described aspects of it. Yet she noted in the meantime, "If we are to believe the majority of writers of Negro dialect and the burnt-cork artists, Negro speech is a weird thing, full of 'ams' and 'Ises.'" She objected that in actuality, "nowhere can be found the Negro who asks 'am it?' nor yet his brother who announces 'Ise uh gwinter.' He exists only for a certain type of writers and performers."

Hurston knew of what she wrote, not only because she was a southern black person but also because she had done extensive ethnographic work among poor black southerners under academic supervision. If anyone knew the truth about the most unfiltered Black English—that is, spoken by people in the South, isolated from whites, and semiliterate, such that Standard English exerted a lesser pull away from their most comfortable speaking styles—it was Hurston. She had the further advantage of hearing and documenting this speech as it still existed in her time. Since then, television, improved education, and highways have diluted what Hurston felt lucky to catch the final echoes of. One reading of Hurston's article is that any depiction of black people using *am* in ways that seem strange to us, or saying "I'se-a" this and "I'se-a" that, is cartoonish, a slur, a goofy version of black speech concocted by whites.

All Language Has History—and History Holds Surprises

However, actual evidence of how black Americans spoke in the past has a way of interfering with the assessment that this was speech concocted by whites. One reads and listens to black people born before the Civil War, expecting them to sound somewhere between Celie as limned by Alice Walker in *The Color Purple* and your favorite rapper. Instead, time and again one finds inconvenient bits of what seems like minstrelsy peeking out here and there. The truth is that minstrelese, while indeed an exaggeration, was also a window into the history of Black English.

Black English has not always been what it is today, and the way black people were depicted as speaking in old plays, skits, and songs was not entirely unmoored from reality. It was one of those cases where stereotype had a basis in fact. This need alarm no one. This perfectly normal human language of the nineteenth century was simply different from the perfectly normal human language that black Americans would come to speak in the century afterward.

To get a handle on how minstrel talk was not purely nonsense, we have to pull the camera back and look into something that may seem only diagonally related to the issue: that human speech is an inherently mutational thing. Alone, that may sound like a fancy way of saying that language always changes. But actually, it's something more specific, because our general sense of how language changes undershoots the reality.

What we usually mean by "language changes" is that:

1. slang changes
2. we always need new words for new things
3. when different people come together, they will exchange words.

That is, we imagine language change as driven by cultural factors, because this is the kind of language change we can hear happening in our daily lives. *Sext, iPad, quinoa*—slang, terminology, and foreign words, respectively—this is the language change we know.

Less obvious is that besides these things, language also always changes just *by itself*. In other words, it is "inherently mutational." Each generation hears sounds a little differently from the previous one and produces them differently. These days in America, in mainstream English, ever more people are pronouncing *aw* like *ah*, so that *caught* and *cot*, *raw* and *rah*, and *hawk* and *hock* rhyme. *Aw* and *ah* are similar sounds, and it happens that people started to hear *aw* more like *ah*– and for no reason. It's just the way the cookie crumbled.

When there are alternate ways of saying the same thing and no specific reason to choose between them, in one era one of them wins out, but in the next one, the other one may take over. A hundred years ago, most people used *dived* as the past tense of *dive*; now many prefer *dove*. The past tense of *sneak*? Most would now, after a pause, say *snuck*. But the Americans you see in starchy clothes barely smiling in old black-and-white photographs liked *sneaked* more. Why? For no more reason than over the past couple of decades, people have started saying "*Based off of* her point, I would say that . . ." rather than "*Based on* . . ." or "*Going from* . . ." These things happen, in the same way as fashions and fonts change.

The reason for dwelling on this at all here is that Black English has changed over time *by itself* in the same way as all human speech has. Old English became Middle English and then became Modern English. Latin became French, Spanish, and Italian. Sanskrit became Hindi. In the same way, Modern Black English is today's version of something that was different two hundred years ago—or even one hundred. Quite simply, there is no way that it wouldn't be. We already know that the slang in Black English of the seventies, when such things were first written down in any detailed way, is now antique. *Jive turkey*, *Right on!*, *boogie*—all of these terms signal a different time, one now associated with synthesizers, Afro Sheen, and gauzy videotape. A few decades before that, Hurston in her discussion of the dialect, outlined some in-group slang of her own time, much of which barely ring bells now. *Battle-hammed*? *Double-teen*? "I'll beat you till you smell like onions"?

It was the same way with the basic *structure* of Black English—how it sounded, how people put sentences together. If a black American were brought from 1850 into our time, we wouldn't have trouble conversing with him, but one of the first things we would notice is that he would *sound* weird to us. This is because sounds in Black English have changed since then in the same way as *cot* and *caught* are sounding more alike today than they did then.

Lost Sounds

To be able to see minstrelese as something other than idiocy—although that was part of it—we have to exercise our Wayback Machine muscles and immerse ourselves in the fact that in 1890, while black America certainly didn't sound like the rest of America, it didn't sound like Mary J. Blige or Jamie Foxx, either. The black American vocal soundscape was vastly different from the one we're used to, simply because it was a different point in time.

We know this because minstrels aren't the only people from a hundred-plus years ago whom we can now hear talking much more easily than ever before. Recording technology was invented just early enough to capture the sound of the speech of some black Americans born in the mid-nineteenth century.

One of the oddest things about the speech of these people is that they sound rather Irish or Scottish, or perhaps like Jamaicans, but never like black people familiar to us today. Today, we know Minnesotans for their "tight" pronunciation of the *oh* sound, such that *so* is not "soh-oo," the way most of us actually say it, but a pure "sohh," with no brief *oo* falloff. Black people in the 1800s pronounced *oh* in that same way. It was the same with the sound *ay*. Americans today pronounce *say* as "say-ee," with an *ee* falloff. But black people in the nineteenth century pronounced it as a straight *ay*, in a way that Americans associate with nonstandard British accents (*Downton Abbey* fans, think of how Anna says the name of her husband, Mr. Bates). Also, most Americans say *me* rather like "mih-ee." Black people of yore really said "mee."

George Johnson was the first black recording star in America, starting in the 1890s, although utterly forgotten today. It doesn't help that his two biggest hits were "The Laughing Coon" and "The Whistling Coon"—Johnson was bound by the expectations of white audiences of his time, which were openly and uncompromisingly racist. Yet recordings he did of those songs are, for better or for worse, the first time we can hear a black American using his voice, ever. And if we weren't told he was black, we would barely know at all, despite that Johnson was born a slave in 1846.

In "The Whistling Coon" (1898), Johnson sings "I had a little lady," pronouncing *lady* as "lehh-deee. . ." and thus sounding almost Scottish. He goes on: "I asked her if she'd marry mee, the answer is nohh," which again reminds us more of tartans or shamrocks (or plantains) than anything we associate with black Americans. In 1906, Johnson even spoke some lines at the end of "The Merry Mailman," and there isn't a hint of a black sound we would recognize in his voice at all.

Of course, Johnson was just one person. Plus, a wrinkle in his biography is that from an early age he lived with a white family. Perhaps their speech (whatever it was like— we can't know from this distance in time and technology) pulled his away from an originally blacker essence. Maybe, but Johnson wasn't alone. Bert Williams and George Walker were America's leading black stage stars in the first decade of the twentieth century. They were so popular that despite their color they were actually sought out to make some recordings—this at a time when the voices of all but a sliver of the most prominent black performers were lost to history.

Walker was the lead singer, and his stage persona was that of the quick-tongued, slick-dancing dandy, based on the minstrel-style expectations of the era. One expects Walker, therefore, to sound like some version of what our modern ears process as black, but Walker sounded nothing like that. He was born in the early 1870s in Kansas, and he sounds more like what we would expect of a white person of that background and period. "My Little Zulu Babe" was one of the songs Williams and Walker recorded, and Walker pronounces babe with the same tight vowel that Joanne Froggatt's Anna on *Downton Abbey* uses when pronouncing the name Bates—on that vowel he sounds more like Craig Ferguson (or a calypso singer) than we would expect any black American man to sound. In another song, "Pretty Desdemone," Walker sings "Pretty Desdemohhhn, I want to call mah ohhhhn," sounding like someone out of *Fargo*.

Walker also gets in the required minstrelly laughs, showing that he considered himself to be singing "blackly" for the audience, and he also sings "**mah** ohhn" for *my own*, with the "mah" for *my* that no one in Minnesota uses. So it wasn't that there was no overlap with modern black speech. One clear ongoing thread between the black sound then and the black sound now is the *ah* for *igh*, which we pick up even amid the ancient crackles and hisses. Bert Williams, in his recordings during the same time, also sounds half modern "black" and half something we can barely define, uses the tight *ay,* and also pronounces a word like *out* more like "eh-oot" ("Where was Moses when the lights went eh-oot?").

Still, couldn't this have been a matter of singing conventions? People don't always pronounce things when they sing the same way they pronounce them when speaking. Today most English-speaking pop singers subconsciously sing with a black dialect sound, whatever their race and however they talk in real life. Could singers like Johnson and Walker and Williams have been singing with vowels tilted toward white speech, in line with the more formal atmosphere of American society at the time?

Recordings of ex-slaves in the late 1930s and 1940s talking rather than singing would indicate otherwise. In them, black people born before the Civil War talk the way the Georges Johnson and Walker sang: kind of like Irishmen, Fountain Hughes (a man) was born in the 1840s in Virginia, in slavery, and was interviewed in 1949. Soberly and casually, he describes his early life with the same vowels as the singers. In one anecdote he says, "I didn't have nohwhere to goh . . . we knew a man that had a livery stehh-ble . . ." This is the general sound of these ex-slaves in one recording after another. Moreover, around the time when these recordings were made, researchers transcribed the speech of other southern black people of this age on paper, Henry Higgins–style, and the results were the same: "cohts" for *coats,* "hee" for *he,* rather than "hih-ee," and so on.

By the late twentieth century, one could even catch the tail end of this difference in generations of living black people. In North Carolina, linguist Walt Wolfram recorded four generations of a black family: a boy, his mother, his grand-father, and his great-grandfather. The great-grandfather did not sound like an old version of the boy: He had the rural white sound I have been describing of black people of his vintage. It's the mother who spoke what we immediately recognize as "how black people talk" in our times; the grandfather's way of speaking was transitional.

This means that movies and plays where black people in the past speak with the same vowels blacks use now—that is, sound like today's black people—are historically inaccurate. This may not be a bad thing—having such characters talk like the ex-slaves on the recordings would sound so unfamiliar as to detract from the artistry, just as otherwise historically accurate films about the early nineteenth century quietly spare the ample facial hair fashionable in the era for male actors cast as romantic figures. However, the black men at the beginning of the 2012 film *Lincoln*, or in the *Buffalo Soldiers* TV movie, or all of the characters in August Wilson's plays set earliest in the twentieth century, such as *Gem of the Ocean* and *Joe Turner's Come and Gone*, would sound to our modern ears, like weird hybrids of Caribbean and Celtic people, more than like the black people in *The Wire*.

Indeed, vowels like the ones we hear in the old recordings are also part of what distinguishes West Indians' speech, and likely, black people had vowels like this in previous centuries because West Indian speech influenced the formation of Black English. The first slaves brought to Charleston, South Carolina, one of the depots from which black America developed, had formerly worked in Barbados and would have spoken that island's variety of West Indian patois, which then became Gullah Creole. Gullah then entered into the mix of regional Irish and British dialects that became Black English, and the "clean" vowels were probably one of Gullah's echoes into what became the speech of black people across the South and beyond.

My older relatives say that my paternal grandfather (whom I never met because he died a few years before I was born) sounded somewhat West Indian, even though he was born near Atlanta in 1901 and had nothing to do with the Caribbean. Likely, what sounded West Indian about him to black people of later generations was that he must have had the residual "ay" and "oh" vowels we can hear in scratchy recordings of black Americans born in the nineteenth century. He was raised by children of slaves, black people just a generation after the ex-slaves recorded in the 1930s and 1940s. It would have been surprising had he not sounded anything like them.

Ye Olde Black English

Now that we understand that *sounding* black in 1890 was quite different from sounding black in the twenty-first century, we are in a better place to know that *putting* things in a black way—that is, Black English's very sentence patterns—was different. As our black time traveler from 1850 got comfortable with us, we'd hear him popping up with strange ways of putting a sentence together, just as white Americans from then would likely talk about how someone dived, rather than dove, into a lake. As disconcerting as this might seem today, some of the ways this man spoke would parallel the way black people were depicted as speaking in minstrel shows. Minstrelese is partly mockery, but partly what Black English actually once was.

A useful example is the use of *am* in place of *is* and *are*. Hurston, recall, ridiculed minstrelese for the *am* fetish, and some scholarly coverage of Black English implies that Black English has never used *am* this way, or that the issue is ambiguous. After all, sentences like "All the streets am just the same" sound very awkward today. Sure, Black English has its differences from Standard English, but "streets am just the same"? Nobody says this. It's hard even to utter it today and feel natural. Certainly this must be just naked minstrel fabrication.

Yet that sentence about the streets is from Harlem Renaissance writer Claude McKay's *Home to Harlem*, a chronicle of lower-class black life in Harlem in the 1920s, with rich and endless depiction of the casual speech of southern black people who had moved north. McKay, of course, was black, and he wrote his book with an almost anthropological intent, wanting to reveal and dignify the lives of a kind of black person who most black litterateurs of the period preferred not to dwell upon in public discussion. McKay was not, therefore, making fun of these people or trying to make them seem exotic. And yet his people use *am* in the way that seems so odd to us:

Oh, these here am different chippies, I tell you.
Lawdy! though, how the brown-skin babies am
    humping it along!
Black womens when theyse ugly am all sistahs of
    Satan.
Niggers am awful close-mouthed in some things.
I tell you, niggers am amazing sometimes.

It's hard to miss that McKay did not hold back in depicting his characters' honest, and often even vulgar, feelings—but that means that this was real speech, not people dressing up their talk in its Sunday best. And the verb *am* is all over the place. But was Claude McKay making these up?

To assess this, there are various things we must consider. One is that McKay was unlikely to have gotten down *exactly* how such people were speaking. McKay grew up in Jamaica and came to the United States only when he was in his early twenties. This means that despite his strong identification with the American black community, he was in no sense a native speaker, or even hearer, of Black English.

Also, if McKay happened to have an explicit interest in getting down on paper *exactly* how black Harlemites from the South spoke, then we might take his rendition as accurate. However, there is no record of his having that intention. Rather, he was an artist depicting the speech of the people around him in a way that seemed faithful to him, but that may have been a secondary concern to the narrative and artistic substance of his novel. The result would have been close enough to the linguistic reality to satisfy—but hardly documentationally pristine. After all, even black Americans can miss the nuances of Black English when writing it down. Human speech is so complicated that no layman (or even linguist) can fully understand the workings of his own language or dialect.

I know of a book in which a black author, to indicate identification with all black people despite some polite criticisms of certain aspects of inner-city culture, occasionally interjects "I be ghetto!" for a note of humor. The point is clear, and harmless, but if one were to *nitpick*—which would only be necessary for making this one point here— Black English speakers don't use *be* in a sentence like that. As we've discussed earlier, that *be* is used for things that are a regular practice, like going shopping, not permanent things, like existence or membership in a category of people. "I'm ghetto!" is the proper rendition of that sentence in Black English, which wouldn't have been of much help to the author, since it happens to be the same as it would be in Standard English. All this is to say that if black people themselves can accidentally distort the dialect when reproducing it, then certainly we wouldn't expect a Jamaican's rendition to be perfect.

This does not mean, however, that McKay's rendition of black speech was a caricature. McKay was aware of actual minstrel distortion of black speech, but it is unlikely that he wrote an entire book, an all-black novel, in which the dialect he put in his black characters' mouths was mere minstrel nonsense. This leads to an inevitable conclusion: McKay's dialogue is a window into the past.

Another way we know this is that no one seems to have called him on the dialect depicted, despite quite a few black critics who reviled exposing the lower-class side of Harlem life to white readers (W. E. B. DuBois famously wrote that after reading it, he wanted a shower). Their problem was that such people were being shown to the larger public, not that they had been depicted inaccurately. Of course, if we go by Hurston's comment in 1934 on the depiction of black dialect in general, McKay's "am" and "I'se gwine" language qualifies automatically as nonsense. But *Home to Harlem* was published in 1928, six years before Hurston's comment. The book was a sensation: We can be all but certain that Hurston, as a member of the Harlem Renaissance group to which McKay also belonged, read it.

Hurston's remarks on the dialect were actually pretty brief—she intended no scholarly investigation of the issue in her article. Here is a reasonable assumption: Hurston had heard black people using the language McKay depicts, or something close to it. Her problem was with depictions of such language that were so inaccurate and clumsy as to qualify as mockery.

Whether McKay was conscious of it or not, there is a systematicity in how his characters use *am*. While I have declared that systematicity cannot convince people that a Black English trait is "correct," that doesn't mean that it doesn't demonstrate that something people say is based on the cognitive coherence of the human brain. Just as modern black people use *up* with a particular meaning, McKay's characters use *am* with a particular intention: jocularly vulgar evaluation of one kind or another. McKay uses the *am* with the word *nigger*—intended in the same in-group love/hate connotation that confuses so many today:

> One thing I know is niggers am made foh life.
> And niggers am got to work hard foh that.
> . . . where bad, hell-bent nigger womens am giving
>   up themselves to open sin.
> Some music the niggers am making.
> You nevah know when niggers am gwineta git
>   crazy-mad.

Otherwise, the *am* is used in references of a certain kind to women, as we have already seen, with the line I first cited ("all the streets am just the same") being the only one in the book that isn't "salty."

As awkward as this particular usage may seem, systematicity in language can be about more than marking things like past tense and plurality. We have seen how *up* is systematic—thus is grammar—in marking intimacy. Another Black English feature is *come*, which can be used to mark indignation, as in "He comes telling me he won't have the money till Thursday" or "Don't come yelling you don't have a broom when you done threw it out with the rest of the trash." As linguist Arthur Spears showed the linguistics community in the 1980s, although one would never think of this usage of *come* as anything but, well, people saying *come*, it actually doesn't mean "approach." It is, of all things, a marker of pique. In the same vein, McKay uses *am* as a marker of what we might call vernacular affection. Today,

Black English does something similar with "brothas" and "sistahs." McKay's characters did it with *am*.

As to whether this kind of usage of *am* is "broken" (systematic or not), Old English comes up again. In Old English, there were two verbs that meant *be*, with separate forms. One *be* meant "being" in a mundane sense—what *is* for dinner—but the other *be* meant being in the sense of embodiment, eternity, like mountains, deities, and the future. One had to distinguish those two kinds of being. To learn Old English means dealing with something like the uses shown below (I have altered the forms a little bit toward how they would sound and be spelled in Modern English to avoid the Teutonic unfamiliarity of Old English itself):

	being just normally	*being* in a godly sense: forever
I	am	be
you	art	bist
he/she/it	is	bith
we/ you all / they	sind	bee-th

So, this was more complicated than the *be* we're used to. Today's *am/are/is/are* have elbowed *bist, bith,* and *bee-th* out of the picture, with no more distinction now between being and Being. Therefore, why is it so barbaric that Black English once spread *am* around a little?

Yet the fact remains that McKay was making his lines up. What did real people sound like? Given that McKay used *am* so confidently and freely in *Home to Harlem*, it shouldn't surprise us that many of the ex-slaves recorded in the 1930s and 1940s used *am* where we wouldn't use it today. Real people said things like these:

> The truth am, I can't 'member like I used to.
> And people says now dat Aunt Harriet am de bes' cook in Madisonville.
> Dey brung massa in and I's jus' as white as he am den.
> Him am kind to everybody.
> Charcoal and honey and onions for de li'l baby am good.

(I, too, am mystified by that last one!) These sentences are not the product of ridicule. Sober, committed people, many of them scholars, transcribed what these people said. Now and then they may have misheard, but there are simply too many occurrences of *am* for all of them to be fiction. Plus, if the people were actually saying *is* and *are*, how much like *am* do those words sound?

So, when minstrelese depicted black people using *am* in a way that sounds fake to us, it was actually based on an earlier Black English reality. Characters speaking minstrelese often used *am* across the board, seemingly ignorant that the forms *are* and *is* even existed. We can be sure that no black person ever talked like that. However, we can be just as sure that early Black English did involve *variably* using *am* beyond the first-person singular. Just as the sound of Black English has changed, its grammar has changed. After all, why would Black English sit still while the English language as a whole kept morphing along in the mouths of everyone else in the United States (and elsewhere). I find it hard to believe that Hurston, for example, never heard anyone using *am* in a way she wouldn't have used it. She was concerned with accuracy and degree.

On what the reality with *am* was, a reasonable hypothesis is that early Black English speakers code-switched. At one pole, they used standard, or standardlike, forms of *be*—no ex-slave or literary character uses only *am* and has no command of *are* and *is*. At another pole, *am* could be used for *are* and *is*. This would have been a symptom of Black English emerging from adults learning English past the age when they could vacuum a new language up perfectly, the way children can. One of the first things adults simplify under such conditions is *be*. Think how irregular that verb is: *am, are, is, was, were, been, ain't*. Why wouldn't grown-ups learning all of that, when needing a break, let one form do a lot of the lifting? The Africans did, and the form they leaned on was *am*.

Those slaves' children however, were born in the United States, and black people born in the United States had enough contact with whites to know the standard forms as well. Worldwide, in situations like that, often people don't simply toss away the old rendition. Instead, they retain it in their speech repertoire but assign it a particular social function. They switch between the standard version and the old rendition, with the old rendition used for more casual or intimate speech and topics. This is how black Americans use Black English alongside Standard English today.

As such, for early Black English speakers, the *am* usage

was colloquial, not ignorant. McKay's usage of *am* suggests that as generations passed, this usage of *am* narrowed even more, being used mainly for emotional effect, such as to express a bluff, levelling kind of cameraderie, or express sexual attraction. The undertone would have been that *am* was old-school and down-to-earth, and therefore handy for striking a note of cultural authenticity. This is the usage of *am* McKay captures. By World War II, it would seem, the old *am*'s day had passed and new generations weren't using it at all.

When we read a line like black writer Pauline Hopkins's in her 1900 short story "General Washington: A Christmas Story," where a black character says "Bisness am mighty peart" (*peart* is a variant of *pert* and here meant "hopping"), only at our peril do we assume that Hopkins was writing minstrelese to appease white readers. Actual black people of nineteenth-century birth, speaking seriously about their lives, spoke exactly such usages of *am* into the historical record. In Alex Haley's *Roots*, he has slaves at the end of the Revolutionary War saying "Freedom am won!" I remember finding that utterance implausible when I read it in the book back in the seventies (Mom made me read the *whole thing*). But given that an actual ex-slave is recorded as having recounted in an interview "Den [Then] surrender am 'nounced and massa tells us we's free," I beg Mr. Haley's pardon. And since a 1973 article was the first to air this sentence beyond the archives, Haley, writing *Roots* around that time, just may have modeled his sentence on this genuine one.

The same lessons come from other items that sound weird now. Hurston's "Ise uh gwinter" gives us all we need. Let's break it down. First, was the "I'se" part just a slur implying that black people can't conjugate verbs? Today, it is easy to suppose that actual black people never said "I'se" at all and that this was just something minstrel performers made up. Yet the case is actually the same as with *am*: McKay made use of it ("Ise gwine to show you some real queens"), Langston Hughes used it in one of his "Simple" stories, "Last Whipping" ("I's a man—and you ain't gonna whip me"), and ex-slaves used it a lot.

What Hurston was referring to, then, was that black people were so often depicted as using it inaccurately. A random but perfect example is in the melodramatic little novel *What Can She Do?* (1873), by Edward Payson Roe, one of those three-named authors who was a bestseller before World War I and yet is utterly unheard of and barely readable today. In *What Can She Do?* Hannibal was a black butler born in the South. Roe's portrait of Hannibal is intended as poignant rather than comical, and one senses Roe trying to get down how such a person actually spoke. However, Roe clearly operated on a basic premise that Hannibal's speech is "ungrammatical," which threw off his ear for how a Hannibal would have used, for example, "I'se." Hannibal uses it not only the way we now know actual black people did but also in ways no actual black people would have. Roughly, for Hannibal "I'se" is practically a replacement for *I* overall, in instances such as "I'se hope you'll forgive me," "I'se isn't," "I'se don't know 'zactly," and "I'se know 'tis" for "I know it is." But no ex-slave is recorded using "I'se" in this way, nor do black authors committed to depicting their people honestly have people use *I'se* in this way. It's depictions like this, which were common, that motivated comments like Hurston's.

One might ask, "Did *any* black people ever actually say 'gwine' for 'going to'?" Today one drops in the word *gwine* to sound like a cartoonish rube, whether a white or a black one; we associate it with *Gone with the Wind* and, at least by my own reading, old plays and probably bad ones. Reading Hurston's dismissal of "Ise uh gwinter" reinforces us in a sense that *gwine* has always been something caricaturists put in black mouths. Yet again, McKay put it in *his* characters' mouths, as in the sentence above, or in "What kind o' bust-up youse gwine to have with me?" Plus, ex-slaves used *gwine* quite freely. Lucian Abernathy, eighty-five, born in Mississippi and interviewed in the late 1930s, said, "I knows you gwine take plumb good care of dem chillun." Boston Blackwell, ninety-eight, and born in Arkansas, was interviewed around the same time. In his narrative, he said, "Here he come, yelling me to get down: he gwine whip me 'cause I'se a thief, he say." The unpleasant subject matter of many of these ex-slave quotations is harrowing, but it also shows that the forms these people were using were real: No one would have distorted his or her speech amid the urgency and intimacy of recounting events like these.

Yet Hurston was still correct that "Ise uh gwinter" was not a legitimate sentence and demonstrated the exaggeration of minstrelese. The use of that sentence to say "I'm going to" or "I'm gonna" is wrong. Ex-slaves are not recorded as saying it, although it pops up often in white people's depictions of black people speaking. It isn't that the "uh"—usually written as *a,* as in *a-rockin'*—didn't exist in itself. It was, like all else, a piece of *grammar* in early Black English (and much other English in the United States and on the other side of the pond). It usually referred to something going on over some time. "Him was a-settin' at a window in de house one night" and "Dey was jus' a-eatin' green apples" are two examples from the ex-slave narratives. That meaning doesn't make sense with *gwine,* as in *going to.*

When you say you are going to do something as in "gonna" do it, you're talking about the future, not describing yourself as in the act of locomotion, "a-going," like "a-settin' at a window" or "a-eating apples." This is why "Ise uh gwinter" (chop some wood, go pick up my daughter, etc.)" doesn't make sense and properly sounded inaccurate to Hurston. Even at a century-plus's remove from a time when anyone would venture that black Americans anywhere said "a-gwineta," it feels clumsy in the mouth and head. There's a reason—it is "bad grammar" in terms of how *a-* is, or was, used. Hence one suspects that even one of McKay's lines, "I ain't agwine to have no Harlem boys seducin' mah man away fwom me," wasn't true to life.

If Black English Never Changed, It *Would* Be Broken

BLACK ENGLISH IS LEGITIMATE LANGUAGE not only because it has nuanced structure of a kind that would challenge the adult learner, just as learning Finnish or Fijian would. It is legitimate language, driven by normal human minds, because it changes over time while always maintaining functionality as a vehicle of nuanced communication, rather than flaking away like slang or some in-group fad. Black English has a history in the *structural* sense, just as Standard English has marched from Old to Middle to its present version and it exists in time as well as in space. Abraham Lincoln would find it odd to hear someone say "A house is being built over there"—since for someone of his time the proper expression was "There is a house building over there," In the same way, a rural black woman in 1850 would find it odd to hear her great-great-great-grandson saying "Folks be tryin' all the time," because in 1850 the unconjugated habitual *be* didn't exist yet—it only came in around World War I. Her great-great-great-grandson would find it odd to hear her say, as she might, "Dose people am your other relatives an' you gwine to town to meet 'um tomorrow." But hear it he very well might, because back then, a great many normal black people spoke in that way.

White minstrel players did not make up out of whole cloth the way they depicted black people as talking, and today's Black English certainly does not trace to a cynical fabrication by those white men. White minstrels made something up by exaggerating what they heard at one point in Black English's time line, and because the white version got so much play, it was easier for many to hear, for a while, than the actual black speech of the time.

Today, though, we're in a better place to understand the reality of the issue. We can hear ex-slaves talking at the press of a button. It's getting easier every year to listen to ancient recordings of black pop—and blues—singers. We can perceive that Black English, like all forms of English, has glided through time, ever turning over, ever challenging our expectations. That's what human speech does.

CHAPTER FIVE

Through a Lens Darkly?

PERCEIVING BLACK ENGLISH AS IT IS: LIFE LESSONS

M Y AIM HAS NOT BEEN SIMPLY to describe some things and make some points, as if I merely wanted to add to the bookshelf of books on black American speech as a kind of exercise. I have sought to help the reader actually hear Black English in a new way, to hear it as an alternate kind of English rather than as bad grammar and a lively slang. I have not succeeded in this goal if my readers perhaps take in what I have tried to get across in terms of some facts and observations but then, back out in real life, are still prone to hearing the speech of black Americans as regrettable errors, cringing at the idea that there is even a such thing as a Black English in any way, quietly equating the whole concept with minstrel shows or other kinds of distortion, et cetera.

I have failed if the reader's response to discussions of Ebonics or African-American Vernacular English or Black English is still, to any degree, a question such as "What's that all about?" or "What exactly do you mean, 'Black' English?" or an impression that anyone described as speaking Black English is necessarily being depicted as incapable of speaking Standard English. I want you to be truly comfortable with the idea that there is indeed a black way of speaking, that there isn't anything wrong with it, that it would be bizarre if such speech did not exist, and that it is spoken alongside Standard English, not in opposition to it.

However, Black English (and there is a such thing!) is spoken in a society in which racism still exists, and the issue of what we do about racism is decidedly complex. On Black English, then, even if we know that there is such a thing beyond slang and perceived mistakes, opinions will differ on where we draw certain lines, where the past leaves off and the future marches on, and where to beware of slippery slopes. The reader may disagree with some of my opinions. That is normal and healthy. However, my intention is to show that even where issues will occasion debate, the debate will be more productive if we understand what Black English is—such as, preliminarily, that it *is* at all.

Barack Obama's "Negro Dialect"

IN 2008, SENATE LEADER HARRY REID occasioned some controversy when he traced Barack Obama's appeal to voters to his being light-skinned, for one, and then also to his speaking with "no Negro dialect unless he wanted to have one." When this got out into the media in 2010, Reid formally apologized to Obama. Technically, he shouldn't have had to, because he had been speaking simple truth—and on more than one level.

The word *Negro* was unfortunate, but more in the sense of being awkward than being a slur. *Negro* is such an antique term for black Americans that we can be sure that Reid switched from *black* and then to *African-American* decades ago. He is not on record as having for some reason continued to refer to black people by a dispreferred name, an insistence that would be odd for a modern politician. Nor is it realistic to suppose that by "Negro dialect" he meant something like the cartoony minstrelese of *Amos 'n' Andy*. First, black Americans don't speak that way, and Reid is a psychologically sane human being who could be under no impression otherwise. Second, if Reid for some reason actually was under the impression that most black people talk like minstrel characters, wouldn't a basic grasp of the sociopolitical tenor of his times lead him to keep that impression to himself? People don't get elected to Congress and stay there for so long without certain basic political smarts.

Rather, Reid was grasping for an official term for Black English. That he had to grasp is not surprising, in that we must recall that black people's speech barely has a widely known official name. To most, the term *Ebonics* has a slangy association with the street, and is also thought of as a passel of mistakes. Naturally, then, Reid, if he was aware of that term, refrained from applying it to Obama. But then, what else was he going to call it? *African-American Vernacular English* is primarily an academic term, alien in any black barbershop or church across the nation. *Black English* is the term I have used, but as we well know, a great many find it difficult to imagine just what this term refers to other than, again, mistakes and slang.

Reid, then, tried something vaguely academic-sounding that he may even have picked up somewhere along the line in the sixties and seventies. Back then, Black English actually was often called "Negro English" in print by those who were beginning to study it; when *Negro* was still current, "Negro English" didn't have the condescending tone that it has today. As late as 1973, to take an example at random, an article that got around among linguists and educators interested in black speech was titled "Issues in the Analysis of Nonstandard Negro English," and this article appeared in the prestigious *Journal of English Linguistics.* Truth to tell, I'm not sure what most people, including Reid, would have come up with as a "respectable" appellation for black speech.

Of course, however, many would contest that Reid should not have been referring to Barack Obama and Black English in the same breath at all. Reid was taken as condescending—and in a racist way—for praising Obama for *not speaking* Black English.

Yet Reid thought he was giving Obama a compliment, as many would have likewise assumed. Here is where this book comes in. Underlying the offense many took upon Reid's remarking upon Obama's *not* speaking Black English was the idea that Black English is simply errors. That is, Reid seemed impressed that an educated, accomplished black man could speak without making mistakes.

It is a safe assumption, given how common the misimpression is that Black English is merely error-ridden, that Harry Reid shares with most Americans the idea that not using the verb *be* or saying "He don't be going" is broken, rather than alternate, English. However, his finding it notable that an educated man doesn't make these so-called mistakes cannot be taken as stereotyping: Most black people, regardless of their level of education, do talk in two ways. One is Standard English, but the other is Black English—which is so widely thought of as merely a flouting of the rules. We now know that such people are bidialectal, not just bad at keeping their linguistic pants up. But we would hardly expect a career politician to be one of those in on the good news.

Key in assessing this issue is that it isn't only whites who have that opinion of Black English. Black people shared the grand old Ebonics e-mail jokes in the nineties as often as whites did. It is a standard experience among specialists in Black English and other nonstandard dialects that people who speak such varieties quite often claim not to, and see the dialect's features as mere mistakes. During the controversy over whether Oakland's school board should espouse using Ebonics as a teaching bridge to Standard English, black journalists were as vehement as white ones in trashing Black English as broken language. In their book *Spoken Soul*, John and Russell Rickford recount:

> This was the fundamental conviction of many of the black journalists who sounded off on Ebonics. Whether liberal or conservative, Black English in their minds represented a dark side, a streak of backwardness that had to be shunned, purged, stripped away, or lopped off like an unsightly carbuncle in order for the race to advance.

During this same controversy, when I was giving my various presentations and making media appearances, black moms quite vibrantly competent in Black English often said. "I would never talk that way to my kids." But frankly, they actually did—alternating normally between the formal and informal poles and using Black English for the latter pole. All of us, when raised in cultures where the standard written language is elevated as "the real language," have a distorted sense of how we actually speak unmonitored. That's a race-neutral truth, and if you don't believe me, set your phone on record mode when you're chatting with friends and listen later. You will marvel at the gap between what you'd write and how you just gab. Around the same time as the Okland controversy, the guy who cut my hair at a black barbershop in Berkeley dismissively referred to the Ebonics in the news as "Oh yeah, that language!" when "that language" was precisely the dialect he was fluent in. To him, "that language" was just weird, incorrect grammar—despite that it was what he had learned on his mother's knee. Black educators who have learned that Black English is a system rather than a disaster encounter an uphill climb in convincing not just whites but also black people of what they have learned. Lesson: Harry Reid's take on Black English is American, not just white.

Reid's statement, taken as a whole, could be read more sanguinely. In describing Obama as having "no Negro dialect *unless he wanted to have one*," Reid was getting at the basic reality that black people use Black English as part of a tool kit when choosing to strike a certain kind of note. The idea that Obama uses Black English when he "wants" it but otherwise speaks Standard English is a more accurate take on how Obama, and many other black people, talk than the less enlightened idea that black speech is merely a matter of stark ignorance, impervious to improvement. Black English is an element in one's tool kit. This is certainly better than the compliment educated black people often get about being "articulate," where the implication is that you speak Standard English as a labored stunt, or that black people other than you talk "wrong."

That impression can truly rankle. Whites are often perplexed that educated black people don't like being called "articulate." The rub is that a white person speaking the same way often would not be called "articulate." The implication is that your not making "mistakes," alone, renders you remarkable, which feels like a bar being set awfully low. It's as if you are thought of as *executing* Standard English, rather than its being as integral to your soul as it is to any white person's. My favorite example of this type of thinking was a remark made by someone who genuinely thought he was giving me a compliment by praising me for how "confidently" I spoke "my Standard English," as if I dream in Ebonics and am ever on my guard for the occasional *aks* or *ain't* to pop up. "But you really are articulate," some people object. And okay, I may have a certain knack with words—but the problem is, you can never be sure how people are really hearing you. So very many articulate white people are never called such, because no one considers it remarkable that they can speak effectively, especially if they have advanced degrees and speak in public a lot.

It's less fraught, then, for Reid to think of Obama as strategically choosing to fail—even though he, along with many Americans, is wrong in what he thinks of as communicative failure—rather than choosing to speak standardly. Reid gets that one can speak two ways and keep them separate. One wonders whether he actually did happen to peruse an article about "Negro English" back in the day.

Whether or not you agree with my analysis of Reid's comment, the proper response to it was not simply to dismiss the idea that there is such a thing as a "Negro dialect" variety local to black Americans, or that educated black people often have it as part of their verbal tool kit. Reid's statement was likely founded in some assumptions about Black English that don't stand up to science, but those assumptions are, alas, commonplace.

Baby Mama: A Touch of Calypso?

Black English is such a phantom concept that certain elements of it now and then strike listeners as isolated peculiarities rather than as integral components of a living and ordinary system of speaking. It's like finding a wedding ring on the sidewalk and assuming it's a little amulet from moon people. We fall into such ideas only because it can be so hard to understand that Black English actually has something worthy of being called grammar.

An example is the proposed etymology of the terms *baby mama* and *baby daddy*, referring to a male or female parent of one's child to whom one is not married. Rap group Outkast's megahit "Ms. Johnson" mainstreamed *baby mama* in 2000, dedicated to "all the baby mamas' mamas," and by 2008 the term was ensconced enough to be the title of a comedy about middle-class whites. Meanwhile, there have been T-shirts reading JESUS IS MY BABYDADDY.

Why *baby mama* and not *baby's mama*? Even *the Oxford English Dictionary* has fallen for a tasty notion that the source is Jamaican Creole (patois), in which there is a term *baby-mother*. However, the chance is infinitesimal that a random locution from the Caribbean would become common coin in black America. Sure, there are Jamaicans in the United States, but black Americans have been no more in the habit of picking up their lingo than other Americans have been in embracing the latest slang from Toronto.

The mistake is in assuming that *baby mama* and *baby daddy* are singletons, isolated expressions oddly letting the possessive *s* go. And that's what they look like when we are denied awareness of the parallel system of speaking English that Black English is. One trait of Black English grammar is that it can do without the possessive *s*—not just when talking about parentage but in general. This is the kind of simplificatory trait in the dialect that I argued against highlighting at the outset. However, this hardly means that the trait isn't real.

"Sometime Rolanda bed don't be made up" is an example from Lisa Green's grammatical description of Black English. At a fast-food restaurant staffed by black Americans, I once heard "That's Brenda drink, not his." In the eighties, the bawdy black comedian Robin Harris did a comedy routine about a woman's naughty brood of children, laced with the catchphrase "Dem Bebe kids!" (for "Those are Bebe's kids!").

It goes back even further. In the 1943 film *This Is the Army*, legendary black boxer Joe Louis appears in a cameo, where he says, "All I know is I'm in Uncle Sam's army and we are on God's side." Or at least that's what the script had, but the way Louis actually rendered the line was, in good Ebonics style, "All I know is I'm in Uncle Sam army." Louis wasn't channeling calypso; he was using the same grammatical regularity that elsewhere yields "Rolanda bed," 'Bebe kids," and "baby mama." To wit: A black person saying "baby mama" is simply rendering "baby's mama" with the rules of Black English instead of those of Standard English, just as they would say "Brenda drink." They are expressing the possessive relation in the same way as legions of languages worldwide that have no possessive marker. In Indonesian, mother is *ibu*, baby is *bayi*, and "mother of baby" is *ibu bayi* "mother baby," used in some places to express the same meaning as "baby mama" is in the United States.

One might ask, though, where black Americans picked up this grammatical regularity. There are two answers. One is that African slaves simplified English somewhat and the next generation modeled their speech partly on their parents'. We know that this did not result in broken speech, because Modern English's possessive *s* is the only one left of many possessive endings that Old English had, and yet no one considers this a threatening matter.

Also, many black people in early America likely heard whites dropping the possessive *s*, too, as hard as it is for us to imagine this today, when it is absent from any white dialect of American English. Remember the indentured servants from schoolroom history lessons who worked alongside slaves on southern plantations? Well, it wasn't elite Brits who wound up laboring in the Alabama cotton fields; it was slaves who worked alongside folks speaking rural brands of English quite unlike that of Henry Higgins. Even today you might hear someone in Yorkshire say among friends "My sister husband" rather than "My sister's husband." Court transcriptions of statements by London prisoners in the sixteenth and seventeenth centuries show that lower-class folk regularly said things like "Goldwell wiffe" instead of "Goldwell's wife" and "Barlowe owne brother" instead of "Barlowe's own brother." Many of these people were due for transportation to plantations in Virginia and beyond. The expression *baby mama* wouldn't have been long in coming.

So, what's up with the term *baby mama*? It's just *baby's mama* with Black English grammar.

Who Dat—What's That?

IT IS TRADITIONAL TO CHANT "Who dat!" at New Orleans Saints football games. In 2010, there was a brief kerfuffle when the National Football League threatened to sue T-shirt owners who were selling WHO DAT T-shirts, claiming that it owned the trademark to "Who dat." For a spell, a question circulated" "What's 'who dat' anyway?"

Unpacking the issue leads in any number of directions, many of interest to fans of ancient pop culture. At the football games, the full chant is "Who dat say dey gonna beat dem Saints?" However, this sentence has still led people to ask, "But what's the *who dat*, by itself, *from*?" It turns out that people have been saying "Who dat?" in any number of pop-culture scenarios since the nineteenth century; the expression has a certain percussive essence that lends itself to doggerel. Chants and exchanges involving *who dat* were staples of old jazz bands, novelty songs, and comedy routines. The source of these, in turn, was minstrel shows, where trading off the question "who dat" was a standard bit.

The pop-culture history of *who dat* is, in itself, interesting. However, the fact that people were saying "who dat" on minstrel stages does not mean that the people in the stands in New Orleans are unknowingly mouthing minstrelese. Just as the Jamaican etymology of *baby mama* strays too far away in space, tracing the Saints chant "who dat" to white men corked up during the Reconstruction era takes us needlessly far back in time. It's like assuming that the Château Lafite wine you're drinking was made in the late eighteenth century because you've read about Thomas Jefferson liking it, but are unaware that Château Lafite is still being made today.

Who dat is simply Black English. In Black English, the verb can often be left out. This means that "Who is that?" Can be "Who dat?" Black culture plays a major part in New Orleans culture, and this includes language—such that a football chant could be phrased as "Who dat say dey gonna beat dem Saints?", as in "Who is that who says they're going to beat those Saints?" A natural step from that chant is to shorten it to the simple question "Who dat?"—meant in a taunting "It's on" way. That's all there is to it. This is something that could easily happen today, even if no one had ever said "who dat" in minstrel shows or songs. *Who dat?* isn't an isolated idiom whose origin requires smoking out like that of *raining cats and dogs* or *dressed to the nines*. "Who dat?" is a vanilla sentence from an alternate English that thrives alongside the standard variety, a sentence using the same construction—linguists call it "zero copula"—that yields sentences like "She my sister" for "She's my sister" and "Where da broom?" for "Where is the broom?" Today's Saints chant arose naturally from the millions of people still using the grammar that produces it.

That grammar existed in the minstrel era, as well, which is why the phrase *Who dat?* could be used in routines then. However, in line with my earlier point about minstrelese, the minstrels didn't make up *who dat* out of thin air. Zora Neale Hurston's characters, carefully and lovingly drawn portraits of the poor rural black people she grew up among and later studied, regularly used "Who dat?" in her works of the twenties and thirties. In *Jonah's Gourd Vine*, Amy asks, "Who dat coming heah, John?"

Also, unlike in the *baby mama* case, where its modern origins make a Caribbean etymology unlikely, *who dat* does likely have some connection to the West Indies. One of the elements in the mix that created early Black English was Gullah Creole, famously spoken by rural black people on the coast of South Carolina and Georgia. Gullah Creole is one offshoot of a family of creole languages. In that family, the most renowned member is Jamaican patois; the creoles spoken in Guyana and Belize are variations on the theme, as are, across the ocean, the Krio language of Sierra Leone and the language misleadingly called "pidgin" or "broken" English by Nigerians and Ghanaians. In many of these creoles, *who* can be expressed as *who dat*, such that "Who dat say dey gonna beat dem Saints" would sound rather familiar to speakers of these varieties.

In sum, many of the people who created Black English already spoke West Indian English, in which *who dat* was basic. Then, the American vernacular that resulted was one where, like those West Indian varieties, it was common to leave out the *be* verb because its multifarious forms (*am, is, were,* etc.) are so hard to learn, and communication works just fine without a *be* verb anyway. The result: "Who dat?" chanted in an American stadium today. It's all about grammar, as human speech always is.

The N-Word is Dead. Long Live the N-Word?

UNDERSTANDING THAT BLACK ENGLISH is something coherent existing alongside standard English also helps make sense of something around which a hopeless debate endlessly swirls: what we are currently to refer to as the "N-word." In discussions of this word in American society, the fundamental snag is the idea that there is a single word *nigger* under consideration, and that the question is merely whether or not a person should say it or not.

To fully understand the mistake in this analysis, it will help to pull the camera far back for a bit—to Scots. In Scotland, the local dialect Scots is not merely a matter of slang, expressions, and an accent. Scots grammar is quite different from English grammar in many ways. When the way to say "I don't know" is "A dinna ken" and "A'll intae the hoose" is "I'll go into the house," it's clear that we are dealing with something other than what most people would think of as English in any familiar sense. Many Scots call it a separate language from English; almost anyone else would surely consider it a different dialect of English than the standard.

In Scots, *home* is *hame*. However, *home* and *hame* do not have the exact same meaning for a Scot; *hame* is not simply *home* said with a different vowel in the middle of it. *Hame* is associated with intimacy, true comfort, close friends— roughly, the home in standard English's *home and hearth*. *Home* is a more neutral or formal term, as in residence, domicile. The reason *hame* has that in-group meaning is that for Scots who speak Scots, Standard English is the formal language, while Scots is the intimate one. The two ways of speaking correspond to different aspects of existence.

Now, often in discussions of the N-word, a black person—in my experience, usually a man—will opine that whether the word is okay depends on how you pronounce it. *Nigger* is a slur associated with disrespect from whites, but *nigg-ah* (and here an audience always laughs warmly) is different. *Niggah* is friendly.

That analysis gets close to the heart of the matter but also reveals how abstract the concept of Black English is to Americans. More economically put, *nigger* is Standard English and *nigga* is Black English. The reason that clean way of parsing it is unavailable to most people is analogous to how hard it is in America to discuss, for example, class. An

American will say, "Well, the difference between him and her is that he went to private schools and had fancy vacations and both of his parents went to college, while although she wasn't *poor*, she went to public schools that were only okay and neither of her parents went beyond high school; they worked long hours." We are often reluctant to simply say of the second person that she was, quite simply, working-class—whereas many British people would readily say the equivalent and are perplexed at our discomfort with acknowledging such obvious socioeconomic distinctions.

Linguistically, reality eludes us in a similar way, in that we can only talk around, above, and outside of the obvious nature of the difference between *nigger* and *nigga* because we have no graceful way of referring to Black English. We don't think of it as a category, a concept. That should change, because this metric neatly resolves the otherwise-eternal tension over who is using "that word" and why. *Nigger* is a standard English slur. *Nigga* is a word in a different dialect, used among black people themselves, usually men, to mean "buddy." It emerged from a common tendency, especially among men, to use mockery and joshing as an expression of affection. There have been Russian men who call one another *muzhik*, which means "peasant." Fans of *Seinfeld* will recall the episode when George Costanza starts spending time with middle-aged white good-time Charlies who call one another "bastard" with abandon; that reflected a real-world kind of language usage among guys. It isn't an accident that these days young men of all colors—including whites ones, as I am now almost accustomed to hearing—call one another "nigga" in warmth. *Nigga* means "You're one of us." *Nigger* doesn't.

There is, then, no single word *nigger*. *Nigga* is not simply *nigger* pronounced "blackly," just as *hame* in Scotland is not simply *home* pronounced Scotly. Nor ought we labor under the impression that this situation is even new, despite notions that the prevalence of *nigga* has some connection to its prominence in rap music, which would date *nigga* (as opposed to *nigger*) back only a few decades. Black men have been using *nigga* in the "buddy" meaning forever; in other words, *nigger* was recruited into a new meaning and function in Black English a very long time ago. We have already seen that Claude McKay used it liberally in depicting his poor black characters in *Home to Harlem* in the 1920s; Hurston also used it a great deal, as did Claude Brown in his *Manchild in the Promised Land,* a novel about growing up in Harlem in the 1940s. *Nigger* isn't the only word that underwent this recasting; *ace boon coon* is familiar to black people of a certain age as a term of affection.

What does all of this mean about the N-word in modern America? Two things. First, the idea that some single word called "the N-word" should not be used by anyone, ever, is not as immediately plausible as it can seem, because there is no single "N-word." It is true that *nigga* sounds a lot like *nigger*, but words are used in context, We can be sure that the black men calling one another *nigga* don't intend it as an abusive slur, just as we know that when someone refers to something as "Cool!" they aren't referring to temperature. Some might object that nevertheless, the word's origins are in the slur, and that this, plus the sonic resemblance, should be enough justification to stamp out even its descendants. That is a reasonable argument, but only when there is a basic understanding that we are indeed dealing with two words, not one. The question is whether there is a reason to ban a word because of its *relationship to* another one. As such, a reasonable riposte could be that we can eliminate the source word while allowing that today's innocent language often has seamy origins. Think of what "that sucks" refers to in terms of its original, literal meaning. Yet who could imagine a campaign against that expression? The debate will go on.

Second, the common question "If we can't use it, how come black people can?" is incoherent. There is no single "it" under discussion. The question is, more precisely, "If we can't use the slur, how come they can use the term of affection?" That makes no more sense than asking "If we can't run red lights, how come they can relax in the park?"

Overall, the confusion over what really could be termed the N-*words* forces us to approach American language with a more cosmopolitan perspective than we usually have to. Without understanding that nonstandard language is an alternate rather than a destruction, we cannot understand that the guy who ventures that *nigger* and *nigga* are different words is not just a comedian but is ahead of the curve. *Nigger* is dead. Long live *nigga*.

In closing, we should return to a story we left unfinished: the one about Shirley, told in perfect Black English. When we left off, Shirley was worried that she wasn't going to get a Valentine from Charles, while the other girls were going to get Valentines from their boyfriends. Well:

> That Shirley, she so worried, she just don't want to be with nobody.
>
> When Shirley get home, her mother say it a letter for her on the table. Right away Shirley start to wondering who it could be from, 'cause she know don' nobody s'posed to be sending her no kind of letter. So Shirley, she open the envelope up. And when she do, she can see it's a Valentine card inside, and she see it have Charles name wrote on the bottom.
>
> So now everything going to be all right for Shirley, 'cause what she been telling everybody 'bout Charles being her boyfriend ain't no story after all. It done come true!

This is the way millions of human beings express themselves in their downtime across the United States. I hope a passage like the one above comes off differently to readers now than it might have when they started this book.

Chapter One: Can you tell why the story has ***don'* nobody s'posed to be sending her no kind of letter** but at the end, *Charles being her boyfriend **ain't** no story after all*? Why not ***ain't** nobody s'posed to be sending*? This isn't random. It's because the sentence about the letter is about an ongoing situation; in negative sentences in Black English, you use *don't* in such cases rather than *ain't*. Black English is not simply unravelled Standard English; it's complicated.

Chapter Two: Note that the narrator of the Shirley story is obviously not a white southerner; in this particular dialect, the narrator is clearly a black American. The passage, in other words, sounds black.

Chapter Three: We assume that the narrator can also speak standard English, just as we need not fear that Shirley is going to grow up only able to express herself in this dialect regardless of context. This is how the narrator, Shirley, her mother, and her friends talk with one another. Like so many people in the world, they speak differently among themselves than when elsewhere.

Chapter Four: It would be hard to say that this sober, touching, and thoroughly plausible tale is merely minstrel caricature, in a dialect no human being actually uses. It is, rather, a slice of real linguistic life honestly recorded on the page.

English hasn't existed long enough to diverge into dozens of starkly distinct regional dialects as it has in Great Britain. Black English is America's only English dialect that combines being strikingly unlike standard English, centuries old, embraced by an ever wider spectrum of people, and represented in an ever-growing written literature. It is worthy of celebration, study, and certainly acceptance. America will never truly grow up linguistically until this is widely understood. This book has been my brick in the wall.

Endnotes

INTRODUCTION

16 "It a girl named Shirley Jones": From the California State Department of Education's *Lesson Plan Handbook* for the Proficiency in Standard English for Speakers of Black Language program, which began in 1981. I am unaware of the author of the text.

19 Southern versus Black English: The handiest presentation is Patricia Cukor-Avila, "Co-existing grammars: the relationship between the evolution of African American and Southern White Vernacular English in the South," in *Sociocultural and Historical Contexts of African American English*, ed. Sonja L. Lanehart (Amsterdam: John Benjamins, 2001), 93–127.

CHAPTER ONE

31 "After all, as much linguistics and anthropological research has shown": H. Samy Alim and Geneva Smitherman, *Articulate While Black: Barack Obama, Language, and Race in the U.S.* (New York: Oxford University Press, 2012), p. 97.

40 *Done* analysis: Elizabeth Dayton, "Aspect and Modality in Grammaticalization of *done* in AAE Filmic Speech," presented at the Society for Caribbean Linguistics meeting, Barbados, August 2010.

42 Jarawara data: R. M. W. Dixon, The Jarawara Language of Southern Amazonia (New York: Oxford University Press, 2004).

42   Narrative *had* passage: John R. Rickford and Christine
      Théberge-Rafal, "Preterite *had* + V-ed in the narratives of
      African-American pre-adolescents," *American Speech* 71
      (1996): 227–54.

48   Black English pronouns and *ass*: Chris Collins, Simanique
      Moody, and Paul M. Postal, "An AAE Camouflage
      Construction," *Language* 84(2008): 29–68.

Chapter Two

58   People identifying speakers as black over the phone: Guy
      Bailey and Natalie Maynor, "The Divergence Controversy,"
      American Speech 64: 12–39; John Baugh, "Perceptions
      Within a Variable Paradigm: Black and White Racial
      Detection and Identification Based on Speech," in *Focus
      on the U.S.A.*, ed. by Edgar Schneider (Amsterdam: John
      Benjamins, 1996) 169–82; Thomas Purnell, John Idsardi,
      and John Baugh, "Perceptual and Phonetic Experiments
      on American English Dialect Identification," *Journal of
      Language and Social Psychology* 18(1999): 10–30.

66   Black speakers' use of sounds differing on the basis
      of class: Consult Walter Wolfram's *A Sociolinguistic
      Description of Detroit Negro Speech* (Washington, DC:
      Center for Applied Linguistics, 1969); and more recently
      Jennifer Nguyen, "The Changing Social and Linguistic
      Orientation of the African American Middle Class"
      University of Michigan (PhD diss., 2006) and Jamila Jones
      and Dennis Preston, "AAE & identity: constructing &
      deploying linguistic resources," in *The Joy of Language:
      Proceedings of a Symposium Honoring the Colleagues of
      David Dwyer on the Occasion of His Retirement*, ed. David
      Dwyer (2011).

70   My description of the vowels in the English of black
      people speaking in the standard dialect is based on studies
      by my students Samuel Heavenrich and Cole Hickman.

75   The effect of gender on speech: Findings supporting
      the difference between black women's speech and black
      men's in terms of grammatical features include Walter
      Wolfram's *A Sociolinguistic Description of Detroit Negro
      Speech* (Washington, DC: Center for Applied Linguistics,
      1969), and Patricia Nichols, "Black Women in the Rural
      South: Conservative and Innovative," in *Language and
      Gender: A Reader*, ed. Jennifer Coates (Malden, MA:
      Blackwell, 1998) 55–63.

84   Black vocal quality study: Julie H. Walton and Robert
      F. Orlikoff, "Speaker Race Identification from Acoustic
      Cues in the Vocal Signal," *Journal of Speech Language and
      Hearing Research* 37 (1994): 738–45.

CHAPTER THREE

106   Recordings of famous black people: Mary McLeod
      Bethune can be heard in an audio recording of her speech
      "What Does American Democracy Mean to Me?" in
      1939. Booker T. Washington's recording of his Atlanta
      Compromise speech is widely available online. A. Philip
      Randolph, who lived until 1979, was recorded often; most
      available is his speech at the March on Washington in
      1963, widely uploaded online.

CHAPTER FOUR

119   Recording of minstrels Leonard Spencer and Billy
      Williams: I heard it on the CD set *Lost Sounds: Blacks
      and the Birth of the Recording Industry* (Archaeophone
      Records, 2005). Since the release of this set, recordings of
      this kind have quite often been made available for listening
      online, as well.

121   "The Negro dialect": Joseph A. Bailey II, at
      blackvoicenews.com, June 29, 2003.

122   "put in a call": Jack White, "Ebonics According to
      Buckwheat," *Time*, January 13, 1997, p. 62.

122   "the Negro dialect, as we know it today": H. L. Menken, *The American Language: an Inquiry into the Development of English in the United States* (New York: Knopf, 1936), p. 71.

124   "we are to believe": Zora Neale Hurston, "Characteristics of Negro Expression," in *Negro: An Anthology*, ed. Nancy Cunard (London Wishart, 1934, p. 6.

129   George Johnson: *Lost Sounds* CD.

129   Williams and Walker: Various online sites include these men's surviving recordings from the first decade of the 1900s.

131   Ex-slave recordings: The Web site for the Library of Congress includes uploadings of these invaluable recordings.

132   Four generations of a black family: This is based on the recollection of linguists present at conference presentations by Wolfram in the past. The recordings are recounted in Sali Tagliamonte, *Making Waves: The Story of Variationist Sociolinguistics* (Malden, MA: Wiley Blackwell, 2015).

138   "Arthur Spears showed": Arthur Spears, "The Black Semi-Auxiliary *Come*," *Language* 58: 850–72.

139   Ex-slave narratives and the use of *am*: Various books and articles present word-by-word transcriptions of interviews with ex-slaves. On *am* specifically, handy for a quick look is Jeutonne Brewer, "Subject concord of *be* in Early Black English," *American Speech* 48 (1973): 5–21. Books on the ex-slave narratives include Federal Writers' Project, *Slave Narratives: A Folk History of Slavery in the United States from Interviews with Former Slaves* (Washington D.C., 1941); Edgar Schneider, *American Earlier Black English* (Tuscaloosa: University of Alabama Press, 1989); Guy

Bailey, Natalie Maynor, and Patricia Cukor-Avila, eds., *The Emergence of Black English: Text and Commentary* (Amsterdam: John Benjamins, 1991). Also useful is George T. Dorrill, *Black and White Speech in the South: Evidence from the Linguistic Atlas of the Middle and South Atlantic States* (New York: Peter Lang, 1986).

Chapter Five

152   "This was the fundamental conviction": John Russell Rickford and Russell John Rickford, *Spoken Soul* (New York: Wiley, 2000), p. 195.

156   "Sometime Rolanda bed": Lisa Green, *African-American English: A Linguistic Introduction* (Cambridge: Cambridge University Press, 2002)), p. 102.

158   Court transcriptions of statements by London prisoners: Laura Wright, "Eight grammatical features of southern United States speech present in early modern London prison narratives," in *English in the Southern United States*, ed. Stephen J. Nagle and Sara L. Sanders (Cambridge: Cambridge University Press, 2003), 36–63.

Index

Negro, 149–50

sentence structure
differences in, 15, 16–17

of southern and Black
English, 19

sub-, in Black English,
74–75

switching, 85, 101–2, 104,
108–9, 111, 123

vowel usage diversity in,
76–77

dictionary, 13, 36, 156

diglossia ("two tongues"),
101–2, 104, 111, 112–13,
123, 167

diphthong, 45–46, 73

discrimination, 26, 117–18. *See
also* racism; stereotypes

dismissive, emphatic, 48, 49–50

done, 40–42

Dumbo, 121

Ebonics, 36, 122
commentary and critique of,
15, 23, 150, 153

jokes about, 12, 152

revival of, 22

teaching, 46, 49–50

education. *See also* schools
black accent and, 66, 78–79,
80

of black Americans, 14, 31

Black English of leaders in,
106–9

Ebonics, 46, 49–50

Egyptian Arabic, 96–98, 117

emphasis, word, 47–51

Empire, 105

employment, 90–93

English, Black. *See also* accent,
black

accuracy in depictions of,
134–36, 144–45

African influence on, 23

aks for *ask* in, 30, 33, 69–70,
114–17

am for *is* in, 134–35, 137–42,
144, 172n139

barriers to understanding,
21

black Americans critique of,
152–53

code switching in early, 141

complexity of, 35–36, 39,
44–47, 50–52

conceptions and
misperceptions of, 12,
20–21, 26–27, 92, 148–52,
154–55

consonants in, 32–33, 67–68

diglossic or dual nature of,
102, 104, 123, 167

The Arno Press Cinema Program

PERSISTENCE OF VISION
The Films of
Robert Altman

Neil Feineman

ARNO PRESS
A New York Times Company
New York • 1978

This volume was selected for the
Dissertations on Film Series
of the ARNO PRESS CINEMA PROGRAM
by Garth S. Jowett, University of Windsor, Canada

Editorial Supervision: Maria Casale

First publication 1978 by Arno Press Inc.

THE ARNO PRESS CINEMA PROGRAM
For complete listing of cinema titles see last pages

Manufactured in the United States of America

———◆———

Library of Congress Cataloging in Publication Data

Feineman, Neil.
   Persistence of vision.

   (Dissertations on film series) (The Arno Press
cinema program)
   Originally presented as the author's thesis, Univer-
sity of Florida, 1976.
   Filmography: p.
   Bibliography: p.
   1. Altman, Robert, 1925-   I. Title. II. Series.
III. Series: The Arno Press cinema program.
PN1998.A3A5764 1978   791.43'0233'0924   77-22906
ISBN 0-405-10752-8

PERSISTENCE OF VISION:
THE FILMS OF ROBERT ALTMAN

by

NEIL FEINEMAN

A DISSERTATION PRESENTED TO THE GRADUATE COUNCIL OF
THE UNIVERSITY OF FLORIDA
IN PARTIAL FULFILLMENT OF THE REQUIREMENTS FOR THE
DEGREE OF DOCTOR OF PHILOSOPHY

UNIVERSITY OF FLORIDA

1976

To Jan,

who somehow lived through it

TABLE OF CONTENTS

ACKNOWLEDGEMENTS

There are many people to thank; you know who you are already. First, my parents who convinced me not to drop out; my grandmother, for caring more than I did; to Charlotte, Tom, my sister Carol, and my other close friends who had to put up with my moods and who seemed to understand; to Dolores and Sid for their concern; to Joy Anderson for being there when I needed her. Also, to Louise Brown and the rest of the English Department for getting the movies; to Diane Fischler for typing this from too many drafts and for forcing me to work; to Jim Flavin, David Dunleavy, and Mark Schwed for running the machines and forcing me not to work; to Russell Merritt for showing me what movies are all about; to my committee members, Dr. David Stryker, Dr. Sidney Homan, and Dr. Alfred Clubok for their time, interest, and signatures.

Most of all, I would like to thank Dr. William Childers and Dr. Ben Pickard. You spent an obscene amount of time helping me and just listening to me complain. Your support has always been appreciated deeply; you deserve the credit for whatever polish and refinement the work has. I wish I could be more eloquent; I owe you both too much.

iii

Abstract of Dissertation Presented to the Graduate Council
of the University of Florida
in Partial Fulfillment of the Requirements
for the Degree of Doctor of Philosophy

PERSISTENCE OF VISION:
THE FILMS OF ROBERT ALTMAN

by

Neil Feineman

August, 1976

Chairman: John B. Pickard
Major Department: English

Robert Altman is one of the most prolific of all the
contemporary American directors; since 1969, he has directed
nine feature films. Although only MASH has enjoyed major
commercial success, Altman has a cult following that includes many of our most respected film critics, actors, and
technicians, as well as countless film scholars and students.
Because he is so respected by his fellow artists and by
visible film people, his influence undoubtedly will be much
greater than his box-office clout. But even without the
framework of his potential importance to film history, his
movies are beautiful, complex, and unusual enough to deserve critical attention. In addition to being its own independent entity, each film draws from and refines the other
Altman films. Because they are so varied in genre and
period but are so similar in style and theme, Altman seems
to be a true American auteur. By treating each film as
both an individual offering and a part of a collective body
of work, this examination of Altman's movies will capitalize

on the structure but avoid the doctrinaire biases of the auteur theory.

Altman's first three films, That Cold Day in the Park, MASH, and Brewster McCloud are artistically uneven; as individual films, they are less successful than his later movies. These three films do establish Altman's basic values of the loneliness of the individual and his inability to succeed and hint at Altman's episodic, non-linear, and emotional way of telling a story. Although each is of some interest in its own right, they are more valuable as illustrations of Altman's as yet unrefined strengths and weaknesses.

With his next three films, McCabe and Mrs. Miller, Images, and The Long Good-bye, Altman develops his visual style and thematic concerns. Each is a reworking of a film genre, but sees the genre through the perspective of the egocentric, isolated individual in a hostile, dangerous world. Each is also a beautifully shot and constructed film, obtaining its continuity and consistency respectively through the narrative and characters, through its editing, and through its music and theme.

Thieves Like Us, California Split, and Nashville all directly relate to the earlier Altman films. Drawing from the other movies, these three reiterate, deepen, and darken Altman's world view and show Altman's increasing skill as a film-maker. They also raise a question: after these nine films, which seem to be a completed body of work, where can Altman go? What can he do that he has not done? The

answer lies, of course, with his next nine movies.

INTRODUCTION

I was not prepared that August 1971 night for what I was to see at the Esquire Theatre in Madison, Wisconsin. After the movie was over, I did not know why I had been so moved; I only knew no other film had touched me so deeply. Hopefully, five years and many film courses since that first exposure to McCabe and Mrs. Miller, I am more articulate about my emotional reaction. And as of this writing, there have been eight other Altman movies, with more on the way, and other directors who have moved me. Still, however, I will always owe most to Robert Altman and, deep down, will always belong to McCabe and Mrs. Miller.

Unlike many analyses of contemporary auteurs, I have made no attempt to disguise my affection for the films or the personal biases behind the discussions. After all, one of Altman's most appealing traits is his insistence on the viewer's emotional reaction. Even when his movies are cold and cynical, like The Long Good-bye and Nashville, he includes us in his design. As Joan Tewksbury, Nashville's scriptwriter, says, "All you have to do is add yourself as the twenty-fifth character and know that whatever you think about the film is right, even if you think the film is wrong."[1]

1

Once my response is added to the other characters,
then, my Nashville becomes complete. More importantly,
since my response is different from anyone else's, it differentiates my film experience from everyone else's. ˉSince
the emotional experience is personal, the analysis must be,
as well. After all, who can better explain my reaction
than myself.

Perhaps because Altman demands this personal and emotional response, rather than an analytical or rational
one, and because his films stress the visual and subtle,
little has been written about Altman's movies. Even after
Nashville, a full fledged media event, much of the belated
attention focused on Altman has taken the form of mild
gossip or superficial summaries of his career and personality. Had there been an extensive amount of research,
however, I still would have concentrated on my reaction
to the movies; Altman's movies are too alive to reduce them
to an academic cataloguing of other people's perceptions.

Keeping this in mind, there have been several informa-
tive articles and interviews that help explain Altman.
These include the excellent article about the selling of
Nashville in the June 13, 1975 issue of New Times, an
interview with Altman in the Chicago Reader of July 5,
1975, and the reviews of Brewster, Images, and The Long
Good-bye in various issues of Film Quarterly. Whenever a
source like these has been helpful or pursues a point differently or more extensively, I have noted the source in

the chapter notes. For the most part, however, this analysis does not pretend to be a scholarly compendium and review of the Altman literature, but deals more directly with the movies themselves.

I have begun my discussion with <u>That Cold Day in the Park</u>. Because I did not have access to Altman's television work, the James Dean documentary, and <u>Countdown</u>, his unsuccessful and mediocre first film, I can only write about the nine films since then. After viewing each of these several times, I found them conveniently grouping themselves into three phases of Altman's development.

The first three, <u>That Cold Day</u>, <u>MASH</u>, and <u>Brewster McCloud</u>, are uneven movies. Failing to develop themselves fully, they function more significantly as illustrations of Altman's as yet unrefined strengths and weaknesses. As a result, my discussions of these three films center on their potential and implications for Altman's future work.

The next three movies represent Altman's first mature efforts; because each is a variation of a particular genre, I examine it against a classic of its genre. <u>McCabe and Mrs. Miller</u>, a complex social study of the settling of the West, a beautiful photographic essay, and an enduring love story, is compared to <u>Stagecoach</u>. <u>Images</u> is juxtaposed against a simpler subjective thriller, <u>Repulsion</u>. Although similarities exist between the two films, <u>Images</u> uses the metaphor of schizophrenia to develop an abstract investigation of the nature of the film experience that forces the viewer to feel Kathryn's madness and accept the film as its own reality. When Altman turns to The Long Good-bye, he amalgamates the essences of The Maltese Falcon and The Big Sleep so that he can present the private eye as he really is, a moralistic, egoistical vigilante. With this film, Altman's style becomes fully developed, refined, and familiar; the overlapping dialogue, the rambling pace, the abrupt and unexplained characterizations and incidents, the unhappy ending, the isolated individual, and the hostile world are by now expected and integrated components of the Altman experience.

Because they have so many other Altman films to draw from, the next three films differ. Thieves Like Us, California Split, and Nashville constantly allude to the earlier films and deal with the same themes of the impermanence of love and the limited power of the individual. Thus, Thieves is more than Altman's gangster film or answer to Bonnie and Clyde; it is also Altman's remake of McCabe and Mrs. Miller, replacing McCabe's tenderness with a chilling bitterness. In the same way, California Split has more in common with The Long Good-bye than it does with gambling movies like The Hustler or The Sting. Finally, a knowledge of McCabe and Thieves makes a viewing of Nashville much easier and richer. In the other films, Altman's social philosophy provides a context for his characters; in Nashville, the characters are used to make a socio-political statement. McCabe has prepared us well, giving us an historical precedent to help judge and understand that statement. Although the last three films are significant and rewarding in themselves, they become even more satisfying and intricate when seen as a continuation of Altman's vision. Thus, these films are treated less as experiments in genre and primarily as parts of Altman's film vision.

Before examining the films, however, I would like to present a collection of statements Altman has made at various times in his career on the way he works.

---

[1] Joan Tewkesbury, Nashville (New York, 1976), p. 3.

CHAPTER 1
ALTMAN ON ALTMAN

"I think I'm more of an impressionist. I think I'm
dealing with atmosphere and impressions more than realism."

Chicago Reader, July 4, 1975.

"I never preplan a shot. Whatever happens almost
dictates itself. Whatever the circumstances are. The
style has already been set, and it sort of dictates itself."

Chicago Reader, July 4, 1975.

"This film follows the script a lot closer than anyone who worked on it will think, including me."

New Times, June 13, 1975.

"One of the things I'm jealous of is your (the audiences's) privilege of seeing the movie for the first time.
None of us will ever know what that's like."

New Times, June 13, 1975.

"I try to get a little over my head, try to get a
in trouble, try to keep myself frightened, do things that
are impossible. It helps me keep fairly straight."

Midwest Magazine, July 27, 1975.

"I don't try to lead you from one place to the other.
I try to put you in a place. I'm not going to tell you
anything; I'm going to show you something. I'm not even
going to show you something; I'm going to let you see something. And if you don't help me, my picture can't be any
good. If I have to do all the work for you, my picture
isn't any good."

Chicago Reader, July 4, 1975.

"I'm looking for surprises. If we had just taken what
was in my head and put that vision on film, it would have
been a pretty lousy movie. Or at least very, very ordinary.
One head, no matter how good - well, it just can't be the
same as everyone bringing something to it. So in that
sense everything is a surprise, but I'm not surprised by
the way it came out. I mean, we knew what we wanted."

New Times, June 13, 1975.

"The son of a bitch doesn't pay me anything. But when
he wants me, I'll be there. He lets me act.

Keenan Wynn on Altman
New Times, June 13, 1975.

"The movies don't fail, the audiences fail."

Midwest Magazine, July 27, 1975.

CHAPTER 2
THAT COLD DAY IN THE PARK

That Cold Day in the Park, Altman's first major feature film, is ultimately uninvolving and pretentious. It
does show, however, that Altman has always been dissatisfied
with passively watched, unambiguous movies. Also, it offers all of Altman's strengths and weaknesses in their unrefined, easily recognizable states.

Perhaps most immediately noticeable is Altman's leisurely pacing. Dealing with the familiar suspense themes
of kidnapping, thwarted sexual desires, madess, and murder,
That Cold Day's genre suggests a fast pace. But as he will
do later in Images, which borrows many of these same themes,
Altman does not generate suspense through tense and increasingly quick editing. Instead, audience involvement
is heightened through the construction of a dense, claus-
trophobic atmosphere and through the slow but threatening
character development.

To achieve this atmosphere, Altman holds the audience
captive in and by the oppressively heavy, albeit beautiful
Art Deco apartment for the first third of the film. Although Art Deco can be light, airy, and amusing, like the
Fred Astaire-Ginger Rodgers musicals that showcased it,

Frances' apartment is a series of stifling, repetitive, and severe geometrical patterns that allow for no movement or deviation. The apartment, like the movie, traps us; since we can go nowhere else, we are forced into the apartment and the film's events.

Unfortunately, however, our involvement is undercut by the characters' lack of appeal and by the events' shallowness. Seeing a boy huddled against the cold rain in the park outside her apartment, Frances invites the boy in. Since the boy does not talk for the first third of the movie, we are forced to listen to Frances' compulsive, constant chatter. Her incessant talking and nervousness, not to mention her initial interest in the boy, are indications of her unresolved, repressed, and unhealthy sexual interest. The boy is equally strange, punctuating his weird and silent passivity with short and unexpected bursts of bizarre dancing and musical explosions. Despite their strangeness, however, they remain curiosities, too mild to be generally frightening or threatening and too remote to be alive. Also, rather than focus and thus create and identification with one of the characters, the camera divides its attention between the two. The characters' lack of vitality and the film's failure to establish a point of view keep us in the audience detached and uninvolved.

The diffusion of focus continues in the next segment. The boy, whose name is never revealed, escapes out of the bedroom window and goes to his squalid hippie pad that he shares with his sexually voracious sister and her drug-dealing, leering boyfriend. Like Garbo, the boy finally talks; his sister explains that he has always retreated into silence, sometimes for weeks. After this information and after an uninspired evening of smoking pot, the boy returns to Frances'. Perhaps he wants to escape from the filthy and cramped pad, perhaps he has nothing better to do, perhaps he is intrigued by the new game. At any rate, the boy gives Frances some hash-laced cookies; they eat them and spend the afternoon playing thinly disguised and unresolved sex games. Before the games become real, however, the boy sneaks into what has become his bedroom and falls asleep.

Had Altman made the boy a more attractive character, our interest and involvement in his fate and the movie would have been heightened. But since he is cruelly tantalizing to Frances and since Frances is becoming increasingly pathetic, we have nowhere to focus our emotions. Because we are not directed, we are not pulled into the movie.

In perhaps the film's best sequence, Frances next goes to the gynecologist. What is important here is not the scene's contribution to the plot, but Altman's execution of it. While Frances nervously waits for the doctor, the soundtrack picks up the disjointed conversation of three other patients. One is quite naive and amuses the other two more experienced women by her confusion over the location of the clitoris and over the size of men's genitals.

The conversation, appropriate for a gynecologist's office, continues the film's recurrent sexual concerns, even though it adds nothing to the plot or the character development. It does, however, add texture to the film. Its humor and absurdity are an unexpected and welcome change from the film's heavy mood; it momentarily disorients us. Catching us off guard, it makes us react emotionally, rather than intellectually. Altman will become increasingly reliant on this non-linear narrative technique; even at this early date, it is startlingly effective.

The following scene reveals Altman's talent for structuring his movies. While Frances is out, the boy's sister, Nina, invites herself into Frances' apartment. Over the boy's protests, Nina draws a bath, freely uses Frances' toiletries, and soon pulls the boy into the tub. They splash and cavort; then Nina tries to seduce her astonished and unwilling brother. Curiously, this scene is the first one that elicits an intense emotional reaction; throughout this scene there is an almost obscene air of destruction and violation. This reaction is caused primarily by the film's structure. Although the characters are not people with whom we identify, the apartment is beautiful. Since the first half hour of the movie takes place in the apartment and since the camera lingers more lovingly on its furnishings and objects than it does on the characters, we become comfortable and familiar with the apartment. When Nina breaks into the apartment, then, it is as if she

is breaking into our apartment; when she mistreats and care-
lessly handles the objects in the apartment, she seems to
be abusing our property. Unfortunately, Altman is not
able to transfer our reaction and concern to the characters;
the scene's impact is, however, proof of Altman's ability
to develop an emotional response through his careful and
almost subliminal structure.

The film's momentum continues with Frances' return to
the apartment. She is unable to prevent the older doctor
who loves her from coming up with her. She checks the
boy's room, sees he is sleeping, and locks his door. While
she is doing this, the doctor begins to tell her that he
wants her. As he talks, she flashes back to the gynecologist's cold and dehumanizing examination, to his rubber
gloves and shiny chrome instruments. The connection between the two doctors is unmistakable and effective. The
scene's beautiful editing and sophisticated handling of
time as non-linear and flexible contrasts with the rest of
the film's straightforward presentation. Because it is so
jarring and not integrated into the rest of the film, the
scene may be considered gimmicky; more importantly, however,
it indicates Altman's as yet undeveloped talent for creative
editing and thematic presentation.

After the doctor leaves, Frances enters the boy's bathroom and tells him that she is lonely and repulsed by the
doctor and the old people around her. As she gets more
sexually explicit in her language, she moves closer to

him and becomes bolder. Lying down next to him but on top of the blanket, she tells him to make love to her. Finally, after he does nothing, she reaches for him. She is shocked to find out that his sleeping body is a blanket and his head only a doll. Although she will later repay the boy with the murder in the bed, for now, she is understandably shaken. She has been cruelly humiliated and mocked, while we have been teased into falsely expecting the sexual confrontation the movie has been building to from its first scene.

Altman has, in fact, been manipulating and then frustrating our expectations from the very beginning. Frances' first locking of the door was an unexpected twist that cut short any early sexual activity; the boy's silence was robbed of truly grotesque implications when it was revealed to be a childish sham. Even Frances' failure to catch Nina in the apartment worked against the cross cutting of Frances' anxious glances towards the window, or at least the direction, of the apartment. These remain little twists; the bedroom scene is the first in which Altman successfully catches us totally off guard and disarms us completely. Later in his career, Altman will become more comprehensive and ambitious in his baiting and then exploiting our expectations. In That Cold Day, however, this reversal of expectations is kept on a smaller scale.

To repay the boy for his trick and to make sure that he cannot leave her anymore, Frances waits until he returns and then locks him in the apartment. Even though he still refuses to sleep with her, Frances will not let him go. Torn between her desire to keep him and her fear of losing him, she decides to get him a whore that will keep him sexually satisfied. As she waits in a barren cafe for the whore, two lesbians visually and physically caress each other. Even though they are not directly related to the plot or characters, they, like the women in the film's other waiting room (the gynecologist's), add atmosphere and dimension to the film. Where the three women are used verbally, the two lesbians are visual, if sordid, relief. Both incidents are free from any intellectual or rational explication, but add to the film's emotional impact.

The remainder of the film is more plot oriented. The boy and the whore try to make love, Frances listens to their efforts, bursts in, plunges a butcher's knife into the bodies under the blanket, kills the whore, and then tries to comfort the boy. By now quite mad, she tells the boy, who is crying now, that everything will be all right. As the credits begin to roll, Altman adds his final touch, Frances' voice whispering, "I want to make love to you."

These final scenes lack the impact of the bar, bed-room, and bath sequences of the middle part of the movie. They do not have the earlier scenes' emotional power; they also do not have much narrative strength. Thus, while they show Frances procuring and murdering the whore, the final scenes fail to explain who Frances is trying to kill. They also do not satisfactorily develop the action; there is a potentially good story here but it is ineffectively presented. As Altman will show in Images, he does not have to explain the events to convey the emotional content of the characters' lives. In That Cold Day, however, he simply does not generate the emotional involvement. By keeping us on the outside of both vapid, unattractive main characters, Altman gives us no human alternatives or dimensions that would emotionally engage us. In addition, by failing to give us a well-developed story, he does not satisfy us on a rational and narrative level either.

When four films and four years later, Altman takes many of the ideas and situations in That Cold Day and makes Images, he has a better control over his technique and a better understanding of the relationship between style and theme. Using the metaphor of schizophrenia for the artistic experience, he broadens his concern from the simpler and narrower suspense thriller. He keeps the emphasis on objects, the soft focus transitions, the shots through glass, the fluid use of time, the creative use of sound. In Images, however, he has an artistic reason for using them. In addition, he adds a strong point of view that enables him to withhold any clinical background information but compensates for the lack of focus and audience identification.

Although That Cold Day looks more like Images than the other Altman films, it resembles all of them. Its

leisurely pace, emphasis on the emotional response at the
expense of the rational one, its careful structure, its
overlapping dialogue, its beautiful photography all will
become Altman trademarks and vehicles in his development
of an artistic philosophy.

That Cold Day also announces some of Altman's recurrent themes. There are no positive elements here. The
rich are empty, bored, and self-indulgent; the poor and
the middle class are prim, naive, inconsequential; the
hippies are a dirtier version of the rich; those in between
are pimps, whores, and older versions of the hippies. Even
the doctors are cold, impersonal, disgusting. There is no
permanent love or even a satisfying temporary escape in
casual sex. From Nina's unbridled heterosexuality to
homosexuality to sex for fun to sex for money, there is
an absence of dignity or satisfaction. Sex becomes a compulsive way to pass the time, to make a living, or to trig-
ger a psychotic reaction. There is no alternative for
lasting happiness or meaning, no hope for the happy ending.
The world in Altman's films, so aptly described in the
film's title, is cruel, hopeless, and cold.

That Cold Day not only contains clues of Altman's
strengths, but also alerts us to the limitations or faults
inherent in his style. The leisurely pace and creative
use of sound can lead to self-indulgence and inspire bore-
dom as easily as they can rapt involvement. The reliance
on emotional moments and atmosphere can create unnecessary

confusion and alienation, rather than increased viewer participation. The attention paid to structure and the de-
light in upsetting expectations may be coldly manipulative
and mechanical, instead of intelligent and fresh. By making the type of movies he does, Altman courts these dangers
and negative evaluations; since he demands a more active
viewer, he invites disappointment, disapproval, disagree-
ment. As viewers of Altman's movies, then, our responsibility is not to like Altman, but to be active, honest viewers
who demand the same integrity and responsibility from
Altman himself.

CHAPTER 3
MASH

Although <u>MASH</u> is Altman's most commercially successful movie, it is also his least interesting and most superficial. It is motivated by a single idea, that the military, religion, and marriage are inhumane institutions
that imprison the human spirit. To convey this theme,
Altman uses effective but stereotypical characters and dis-
arming visual tricks. For all its cleverness, however,
<u>MASH</u> is an empty and shallow movie.

The film begins as Hawk-eye comes to Korea and is mistaken for a jeep driver by Duke, another arrival. Sensing
the potential humor, Hawk-eye throws himself into the role
of chauffeur and drives Duke to their camp. Immediately,
his character and the film's values are established.
Rather than be imprisoned by false roles and status, Hawk-
eye mocks the roles and the system they legitimize. His
theft of the jeep and his impersonation of its driver reveal his quick and playful wit, his innate rebelliousness,
and his lack of seriousness.

Trapper, the other ringleader, displays an even
greater aggressiveness than Hawk-eye, as shown in his at-
tacks on Frank Burns and in his maneuvering to get a free

trip to Japan. Sharing the same irreverence and tastes,
Trapper and Hawk-eye are the ideal team. Each knows what
the other is thinking; they spontaneously act in unison.
Because they are so flexible and so quick, they are able
to seize control over any situation and defeat the more
rigid military establishment. They totally ignore, for
example, the military conventions and are thus untouched
by the military restrictions. When they go to Japan, they
do not acknowledge any of the military hospital's rules;
since they are not bound by any prescribed pattern of action, they constantly outwit the hospital staff and thus
are sure of getting what they want, be it food, a golf
course, or an operating room.

The film's other characters are also defined by their
ability to get around their roles and function humanely in
dehumanizing situations. Colonel Blake, for instance, is
a positive, decent character because of his complete indifference to his role as base commander and his incompetence in his enforcement of military regulations. Rather
than the military, the Colonel loves fishing and nurses.
His assistant Radar, on the other hand, is so efficient
that he can anticipate the Colonel's instructions before
the Colonel even gives them. Radar is positive because
he uses his efficiency to twist the Colonel's instructions
to the group's advantage. Radar, as his name implies, is
a key figure in keeping the MASH unit going, be it by
stealing the Colonel's blood or hooking the loudspeaker

to Hot Lip's tent. The priest, Dago Red, is also sympathetic, primarily because he listens more to the men than to
God. Kindly and devout, Dago never pushes his role as a
man of God but abdicates it whenever challenged. When
giving last rites to a soldier who has just died, for example, he obeys a doctor who tells him to stop paying attention to the dead and help assist a patient who is still
alive. Also, when he learns of Painless's problem of impotence, he realizes his personal inability to help and
turns the matter over to Hawk-eye. Even though he ultimately is reduced to blessing a jeep, he is a flexible and
unceremonious person.

Like these three, the rest of the characters are likeable and positive, primarily because they are pleasant
components of this zany group. Painless, for example, has
the biggest penis in the Army; Duke is Trapper's and Hawk-
eye's friend and tent-mate; Dish forgets her vow of fidelity
to her husband and her desire for Hawk-eye by going to bed
with Painless's enormous organ; Colonel Blake's girlfriend
keeps his mind off military matters; even the General is
an overgrown college boy, unable to concentrate on military
affairs when football is mentioned. These are happy, fun-
loving people, with whom we identify.

There are only two sustained negative portrayals in
the film, Frank Burns and Hot Lips Houlihan. Of the two,
Burns is the more threatening. His religious fanaticism
is cued by his teaching Ho John, the Korean gopher and

camp mascot, to read the Bible, his ostentatious and lengthy public prayers., and his unwavering seriousness and superficial righteousness. Despite his faith, however, Burns bullies a male nurse into falsely accepting responsibility for a soldier's death. Also, Burns, unlike the other MASH doctors, is professionally incompetent, even though he is the only one that is impressed with the title and implied status of his roles of doctor and major.

The Burns' saga is continued in his relationship with Hot Lips. Kindred spirits, they decide to write a letter to their superiors that will expose the nonmilitary character of the MASH unit. In effect, they are "squealing" to the authorities because no one is playing by the rules. As they become involved in their conspiracy, they also become involved in each other. They look at each other, suddenly and passionately and noisely kiss each other, and just as suddenly straighten their clothes and rush to the mess hall. For them, sex is like the military; they have respect for the form and look of the act but miss its emotional intensity and feeling. Later, when they finally make love, it is only after agreeing that God brought them together and that his "will (must) be done." Unlike the rest of the camp, then, they must hypocritically rationalize their nonreligious desires through the misapplication and emptiness of their religious doctrines.

Even their lovemaking is indicative of their absurd personalities. Devoid of any grace, naturalness, or dignity, it consists of clumsy grabbing and overly loud and heavy moaning. "Kiss my hot lips," she begs him repeatedly. Unknown to them, their noisy coupling is being piped through the camp's sound system for the entire base's amusement. Although the humor in this sequence stems from Hot Lips' and Burns' humiliation and is thus ugly, they are so unsympathetic that the cruelty becomes humorous.

When Burns is taunted into a nervous breakdown by Hawk-eye the next day and is carried out of the camp and film in a straight jacket, the loudspeaker plays "Sayonara" and the audience laughs. Because Burns is so absurd and because the rest of the MASH unit is so likeable and happy, Burns' mental condition and mistreatment by Hawk-eye is minimized. Even at the end, he never becomes sympathetic but remains an object of ridicule.

Altman's tacit approval of the camp's treatment of Burns is continued with Hot Lips' transformation. When she arrives, she is a ridiculous character, making small talk in the operating room, referring to the military as her home, and thinking that Frank Burns is the fine specimen of military excellence. Her mating with Burns gives her a nickname and continues her degradation. The shower scene adds to it; she is forced to shower nude in front of the camp so that a bet over her natural hair color can be ascertained. Once again the unit's cruelty is disguised and endorsed by the film's structure of heroes and villains. Because her unflagging devotion to the military

and her resulting disdain for the MASH people have caused
an alliance with Burns, she becomes a target for laughs,
regardless of the joke's underlying brutality.

Hot Lips is, however, different than Burns; although
she too has a misguided loyalty to the military, she does
not share his religious fanaticism. She is also different
because whatever her faults, she is a "damn good nurse."
When she breaks down in front of a bewildered Colonel
Blake, she does not get carried out but instead begins her
acceptance into the group. Soon she and Duke will go to
bed, signaling her certification as part of the MASH team.
And shortly thereafter, she will become head cheerleader
for the football game, the traditionally prestigious symbol
of female leadership. Unlike Burns, then, she has the
ability to change and adopt a new set of values that give
her greater happiness.

When Hot Lips changes her values, she changes from a
"bad" or ridiculous character to a more likeable and happier one. Burns, however, is less flexible; because he
never changes, he is destroyed and sent away. Although
Hot Lips changes her code from an oppressive reliance on
empty authoritarian roles and institutions and becomes
freer and healthier as a person, her transition from bad
to good character must be looked at skeptically and carefully. As long as she and Burns do not have the correct
standards, they undergo much humiliation, which seems both
humorous and justified because of the inhumanity and

boorishness of their beliefs. The humor of the film is, then, in great part based upon the intolerance and insensitivity of the MASH unit and, by implication, the laughing audience.

Burns and Hot Lips can be laughed at with immunity because they are charicatures and stereotypes, too broadly drawn to the fully human. The stereotypes give us a distance and superiority that dehumanizes them and thus makes them safe targets. In the same way, the good guys are stereotypes; we like them because of external conditions, not because they are good individuals. We see Hawk-eye and Trapper battle hypocrisy and bring life to any situation they enter; their fundamental honesty and refreshing rebelliousness, plus their expertise as surgeons, make them likeable and identifiable, even despite their cruel streaks. The other characters, however, are defined primarily by their integration with the group; if they do not detract from the free-wheeling values of the MASH unit, they are positive characters. When they threaten to upset the maintenance of the group, however, they are ostracized and humiliated and scorned. MASH is more like a summer camp than an adult military establishment; its anti-authority values, emphasis on fun and games, absence of relationships that entail responsibility, and power of the group norms give MASH an adolescent quality. This immaturity is reflected in the puerile nature of many of the jokes and the hidden degradation and superficiality of much of the humor of MASH.

Both the characterizations and the humor of MASH, then, depend upon our unambiguous identification with the obviously right values and with our acceptance of their broad, fast presentation. The situations with Hot Lips and Burns have, had they been treated humanely, an inherent sadness and cruelty to them. If Dish had been a more fully defined character, Painless' suicide and its underlying sexism and anti-homosexuality would be patently offensive. If the importance of winning and the rampant cheating in the football game had been treated with more subtlety, the football game could have become a serious satire rather than a hilarious lark. MASH, however, is so sure of its values that it is oblivious to these ambiguities, intolerances, and weaknesses. Rather than aiming for important insights, the movie settles for a broad, easy, slapstick presentation.

The Last Supper sequence illustrates the adolescent quality of MASH's humor. Painless decides to cheat on his three fiancees; this is the first cheap joke - Painless is so well endowed that he needs and is able to satisfy three women. He then is unable to perform, which he interprets as evidence that he is a latent homosexual. Rather than accept this, Painless decides to commit suicide, which explains the film's title song, "Suicide is Painless." The rest of the group understandably do not share Painless' panic and depression, but decide to humor him. They plan to stage his suicide and then provide him with a woman who will unexpectedly disprove his fears. After an

elaborate satire on "The Last Supper," everyone gives Painless his last regards and he solemnly takes the big black
pill that will kill him. It is, of course, a fake pill;
as he sleeps, Hawk-eye and Painless' equipment convince
Dish to go to bed with him. As she snuggles next to him,
Painless wakes up and regains his form. The next day, he
has forgotten his troubles.

This scene is undeniably funny; the religious parody,
the elaborate and meaningless ceremony and seriousness, and
the group's sincere if irreverent concern for Painless'
mental condition all contribute to the scene's success.
The idea, however, is devoid of any subtlety or insight;
it does not reveal anything about the plot or the characters. Regardless of the charm and humor of the scene, all
its details reinforce the final effect. Once that is obtained, the idea loses its freshness; on the second or
third viewing, the scene becomes tedious.

In addition to the lack of subtlety, the scene is
fueled by an adolescent assumption, the idea of a large
penis and sexual pleasure. Painless is defined in the
film solely by the size of his penis; his size and subse-
quently his prowess make his impotence and his depression
more notable, just as it makes Dish's reactions explainable
and humorous. Again, although it is funny, especially on
a first viewing, the scene rests upon an adolescent preoccupation with the size of Painless' penis. And like all
adolescent jokes, the humor wears thin after a while.

Even Altman's stylistic devices, usually used to add diffuseness, ambiguity, and texture, are used in MASH to single-mindedly add to the unambiguous statement on the inhumanity of war, the military, and religion. The overlapping dialogue, for instance, does not add levels of structure and contrasting detail but merely reinforces already apparent relationships. At the film's beginning, for example, the women officers are almost inaudibly talking about soap and sex, foreshadowing their definition by sexuality. When the doctors in the operating room mumble about the nurses' "boobs getting in the way" or about a particular nurse's figure, they only reiterate the loose and prevalent sexual atmosphere of the camp. And when someone asks if a patient is an enlisted man, who get bigger stitches than the officers, the satire on the military is repeated. Like the cheerleaders' chant, "69 is Divine," the comments are funny but, if missed, leave no gaps or ramifications in this film experience. If they are caught, they add another laugh, a slightly different version of the same joke.

The loudspeaker is no different. It adds to the noise on the soundtrack, is an editing device, and provides structure and foreshadowing with its announcements of missing drugs, VD epidemics, absurd regulations, and medical warnings. It predicts Ho John's attempt at draft evasion by taking handfuls of amphetamines and also the pot smoking at the football game; both by now dated attempts at topicality and courting of safe and predetermined audience responses. Again a device is used not to add depth but to further an already clear statement.

The loudspeaker is used in another way as well. In addition to playing music that directly comments on the visuals, as with the "Sayonara" to Burns' exit, it announces the showing of movies on the base. The films are usually war movies like The Halls of Montezuma and are announced by the reading of the films' press releases. At MASH's end, the loudspeaker tells us the film is over by reading MASH's own press blurb and introducing the cast. There are other movie allusions as well. Hawk-eye's first appearance in the film is accompanied by the traditional and unmistakably dramatic movie music of the hero; Burns' and Hot Lips' first kiss is a parody of the old movie kisses; Dish's and Painless' lovemaking to a Handel-like choir and a shot of the sun rising over the tent are satires of Hollywood's traditional inability to treat sex naturally; Hawk-eye's and Trapper's roles when they deal with the military police in Japan are stolen from countless American "B" movies. Unlike the later Altman films, however, these allusions do not seem artistically purposeful. Instead, they resemble Mel Brooks' self-conscious attempts at drawing attention to the medium for a laugh. Rather than expand the film's focus, the allusions are cute but superficial and thrown away.

The blood in the operating room is still another successful gimmick. Veins pop and guts flow amidst wise-
cracks and sexual games. The juxtaposition of humor and
gruesome blood is effective, making real the human waste
of war, exploiting the potential for black comedy, and
breaking new ground for the film. Its repetition in the
film wears thin, however; since it never really develops
beyond the obvious contrast between gore and laughs, it
becomes a predictable and easy device.

MASH, then, is an explicit and savage attack on the
abuses and hypocrises of the military and religion, empty
forms that shackle people to false values and legitimize
inept leaders. Impulses and spontaneity, MASH says, are
more important and more beneficial; if followed, they will
lead to at least temporary happiness. Thus, Hot Lips
learns by the end of the film to love, laugh, jump, and
scream; even though her relationship with Duke is only
temporary, she does have the moment.

Despite the humor and superficial good will generated
by the movie, much about MASH is ugly and questionable.
The portrayal of Frank Burns is callously one-sided, as is
Hot Lips' transformation. They exhibit an almost frightening reliance on the group norms and on conformity, even
though the MASH group has understandable and identifiable
values. There is also a smugness to the anti-military,
anti-religious, and pro-drug references that seem to capitalize on already prevalent audiences' prejudices. When

MASH was released, the climate of the time disguised and
perhaps justified MASH's style. Now, seven years later,
however, the sexism, condescension, adolescence, and cruelty
of much of MASH detracts from the movie and badly dates it.

As we are to learn from Images, we must take a film
on its own terms. And MASH is so single-minded, unambiguous,
and broad that we must admit that yes, it is a broad, single-minded, unambiguous - and funny - comedy. On its own
modest terms, it succeeds. But because it set its sights
so low, because it traded art for a quick laugh, it has
dated itself and lost much of its effectiveness. Instead
of the timeless work of art it might have been, MASH now
is only a reminder to those who share MASH's values that
we too are capable of intolerance, sexism, and dehumanizing
behavior.

CHAPTER 4
BREWSTER McCLOUD

Although Brewster McCloud is as broad, excessive, and
reliant on stereotypes as MASH, it is also a more whimsical,
innocent, and personal movie. Rather than aim for MASH's
realism, Brewster is a fantasy, developing its own world
that works on its own values.

The first scene establishes Brewster's tone. After a
brief speech by the lecturer, who tells us that man has always wanted to fly or at least wanted "the freedom that
true flight seemed to offer," we see Miss Daphne rehearsing
"The Star Spangled Banner" in the empty Astrodome. As the
opening credits unfold, we hear her scream that the band is
off key. "And I want that scoreboard lighted...." As the
band begins again, the credits also reappear; this time, the
scoreboard has rockets bursting everywhere. As the credits
continue, we read "title song - Frances Scott Key." Rather
than sophistication and subtlety, then, the humor is obvious
and pointed.

The next scene continues this broad style of comedy.
Brewster drives Abraham Wright, the invalid, almost senile
brother of Wilbur's and Orville's, on his weekly collection
of the rents from his chain or rest homes. Obscenely ugly,

Wright obviously enjoys himself; he hideously giggles, insults everyone, and demands rent from patients who have
died during the week. A contemporary Scrooge, his inhumanity and grotesque personality make him an absurdly unbelievable and comic villain. So when he and his wheelchair
are pushed onto the freeway, when his body lands on the
pavement, desecreated by bird droppings (an integral part
of the killer's modus operandi), we laugh. Too broadly
drawn to assume human dimensions, Wright becomes a caricature, a cardboard villain created only for our amusement.

Underneath the scene's absurdity, however, lie subtle
details that increase the discerning viewer's enjoyment.
Reflecting the film's concern with birds, the rest homes
have bird names like the Feathered Nest Rest Home and the
Blue Bird of Happiness. In addition, Wright's license
plate reads OWL, another detail reinforcing the aviary
theme of the movie. In the shots of Brewster and Wright
in the car, Altman adds an arresting visual pattern by
shooting the action through the colored automatic windows.
As we hear the two characters, we watch the playful motion
of the window, which goes up and down, reflecting, obscuring, or revealing Brewster, Wright, and Houston. Finally,
the dialogue, often lost in the visual confusion and quick
pacing, is surprisingly funny. As an old woman gives
Wright the week's rent, for example, he asks her if she
has given him everything. As she tells him he has "every
last penny," he reaches into her blouse and grabs two bills.

As he drives away, he excitedly cries, "Two big Georges."
Although a funny line, it is relatively hidden; the line
may not add any ramifications or refinements to the overall
situation, but it rewards the more attentive viewer unsatisfied by the farcical nature of the scene. In the later
films, the details will do more than just support and reinforce the main idea. In Brewster, however, the hidden
details add to the film's single-minded, broadly comic mood.

Even the movie allusions, usually Altman's most subtle
device, add to Brewster's outrageous absurdity. Margaret
Hamilton plays both the witch in The Wizard of Oz and Miss
Daphne in Brewster. She dies in Brewster when a black
"nigger" bird opens her giant bird cage (shaped like the
Astrodome) and it falls on her. The wicked witch, of course,
was killed when Dorothy's house fell on top of her. As the
camera pans across Miss Daphne's body, we hear an AM radio
news report of her death. While the radio announcer describes her red, white, and blue acrylic knit dress and
red rhinestone shoes, we see that she is wearing the ruby
red slippers of The Wizard. Thus, all of the scene's
visual and verbal components combine to make its single,
absurd, unrefined joke.

Unlike the later Altman movies, the sound and background visuals do not extend the scene's boundaries, but
merely reinforce the primary idea. When the radio announcer tells us about the red shoes, for example, we also
see them. The lecturer describes a Crested Peacock; we

then see Frank Shaft, the strong, silent, professional detective, wearing shoes that match his luggage. After that,
we see him open a suitcase full of turtleneck sweaters of
different colors. Since Altman had already made his
point, this second illustration is repetitive and unneces-
arily obvious.

As befitting the humor, the characters remain broadly
drawn parodies.[1] Had Brewster been a realistic film, the
use of caricatures could have detracted from its effectiveness. Since Brewster is a fantasy, however, the characters
need not be realistic, only recognizable. Frank Shaft, for
example, is defined by his serious and vain self-consciousness and his intimidating, if meaningless, professionalism.[2]
He is a villain and his suicide is laughable not because he
is the most serious threat to Louise and Brewster, but
primarily because of his tiresome pomposity. Johnson, on
the other hand, has the same job as Shaft, although he does
not have the title or the reputation to uphold. Unlike
Shaft, Johnson bumbles his way through the job; he whispers
into the microphone, speaks into its wrong end, and enjoys
Captain America comic books. Because of his incompetence,
his sense of humor, and humanity, we like him, even if he
is a cop.

Louise works the same way; she murders and steals, but
she also laughs and protects Brewster. A cross between a
bird and a person, she bathes like a bird, has scars on
her back from her raw shorn wings, resorts to bird sounds

when under emotional stress, and understands the true importance of flying. She tells Brewster that "people....accept
what's been told to them. They don't think that they can
be free. They don't even believe they can be free....some-
thing happens to them as they grow, and then they turn more
and more towards earth. And when they experience sex, they
simply settle for it."

Because she understands the value and elusiveness of
freedom, Louise acts like Brewster's mother, making sure
he obeys training rules, warning him that sex will sap his
energy and destroy him, rocking him to sleep by singing
lullabies, and protecting him from strangers wishing him
harm. Like most mothers, Louise can seem unduly repressive and overprotective.

Louise, then, offers Brewster the knowledge and ability
to fly. She has the film's secret; she alone has refused
to compromise and knows where freedom can be found. Loyal
to Brewster, she represents his chance to be free; when she
kills Wright, Miss Daphne, Breen, Billy Joe, Shaft, and
Weeks, she is protecting Brewster. She does not kill anyone who in the context of the film does not deserve his
fate; thus, she still keeps our empathy and admiration.

In a similar vein, Brewster becomes a positive character because he is, by definition, the hero of the film.
The archetypal individual, Brewster does not have personality or individuality; he is more like a blank face that
each of us can identify with and substitute ourselves.

Because he has Louise to look out for him and because he attempts to fly and thus be free, Brewster is the hero, the character we would like to be.

As a fantasy, then, Brewster establishes its own world with its own code of values. Since the characters do not have to function in our everyday real world, they have no responsibility to behave like real poeple. All they have to do is present their characteristics and roles in a re- cognizable manner; once we understand their function, we know how to react to them.

Thus, Shaft is the typical professional; Wright, the all too familiar money-mad absentee landlord; Louise, ma- ternally loyal and perceptive. We can identify their roles and, within the context of the story, believe them. In- terestingly, the only unbelievable character in the film is the most original, the least developed, and the most typical of the later Altman films. Hope, the health food cashier, knows nothing about health foods. In addition to supplying Brewster with health foods, she crawls under a blanket and thrashes herself into sexual ecstasy. Unlike the other characters, she is not grounded to a recognizable type. We cannot believe her here because our imaginations are already engaged in making the larger fantasy work; al- though a minor and specific character, her strange actions overload our imaginations by drawing attention to the artifice of the entire fantasy. Because she violates the internal consistency of the fantasy, then, Hope becomes an ineffective and distracting character.

Brewster's plot also depends on the suspension of our disbelief. As a fantasy, it depends on our compliance. We cannot demand realism and cannot ask usually normal questions like how Louise got out of the camera store, how Haines and Mrs. Breen got to Lost World's River Adventure, how Shaft knew where Brewster and Susan would drive to, or what Louise did with Johnson. If we ask those questions, the movie obviously would not work. Instead, we accept the film's events at face value. Like the humor, the story either works for the individual or it does not.

Although this demand forces the viewer to accept a very broad style and an implausible plot, many original and satisfying details remain in the movie. The lecturer, who hilariously turns into a bird, may not be subtle, but he does break the plot's linear motion. Although his comparisons of the characters with birds only reinforce our perceptions, like Shaft's vanity or Louise's maternal protectiveness, and thus become repetitive and unnecessary, the lecturer is original and very funny. Another effective and more peripheral scene is introduced by the lecturer. While the lecturer talks about the bathing habits of certain species, Altman cuts to a shot of Louise frolicking in the Astrodome's fountain. Suddenly, she becomes aware of the camera, smiles, and covers her breasts. Although it has nothing to do with the rest of the movie, her action convincingly conveys her exhuberance, joy, and dignity. Three movie allusions are also handled with subtlety. When Shaft

checks into the hotel, he notices the incessant sirens.
Johnson explains that a group of doctors from Boston who
do heart transplants "just sit around and wait until a
stiff dies." Could Johnson be talking about our Boston
doctors from MASH, the pros from Dover? Altman teases us
with his next allusion, a poster of the film The Decline
and Fall of a Birdwatcher. Although shown three times, the
full title is visible only the first time; by obscuring the
last three words of the title, Altman playfully frustrates
the viewer who did not read the poster that first time.
The MASH poster in Suzanne's apartment, also only fleetingly
seen, makes another pleasant contrast with most of the
film's pointed approach. The scene in the amusement park
does not really further the story, but provides a comical
visual aside. The Lost World River Adventure has a native
god with rolling eyes; the tour guide explains that it is
called Shirley's temple. Should they paint Shirley's temple
black, she wonders. Perhaps more than any other detail,
Shirley's temple foreshadows Altman's eye for the cinematically absurd and his willingness to make a place for it in
his films.[3]

More interestingly than these details, isolated from
the rest of the film, is the flying sequence in the middle
of the film; it compresses the entire film into a single,
short episode. Louise lulls Brewster to sleep; he dreams
of rolling clouds, beautiful vistas, and the true freedom
of flight. His brief dream ends, however, as a swish pan

brings us from the clouds to a dead white bird lying on the
ground. The camera then moves to the funeral, which quickly
becomes a circus of multi-colored umbrellas. Brewster, of
course, will suffer the same fate; after a brief flight, he
too will plummet to the ground and lie there, encased in
white. And as soon as he hits the ground, the circus will
arrive. More than a mere interlude in the film, the dream
sequence acts as a surprisingly subtle microcosm of the
film. As such, it hints at Altman's increasing concern and
skill with his films' structure.

Even with these inventive, subtle details, Brewster
remains an obvious and simple movie, a fantasy. Because
it is a personal little fable, the individual viewer must
decide for himself whether it successfully captures and
holds his imagination. More universally demonstrable, however, are the values that structure the fantasy. Since
Brewster operates in an imaginary world created by Altman,
his values can be seen in pure, discernible states.

"The desire to fly has been ever-present in the mind
of Man," the lecturer begins, at once establishing that
Brewster's quest is primal and universal. But, Louise
cautions Brewster, the ability to fly and to be free becomes possible only after intensive training, discipline,
and sacrifices. As an archetypal individual, Brewster is
warned about sex and passion, which hinder discipline and
obscure the vision of freedom. Sex causes people, Louise
tells him, to rationalize their lives and to ultimately believe what society tells them.

Brewster's temptation, of course, is Suzanne. (Hope seems quite happy without Brewster's active sexual participation and is, therefore, no real temptation.) Susan proves irresistible; to Brewster's surprise, sex with her feels good and does not appear to sap his strength or resolve. Hurt because Louise has lied to him, Brewster tells Suzanne about his ability to fly. And although Louise's advice has seemed typically unreasonable and maternally overprotective, she does know best. Before Brewster has even finished telling Suzanne about his plans to fly away, she is happily merchandising him into a mansion in Houston's most fashionable neighborhood. As soon as he tells her of his responsibility for the murders, Suzanne drops her pose of "feminine" stupidity and becomes a coy schemer. She quickly gets Brewster out of her house, reports him, wins back her old boyfriend, and transforms a case of premature ejaculation into a marriage proposal. In almost any other film, her reluctance to lie next to a confessed mass murderer would be understandable. In this movie, however, Brewster is the harmless hero; when Suzanne turns him in, she betrays him and the film's positive values. As such, she proves Louise's advice. Brewster's indulgence in sex does destroy him; a passionate woman does betray him.

The climactic scene is at once heartbreaking and exhilirating. Louise, who has grasped the situation, has already left (but not before doing one final favor, murdering Weeks). Brewster knows he must fly. He puts on

his wings and, in full view of the Houston Police Department, triumphantly soars to the top of the Astrodome. As
he rises, we remember the lecturer's initial warning, "It
may someday be necessary to build enormous environmental
enclosures to protect both Man and Birds. But if so, it
is questionable whether Man will allow birds in....or out,
as the case may be." Although we hope for Brewster's escape, we know he cannot. As the lecturer screams that man
will never equal the natural flight of birds, Brewster plum-
mets to the ground. As soon as he hits the astroturf, Altman cuts to a tiny section of the Astrodome, which is filled
with politely applauding spectators. The scoreboard lights
up and the Greatest Show on Earth, a circus of sorts, pours
into the arena. We realize that the circus is Brewster's
costumed cast taking a curtain call; even the dead characters are resurrected and take their bows. Only Brewster,
the individual who has tried to be free, remains dead. His
insistence on remaining dead reinforces his failure to be
free.

Although Altman has prepared us for Brewster's death,
the movie might have supported a happy ending. Had the
dome opened and Brewster flown out, he could have been a
comtemporary Peter Pan. Even at the risk of sentimentality,
we would have believed it. But Brewster does not break
away; he fails. This inability to escape reveals how deeply
Altman believes in man's inherent limitations.

Perhaps Brewster does not deserve to escape because he ignored Louise's advice; in any case, he was doomed from the start. Louise told him he must remain pure and dedicated, if he were to succeed; the professor told us at the beginning and end of the film that he was not going to get out of the dome; Brewster's own dream ended with the death of the white bird; most importantly, the freedom of flight was never even verified. Freedom is not only attainable, then, but may also be illusory.

The refusal to let the individual exist in a state of freedom connects Brewster, which superficially seems so different, with Altman's other, more realistic films. Not only are the values the same; some of Brewster will be used in other Altman movies. Abraham Wright's priorities and speech about his money will be repeated by Marty Augustine in The Long Good-bye; Shaft's slow motion death in water will reappear in McCabe and The Long Good-bye; his repeated use of "Jesus Christ" will characterize Images' Hugh's speech pattern; the climactic death by betrayal will resurface in Thieves Like Us. But most importantly, all the films will concern themselves with the individual's inability to be free.

Although Brewster is more successful than That Cold Day, which was a collection of techniques in search of a theme, and more original than MASH, which was an adolescent collection of stereotypes and slapstick comedy, it still does not have the tightened structure, totally integrated

design, and depth of Altman's later films. With his next
film, McCabe and Mrs. Miller, Altman will gain that control,
eliminate the ragged edges, and work with more subtlety.
And although his movies will be better, his assurance,
talent, and visibility will hamper his ability to make another personal movie like Brewster, which is both his and
our loss.

---

[1] For a more detailed and socially oriented treatment
of Daphne and·Wright, see Roberta Rubenstein's excellent
review of Brewster in the winter 1971 Film Quarterly.

[2] More specifically, Shaft is a parody of Bullit, the
blue-eyed San Francisco detective played by Steve McQueen.

[3] Another nice touch to Brewster is its patriotic use
of color. In addition to the allusions to the astronauts
landing on the moon is the profusion of red, white, and
blue. Almost everyone wears some combination of the colors,
no one more spectacularly than Daphne, who dies in a red,
white, and blue acrylic knit and Suzanne, who wears a
white blouse, blue skirt, and red lipstick to snare Bernard.
There are also mammoth red, white, and blue banners in
Brewster's lair. Although the motif remains undeveloped,
it is noticeable and amusing.

CHAPTER 5
McCABE AND MRS. MILLER

McCabe and Mrs. Miller, says John Huston, is the great
forgotten movie of our time.[1] It is a serious and comprehensive statement about a younger America, a tender love
story, and a stunning photographic essay. Finally, McCabe
is Altman's western. Like his other films that deal with
a particular genre, McCabe does not just refine the western
but carefully uses the genre's conventions to expose its
false underlying assumptions.

Until recently, the western was probably the film genre
closest to people's hearts. One explanation of this appeal
may be that the western directly and positively deals with
the myths and legends surrounding America's development.
These films told of simpler times when values were less ambiguous, roles more certain and secure.

John Ford's Stagecoach is probably the best example
of the genre. Of the many characters in the film, all are
immediately identifiable. The whore with the heart of gold
is there, as is the doctor who cares for people no matter
how drunk he gets. The driver is, beneath his cowardly
and comical exterior, solidly dependable; the serious and
responsible demeanor of the sherrif disguises a perceptive

44

and humane flexibility. Also stereotypical are the gentle
lady of breeding, the misguided but loyal Southern gentle-
man, the meek and ineffectual liquor salesman, the prim
and repressive society matrons, the hypocritical banker
turned thief, and the evil and ruthless killers. And, of
course, there is the hero, Ringo, played, not surprisingly,
by John Wayne.

Ringo is a living representation of moral goodness.
He has the right dream of a simple, rural existence on his
ranch, surrounded by his family and crops. He realizes,
however, that his dreams may be postponed or shelved when
they conflict with his civic and familial responsibilities,
which he must accept. To maintain his self-respect and
his moral superiority over his brother's murderers, for example, he must revenge the murder, even though it means
facing the three killers by himself. His failure to stand
up to them would be sanctioning the rule of the gun and
terrorism as a way of life. Given the situation and Ringo's
personality, he has no real choice but to accept the responsibility to act in a traditionally moral fashion.

In addition to being moral, Ringo is physically strong
and has unpretentious and accurate instincts. His strength
is important because it gives him credibility and the
ability to fight for his values. His instincts are helpful because they enable him to see through the facades of
false authorities and values and recognize true quality.
Thus, he knows immediately that Dallas, despite any reputation, is kind, generous, decent, and worthy of his love.

Ringo, then, is a man of superior moral and physical strength and of unerring instinct. He is not, however, the only admirable character; others in <u>Stagecoach</u> are "good." Doc, for instance, may be a drunk, but when needed, is able to sober himself up and successfully operate. The cavalry, who have been eluding the stagecoach for most of the film, miraculously appear at the last possible moment and avert a massacre. Even the sherrif is humane enough to realize that, despite Ringo's legal problems, he is morally justified and thus allows Ringo and Dallas to ride off and live their kind of life. Despite societal roles and personal eccentricities, then, the "good" characters are solidly dependable and successful.

The vindication of the morally good characters goes further than their receiving rewards. As in all truly benign worlds, the bad people are punished, often by the same good people. The banker gets caught with the stolen money and will be returned to the town, where the investors will try to punish him. The three murderers will not just die, but they will be killed by Ringo himself. Ringo's avenging of his brother's death and his subsequent reward is, in fact, typical of the western's values. Because of the physical roughness of the terrain and society, the good people must endure much testing. In the end, however, they will be rewarded, just as the evil ones will be destroyed or rehabilitated. For the movies, then, the West is a secure place where values and identities are clear cut and invigorating.

As shown in McCabe and Mrs. Miller, Altman's West is
much different. He simply does not see the pioneer romance
or the thrill of the frontier. The people who settle in
Presbyterian Church seem no different from the residents of
any other American blue collar neighborhood. Growth is
not a noble and inspiring process here, but is spurred by
commerce and projected profits and is accompanied by its
attendant hypocrisies, dehumanization, and racism. The
West, Altman is saying, was not won but was merely an early
example of suburban sprawl.

Like countless other westerns, McCabe opens with the
mysterious stranger riding into town. The stranger would
like to give the impression of class; he carries his own
linen tablecloth and silver whiskey flask and pays much
attention to his sophisticated, if inappropriate, hat and
coat. Even this pose, however, is enough for Presbyterian
Church. The town's one bar-hotel-restaurant, Sheehan's,
is overcrowded, unfinished, dirty, poorly lit, and uncomfortable. It is peopled with unshaven, undistinguished
white men, including a messy drunk, a self-conscious dandy
and his slavish admirer, a faceless group of card players,
and Sheehan, a physically repulsive and nose-picking small
time entrepreneur. This motley and unromantic group of
original settlers represents quite a change from the group
in Stagecoach, who made a much greater and individualistic
impact than McCabe's characters.

Although McCabe looks more like the hero than any of
these others, he is still no John Wayne. Although he seems
cool and self-assured and although Sheehan says he is the
well-known gunfighter who killed Bill Roundtree, Sheehan
also says that McCabe's nickname is Pudgy. McCabe's de-
fensiveness and refusal to talk about his past and his insistence that he is a "businessman" give some believability
to Sheehan's story. The nickname Pudgy and McCabe's ridiculous aside to Sheehan, "if a frog had wings, he wouldn't
bump his ass so much," indicate that McCabe's reputation and
ability as a gunfighter are considerably exaggerated.

At any rate, McCabe is a businessman of sorts, even if
his business is pimping and gambling. Realizing that the
town of men is a major and captive market, McCabe buys
three prostitutes and three tents and then begins building
a more permanent house for his business venture. Even before the building is finished, however, the whores are stab-
bing customers and giving McCabe trouble.

Unlike Dallas who is getting run out of town, Mrs.
Miller is seen arriving at Presbyterian Church. She immediately proves herself a more astute businessperson than
McCabe. She tells the skeptical McCabe that he could make
a great deal of money if he would only expand his vision.
"You've got to spend money to make money," she tells him.
Her plans involve "a proper sporting house with clean linen
sheets and class girls." McCabe, thinking of the men of
the town and of the expense of such a house's construction,

tells her that she does not know the men's tastes. "Once
they get a taste of it," she answers, "they'll like it all
right." Mrs. Miller convinces McCabe that he does not have
the experience to run a decent whorehouse and prevails;
they form a partnership that will bring an expensive, sophisticated business establishment to town.

Another sign of encroaching civilization arrives with
Mrs. Miller. Ida, a mail order bride, has come on the same
train. Like many of the men, she is ordinary and relatively
nondescript in appearance. Although her hair is frazzled
like Mrs. Miller's, she is frail, frightened, and apologe-
tic. Nonetheless, she represents respectability and the
potential for a family and a middle class in Presbyterian
Church.

The whores and the Jeffersons constitute the next in-
flux of growth and the next increment of civilization. The
whores are cosmopolitan, lively, proud, and eager to enter
into the town life. They are not degenerate or vulgar,
but are decent, religious people accustomed to a relatively
comfortable standard of living. Rather than sabotage the
town's moral character, they complement its developing middle class atmosphere of hard work and clean living. With
the whores come the town's first black family, the Jeffersons. Immaculate and polite, they are the town's second
most interesting looking couple (after, of course, McCabe
and Mrs. Miller) and sound like the most educated. The
Jeffersons, being black, add another ethnic group to the
town's population and also another level to the class system.

With this arrival, the permanent population of the town
is complete; everyone else who comes is temporary and tran-
sient. First are Sears and Hollander, representatives of
the conglomerate Harrison Shaunessy, who want to buy the
businesses in Presbyterian Church. The stereotypical hypocrisy of the banker and the comic ineffectiveness of the
liquor salesman in Stagecoach have been changed, then, to
one of a bland, rather petty organization man. Despite Harrison Shaunessy's low offers and tendency to capitalize on
other's hard work and to avoid risks, there is one good
reason to sell to them: "They'd as soon kill you," says
Mrs. Miller, "than look at you." Because he is drunk and insecure, however, McCabe fails to deal with them, thus con-
juring up a different group of company representatives.

Before they come, however, the cowboy wanders into
town. Like Ringo, the cowboy is primarily a rural creature
who comes to town to stock up on supplies from the general
store and to have fun at McCabe's whorehouse. He relies
on Presbyterian Church as a city and a service center; he
is yet another indication that the town is on its way to
becoming a metropolitan area. Unlike Ringo, the cowboy, as
we shall see, is no hero.

The final group who ride into town are the three hired
killers who are to remove McCabe. Although these three are
as dishonorable and ruthless as the three in Stagecoach,
there is a major difference. McCabe's killers are company
agents who want to kill McCabe because he is an obstacle

to the company's plans for the area. Even though they are sanctioned by one of the largest companies in America, as hired killers, they are the least moral of all the characters. Ironically, the completion of their mission will make consolidation of the town's resources possible and will facilitate real growth and progress. Its cost, unfortunately, will be intimidation, terrorism, and murder.

In an effort to survive, McCabe goes to Bear Paw, still the major city in the area, in a futile search for someone to make a deal with. When he realizes no one is there, he seeks the sherrif. Instead, he finds a lawyer, an ex-Senator, who is the film's most articulate, most civilized character. Rather than help McCabe, the lawyer sees an opportunity to boost his own reputation and political career. Thus, he inspires McCabe with talk of noble principles and heroic dreams and sends him back to Presbyterian Church and certain death. The lawyer, like the company, is the product of civilization, indifferent to another's individual's plea for help unless it can directly further his own ends. Stagecoach's innate sense of community and justice has no place here.

The final civilizing gesture occurs at the end of the movie. In the hunt for McCabe, the church is set on fire. Although the winter landscape mutes the sound of gunshots, the fire is seen and draws everyone but McCabe, the surviving killer, Butler, and Mrs. Miller (who is in an opium den) into a joint effort to save the church. As McCabe lies yards away, freezing to death, the townspeople save the building, a hollow symbol that has never even been used. And while they celebrate its salvaging, McCabe dies.

Altman's comment is clear; civilization is achieved at the expense of individualism and humanity. McCabe and Mrs. Miller, then, is a comprehensive indictment of the winning of the West.[2] From the beginning, this film states, there has been social, religious, and racial hypocrisy and abuses; from the beginning, the corporation has terrorized and oppressed the individual. There have never been any heroes or any romance, just people trying to cope as best they can with forces bigger and more dominant than themselves.

Equally important is the essential bankruptcy of the forms and institutions that appear so important to American society. According to McCabe, the idea of racial equality, the functions of the church and the social importance reserved for marriage, and the notion of the supremacy of the individual have always been lies. The belief in the forms may help keep people satisfied or ambitious, but will not help them transcend the basic conditions of life.

The first fact of Altman's West that is different from the more traditional presentation is his presentation of racism. Sheehan's first conversation is full of racist overtones. "Turn over a rock and you'll find a Chink," Sheehan mutters. All they do is smoke opium, which is not tolerated in the white part of town. In addition to the

existence of a ghetto, there is also another type of segregation. In the mines, the dangerous and difficult work is
done by the Chinese. This theme is reinforced later in the
film in a callous speech of Butler's. In it, he argues for
the introduction of a profitable new mining technique. Its
only drawback is the certain death of many of the miners;
but since they will be Chinks, the hazard seems of small
importance.

Mrs. Miller is the only character to violate the color
line. First she brings in an Oriental whore, who is the
source of much curiosity and crude jokes ("If her eyes are
slanted....") and business. She seems, however, a token,
acceptable only because she is under Mrs. Miller's auspices.
More importantly, Mrs. Miller goes to the Chinese section
to smoke her opium. She does not go for companionship or
out of a belief in social justice, however, but to escape
into oblivion.

The black people, the Jeffersons, are also illustra-
tive of the segregated nature of early America. The Jeffersons are astonishingly good looking, well-dressed, and
well-mannered. More than any other characters except
McCabe and Mrs. Miller, they hint at interesting pasts and
potential development. Although they meet with polite
acceptance and live in the white part of town, they never
enter into its social fabric. No one makes an effort at
winning their friendship. When Coyle is killed, they are
by themselves and remain so; when the church burns, they

help save it but are not a part of the celebration. Instead, they slink away, alone and unnoticed. Despite their
obvious assets, the Jeffersons never really integrate into
the town, functioning only in a business role and in emer-
gencies.

The myth of racial equality is not the only empty concept; another is the institution of organized religion.
To deal with this issue, Altman uses one of the film's most
interesting characters, the preacher.

The preacher seems a little strange from the beginning.
His eyes are beady; he shuffles; his presence makes the
other characters uncomfortable. Ill at east among other
humans, he only once is shown with dignity. In a long
shot, the preacher is shown working on the church's steeple.
Even in this shot, however, the dignity is derived from the
beauty of the natural setting; when juxtaposed against his
apparent indifference to people, his solitary efforts at
building a structure loses their nobility.

The preacher's character is definitely established by
his actions in the scene where Coyle is struck on the head.
Coyle is clearly in need of medical and spiritual help; as
everyone rushes to Coyle's aid, the preacher pulls his
collar up and sneaks away unnoticed. Although he has supposedly dedicated his life to doing God's will and helping
people, his only real dedication is to his unfinished, un-
used building.

The following funeral scene is an amusing yet poignant
counterpoint to the preacher's behavior. Armed with the
knowledge of the preacher's conduct and Mrs. Miller's early
remark that "nine times out of ten a good whore with time
on her hands will turn to religion," we see the choir, composed of the whores and the Jeffersons. Their tuneless
screeching and religious fervor seem at first incongruous
and humorous, but their basic decency and fundamental respect for life and death become moving. Although their
faith significantly is not shared by the more worldly Mc-
Cabe, Mrs. Miller, or the dandy and although their vision
is both misplaced and deluded, their essential goodness and
humanity shine.

In the film's final moments, however, the beauty of
this scene turns on itself. The preacher's mania becomes
more dangerous when he forces McCabe out of the church and
into near certain death. Ironically, this action leads to
the preacher's own death and to the burning of his building. And when the citizens work together to save the
structure and then celebrate their success as McCabe dies,
they seem shallow and foolish and their victory seems hollow and unimportant.

Like organized religion, which reveres material goods
rather than human life, the concept of marriage and social
respectability is false. Ida comes to Presbyterian Church
to marry a man she has never seen. Unlike Dallas and
Ringo who meet and fall into the deepest, most romantic

type of love, Ida is ordered like a piece of merchandise.
Love has nothing to do with Ida's marriage, which is a legal
transaction and an economic arrangement that is somewhat
meaninglessly sanctified by society.

As Ida is walking with Coyle one night, a man asks if
he has seen her at Mrs. Miller's. Coyle forgets that since
their marriage is essentially a business transaction, Ida
is no different from Mrs. Miller's whores. Also, Mrs.
Miller's girls are respected members of the town. The remark, when considered reasonably, is not that offensive.
Coyle, however, reacts blindly; now that Ida is his wife,
he must defend any slur against her honor. He does so in
the traditional manner - with his fists. In the fight,
Coyle is pushed down, strikes his head on a rock and dies.

Coyle's death is the first serious violent incident
in the film and as such is its first documentation of the
waste and foolishness of social violence. Like many violent
occurrences, the fight happens spontaneously and has unfor-
seen tragic consequences. Also like other violence, it is
self-indulgent, shortsighted, and meaningless. The remark
that triggers the fight is almost inoffensive and certainly
not worth dying for. Coyle, however, reacts according to
the best western tradition, a manly defense of his property.
In his childish efforts to defend her (and ultimately his)
honor, he is killed and thus places Ida's survival, rather
than her honor, in jeopardy. Once again, the empty form
is pursued at the expense of human life.

In an ironic twist that makes Coyle's death doubly meaningless, Ida ends up at Mrs. Miller's. Because she has no
other alternative, she must become a whore. Still, she is
nervous about her new calling; she never really liked sex
but did it because it was her duty. "Maybe I'm just small,"
she tells Mrs. Miller.

Mrs. Miller tells Ida to relax and that soon she will
learn to enjoy sex and "do just fine." She also explains
that Ida's status has not changed. "You did it with Coyle
to keep a roof over your head. Here you'll be doing the
same thing, only get to keep a little (money) for yourself.
It's more honest, to my mind." And she is right; within a
few days, Ida is smiling and enjoying herself. Of all the
whores, she is the sorriest to see the cowboy leave; she
stands in the snow waving and calling after him longer than
any of the others. She finds honor and fulfillment, then,
not in a loveless marriage, but in Mrs. Miller's whorehouse.

The false glorification of violence in American society
and in the typical western is more brutally and devastatingly
dealt with in the killing of the cowboy. Despite his menacing entrance into the film, he is a good-natured innocent
without any violent tendencies. While he is enjoying himself at the whorehouse, the three hired killers come into
town. Unlike the easy-going cowboy, the killers enjoy hu-
miliating people. When the cowboy leaves Mrs. Miller's, he
meets the youngest gunfighter, who is embarrassed because he
missed a bottle he was shooting at. To save face, the

gunfighter goads the cowboy into a gunfight. Claiming that
he cannot hit anything and just carries his gun for show,
the cowboy backs away. As he turns to leave, he listens
to the gunfighter's offer to inspect his gun; perhaps the
gun, not the cowboy's aim, is at fault. As the cowboy
stupidly reaches for the gun, the gunfighter draws his and
shoots and kills the cowboy.

As soon as the shot rings out, Altman shifts to slow
motion to show the cowboy fall into the ice, bleed, and
die. The shift in the film's pace is brutally and cruelly
jarring. As Altman cuts from the dead cowboy to the re-
pulsively smug boy/killer, we feel anger, hatred, waste,
and powerlessness. We see the gunfighter as he really is -
not a romanticized hero, an honorable man of courage, or
even a misunderstood social problem, but a vicious murderer
who preys on innocent, unaware, ordinary people. And because the gunfighter kills coldly, whether for sport, money,
or ego, he is able to terrorize the more decent people into
submission. Because he makes all the rules, he holds all
the cards. Unlike the traditional western, there is no
necessary punishment or avenging of the gunfighter; he may
or may not be killed himself, but nothing can happen to
make his victim's death meaningful. Rather than being an
object of adoration, then, the gunfighter and his violent
code are treated with disgust and hatred.

The three gunfighters are not, it must be remembered,
after McCabe and in town by accident; they are employees

of a major company on a business assignment. Too big, powerful, and anonymous to worry about conventional morality, Harrison Shaunessy routinely engages hired killers to get rid of difficult businessmen. That a corporation would act this way this early adds a new dimension to violence in America. In fact, the corporation is seen here as the central guiding and omnipotent force in early America.

The corporation, according to McCabe, has been with America from the very beginning. It waited and watched; as soon as the groundwork and initial efforts of an ambitious individual proved to be successful, the corporation moved in, assuming total control at any cost. Because of its size and power, the corporation was able to operate with impunity and ruthlessness, co-opting everyone and everything in its path.

The corporation's power explains the faceless, small nature of the film's individuals. The corporation is so big that the individual must manage to make a life for himself around or through it, almost always serving it as deal maker, hired killer, manager, clerk, construction worker, or supplier of goods and services to it and its employees. Rather than translate the idealistic superiority of the little people's numbers into realistic power, the individuals acknowledge the corporation's strength by not questioning its tactics or power. When the Company is not around, the individuals are decent, cooperative, and morally responsible. As soon as the Company is involved,

however, the individuals become frightened and servile participants in its games.

This change can be seen in the townspeople's behavior.
When they are involved, they are capable of instinctively
good and generous behavior. When Coyle is hit and hurt,
for example, everyone but the preacher rushes to his aid.
When Birdie has a birthday, everyone but McCabe shows up
to wish her well. Most importantly, when the church catches
fire, everyone is capable of working in harmony towards the
common goal. And when the corporation moves in and Sheehan
sells out, no one blames him or resents him for selling out
to the mob. When McCabe, on the other hand, is drunkenly
arrogant to the corporation and tempts its wrath, the townspeople do not respect his courage, but feel he is a fool.
Later, when McCabe is humiliated by Butler, the townspeople
do not try to ease McCabe's humiliation. The dandy is
openly contemptuous of him; the lawyer is condescending;
the rest are made uneasy. Rather than involve themselves,
they look away and mind their own business.

Indeed their reaction is understandable. When the cowboy is killed, the townspeople are forced to witness the
murder. As in the scene with McCabe and Butler, no one
comes to the cowboy's aid; no one makes a moral stand. If
they had, they too probably would have been killed. Although the townspeople want to help, their desire to live
is understandably stronger. Although each is resigned to
hoping he is not the next victim, he cannot be blamed for
not taking on the corporation by himself.

The perception that America is a corporate wasteland peopled by a sheepish mass is not new; for anyone living through the last decade, it seems almost taken for granted. What is new is Altman's insistence that America has always been this way, that the tales of the frontier pioneers who had control over their lives have been lies and distortions used to socialize us into more of the same. Unlike Stage-coach, the real enemies were never Indians or outlaws; the only Indian in McCabe is a chippy and outlaws are so non-existent that McCabe and Mrs. Miller keep all their money in portable boxes and heart-shaped tins. Not even storms and fire pose a real threat; through cooperative action, they are conquered. No, the only realy enemy is the Company, which will lie, steal, and kill "as soon as look as you."

Because the villain is so pervasive and so omnipotent and because there are such a limited number of options open to the individual and because traditionally heroic action leads only to death and waste, there can be no traditional hero in McCabe and Mrs. Miller. But because McCabe does not have to be a hero, he can be a human being. Because he can be flawed and even somewhat ordinary, his story and his relationship with Mrs. Miller can be more realistic and more moving.

When McCabe arrives in Presbyterian Church, he seems self-assured, sophisticated, and successful. Establishing himself as a businessman, his immediate plans for a gambling casino and whorehouse overshadow his obvious shortcomings as an operator and thrust him into the additional role of the town's leading citizen. Sheehan confirms this status when he tries to form a partnership that would prohibit any other establishment's opening without their approval and subsequent cut. McCabe turns Sheehan down, telling him that he has come "to get away from" partners, even though he does not mind deals. (In the course of the film, however, he will profit from his partnership and die because of his failure to make the right deal.) "Sheehan," McCabe characteristically concludes, "if a frog had wings, he wouldn't bump his ass so much."

Although their conversation is interrupted by one of McCabe's whores who is slashing a customer with a knife, much has been said. McCabe states that he does not like partners but is amenable to deals. He is soon, however, to make Mrs. Miller a partner, which is wise because he is generally incapable of running a business. And ultimately he will be killed because he does not make a deal or even understand the deal making process. Rather than act like a businessman, he treats Sears and Hollander rudely.

Sheehan is right when he tells McCabe that a businessman has to know how to make deals. He is also right in understanding that there is a safety in numbers. McCabe, however, never really understands the power of the corporation; when he lets his drunkeness and personal problems interfere with his business conduct, he ruins himself.

McCabe's frog joke is the first concrete indication that
he relies on instinct rather than intelligence. He obviously meant the joke to be a witty, incisive remark that
would make him look intelligent and urbane. Instead of
making him look smart, however, it reveals his stupidity.

McCabe's pretensions are evident during his first meeting with Mrs. Miller. Ill at east because of her self-confidence and as yet unannounced reason for approaching him,
McCabe takes her to Sheehan's and clumsily buys everyone
there drinks. After this transparent attempt to impress
her, he dramatically drinks his usual raw egg in front of
her. To let him know that she sees through his actions and
that they are unnecessary, she playfully pulls him close
and whispers, "If you want to make like such a fancy dude,
you ought to wear something besides that cheap Jockery
Club perfume."

With one sentence, she deflates his airs and poses;
never again can we think of McCabe as suave or sophisticated. Mrs. Miller, then, exposes his image of a cool, shrewd,
and fast thinking businessman. His inexperience, lack of
imagination and foresight, and reluctance to take chances
are revealed by his inability to answer even one of Mrs.
Miller's many questions and by his hesitation at becoming
her partner. In the end, however, Mrs. Miller's confident
and intimidating recitation of the obvious advantages to
the partnership and her demand for an immediate answer
railroad McCabe into acceptance. But even though the

partnership is financially and personally successful, McCabe never loses his initial reservations about the arrangement.

These reservations stem from McCabe's concern for his reputation. Extremely insecure, he places an inordinate amount of importance on what others think of him. As such, he feels the need for others to regard him as sophisticated, successful, and urbane. Mrs. Miller, however, not only sees through his facade, but also understands his need for one. But because she knows so much about him, she is threatening to him.

An even greater concern for McCabe is his partnership with a woman. He cannot escape the feeling that his partnership with a woman involves a compromise of his masculinity, a public admission of insufficiency, and a resulting loss of respect from her and the community. He is also unable to reconcile her business and professional acumen as a whore with their personal relationship as lovers and remains continually frustrated over the two roles.

Because McCabe is so acutely concerned with the way others judge him, there is a large gap between the public and private McCabe. He has hidden his inner thoughts and kept them non-verbal for so long, he has forgotten how to articulate them. "I've got poetry in me," he tells himself, clearly wishing he could release it to Mrs. Miller.

Actually, McCabe's worries about revealing himself are unnecessary. Although his dreams are not great, they are decent wishes for an honorable reputation, a successful business, and an ability to provide for his woman. Although not an intellectual or even particularly intelligent, he is sensitive and alive. After all, he was the one to develop or at least recognize the opportunities in the town and was able to get the men to work for him. More importantly, he is never cruel or jaded, but innocent and charming. These private virtues excuse the obnoxious elements of his public personality, notably his incompetence and delusions of sophistication and resulting need to constantly prove himself. Had McCabe been less concerned with trying to seem like a successful businessman and more concerned with being John McCabe, he would have been happier and more successful. He also may have lived longer.

Instead, of course, McCabe tries to maintain his public image, even though his attempts lead to increasingly greater frustrations. McCabe releases these frustrations through his drunken binges. Unfortunately, Sears and Hollander arrive during one of these binges. Driven into drinking because of his feelings of inadequacy, McCabe overcompensates by trying to impress the two agents with his women, whiskey, and wit. His patronizing behavior insults the already irritable Hollander, who feels the corporation mistreated him by sending him on such a simple and remote assignment. "That man is an ass," he tells the more patient Sears, "I'm going back." As soon as Hollander leaves, he triggers the film's remaining events. Once started, the events cannot be stopped. Thus, McCabe's inability to be himself and his failure to control his public personality drive away the people he cannot afford to alienate.

When Sears and Hollander leave and the deal falls through, Mrs. Miller begs him to sneak out of town. Not only does McCabe refuse to consider her suggestions, but he gets offended by it. "Go into business with a woman," he mutters, "and you can't expect her to have reason to respect you." Thinking he will not sneak away because the townspeople will think him cowardly, Mrs. Miller loses her patience. "What are these people to you?" she yells, "Why do you care what they think?"

McCabe's refusal to run away involves more, however, than simple pride. After all, McCabe suffered humiliation in his dealings with Sears and Hollander and then was willing to grovel to Butler in front of his former employees, friends, and customers. He is also willing to go on a desperate search for anyone who can make a deal with him. Something in McCabe, however, will not let him run away completely, leaving his property and efforts and dreams to the jackals.

McCabe may not be taken in my the lawyer's high principles and may be using them in an attempt to impress Mrs. Miller and to inflate his own importance, but he does believe that he should "stick his hand in the fire and find out what he's made of." He is no longer thinking about other people's opinions, but is acting out of his beliefs

and for the maintenance of his self-respect. Although he
is like Coyle because he is acting out of a misguided, futile, and wasteful code, he has finally reconciled his
public and private selves. And perhaps because he believes
in what he is doing, he is able to move purposely and re-
sourcefully for the first time - even though he is killed,
he does elude the killers for a surprisingly long period,
manages to kill all three, and almost escapes. Although
his death is still a waste, he does achieve a dignity of
sorts.[3]

While McCabe may put on airs of sophistication, Mrs.
Miller is genuinely sophisticated. She is also witty and
intelligent. When she tells McCabe that his cologne is
cheap, she is not being malicious. Instead, her eyes and
voice sparkle; she is both teasing him and telling him
that she is different and that he does not need those airs
with her. Despite her aggressiveness, she is not emasculat-
ing; even though she devours four eggs and a plate of stew,
she never becomes slovenly or gross like the woman in the
famous eating scene from Tom Jones. Totally self-confident,
she is intriguing, sexy, independent, and fascinating.

Because Mrs. Miller has so much self-respect and confidence, she feels no shame in her profession. Unlike Mc-
Cabe, she is an excellent businessman. Also unlike McCabe,
she does not need to hide behind the title "businessman."
"I'm a whore," she tells McCabe. Not only is she a whore;
she is one of the best. While the other women charge one

and a half dollars, Mrs. Miller charges five dollars for her services. And everyone, including McCabe, must pay.

The first time we see McCabe in bed with Mrs. Miller is the first time their relationship is clarified. Mc-Cabe's repeated solitary complaints and frustrations with Mrs. Miller ("Money and pain....") and her impatience and disappointment over his inability to manage his affairs are intense enough to suggest a deeper personal relationship than a simple business partnership. Also, the delicacy with which Birdie tells McCabe that he cannot talk to Mrs. Miller because she has "company" and his uncomfortable, embarrassed response hint at his personal involvement. Thus, when the two are shown in bed, we are not really surprised.

What is surprising, however, is that Mrs. Miller stops to remind him that he has not paid. Smiling, McCabe gets out of bed and puts his money in the box. But Mrs. Miller shows that he is no ordinary customer; she curls up under the covers and pulls the blanket up over her nose. All we see is her eyes, excited, radiantly alive, and happy. Before McCabe came in, she had smoked some opium; for the first time, the drug enhances her mood of pleasure and activity rather than dragging her into oblivion. Her response to McCabe and his presence is not mercenary, then, but loving.

Mrs. Miller's charging McCabe is consistent and crucial to her character. As she says, she asks nothing from no one. And she knows she cannot be a whore forever; someday she hopes to run a proper boarding house in San Francisco.

Living alone in the present and preparing for the future takes money. Since she is independent, she has to be concerned with her own welfare. The price of independence, after all, is the responsibility of caring for oneself. More importantly, Mrs. Miller, unlike McCabe, has enough self-respect and awareness to separate her business and professional lives. In her case, this means separating love from sex. If McCabe and Mrs. Miller are in love, all McCabe can expect is her love. This love cannot include her abandonment of her welfare for his pleasure. To remain independent and to keep her self-respect and equality in their relationship, she cannot give him free use of her body. Until both decide and desire that he should be responsible for her, she must remain responsible to herself. She must, then, charge McCabe or enter into a one-sided, unequal relationship.

When McCabe returns from Bearpaw without the deal, Mrs. Miller reveals the depth of her self-awareness. She realizes that the lawyer's principles are empty and that McCabe's death is inevitable. She leaves the stove (the only time in the film that she performs a domestic duty), turns her back, and begins to cry. McCabe looks relieved; at last she is conforming to a feminine role. Soothingly, masculinely, McCabe falls into his role. "There, there now, little lady, don't you cry." Mrs. Miller's reaction is explosive and immediate - "Don't give me any of that little lady shit!"

She stops crying and pleads with him to leave town.
When she sees that McCabe will not be swayed, she composes
herself and closes the discussion with an abrupt "eat your
meal." She knows that everything has been said; she com-
passionately drops the subject without any whining, complaining, or self-pity. She never even reminds him that
she told him so.

Immediately preceding their final scene together, Mc-
Cabe admits to himself that he hates the thought of other
men sleeping with Mrs. Miller; if only, he wishes, she
could be tender and free just once. McCabe does not understand Mrs. Miller and does not realize she hears the poetry
he has locked inside himself. Instead, he thinks she is
"freezing his soul." When he finally comes to her for what
they both know is their last night, he tries to verbalize
his feelings but breaks down. Rather than have him be
further embarrassed, Mrs. Miller tells him that there is
no need to say anything else, that she knows and feels the
same needs. She pulls him to bed without a glimpse or
possibly even a thought of the money box. She is tender,
giving, and human. Regardless of her future or welfare or
situation, she and McCabe have an intense moment of true
oneness.

Before McCabe wakes up, Mrs. Miller sneaks off to the
opium den. Both know what is to happen that morning; her
presence there would be both uncomfortable and painful.
Soon thereafter, McCabe will lie alone in the snow freezing

to death; Mrs. Miller's soul will be temporarily frozen in the opium den's oblivion. It is a depressing ending for we are forced to watch the destruction of two people whom we have learned to care very much for.

Although there is no way to see McCabe's ending as a happy one, there are elements of optimism, hope, and beauty in the film. If at the end McCabe and Mrs. Miller have to face their fates alone, they are no different than any of us. And before that end, they are able to build a relationship based upon mutual respect and care. Neither is forced to compromise a belief or stance; each recognizes the other as an individual with feelings and integrity. Although they do not have a very long relationship, it is intense and beautiful, punctuated with moments of happiness and total commitment. Because they attain these moments, they do create that "momentary stay against confusion"; they really live. And that is a major accomplishment.

Because of the leisurely pace, overlapping dialogue, and large number of characters, McCabe appears to be a loosely structured, dissonant film. The appearance is, however, deceptive; the movie is tightly controlled, direct, and coherent.

There are many characters in McCabe: the original townspeople, the whores, the Company men, the cowboy, the lawyer, the killers, McCabe and Mrs. Miller. Not every character is developed, however; the facelessness of many preclude the necessity for any development. The others are defined primarily in terms of their occupation as politician, gunfighter, company lackey. Only the dandy and his slavish admirer do not seem related to the rest of the film; their feud over the moustache is funny but peripheral and independent from the rest of the film. Every other character, however, exists primarily to further the film's central characters and theme. McCabe's first three whores, for example, exist primarily to illustrate his incompetence and limited vision, especially when contrasted with Mrs. Miller's ladies. The black couple comment on the racist nature of early America; the lawyer is a caricature that closes another avenue of individual control and exposes as a myth the idea of an unbiased and helpful legal system in America. These characters are all visually interesting but are not allowed to exist independently. Instead, they all are used to serve a specific function.

This is especially apparent in the cases of the preacher and of Ida. The preacher's initial appearance in the film is arresting and provocative; his refusal to help Coyle and his inching away from the accident is an unmistakable indictment of religious hypocrisy. He is also used as the agent of McCabe's destruction; as such, he becomes a major force in the development of the plot. As soon as he assumes this important function, the function becomes more important than the character. The statement Altman is making with the preacher becomes more straightforward and more direct. Its content does not really change but the preacher as a character becomes dwarfed by the point. In addition to diminishing the preacher as a character, the change destroys the subtlety and diffuseness the preacher brings to the earlier part of the film.

Ida suffers the same treatment. Unusual and haunting, Ida initially shies away from the camera and exudes fear, timidity, tension. When Coyle dies and leaves her without any means of support and without anyplace to go, her logical alternative is Mrs. Miller's. One or two shots, culminating in her waving good-bye to the cowboy, would have explained her adjustment. Rather than do that, however, Altman has Mrs. Miller calm her down and explain how whoring is as, if not more, honest as marriage. Through this conversation, Altman explicitly justifies Mrs. Miller and the other whores. Since throughout the film they have acted with decency and pride, their honesty need not be questioned. When Mrs. Miller talks about her position, her speech seems unnecessary. Also, because of this conversation, Ida becomes more than a character; her transformation from a scared girl to a mature, sensual woman becomes more than a happy change. Instead, Ida is turned into a before/after advertisement and proof of Mrs. Miller's argument. Although she becomes a more important figure in the film, she does so not because of her individuality but because she is a connection and key to the larger message.

In McCabe, Altman does not seem ready to let his minor characters stand alone as individual characters. He is

expecting less of the audience than he later will; he seems
here careful to make every connection explicit, to tie
every loose end, to make every detail direct and functional.
Because he does this and also because of the socio-political
nature of his message, McCabe remains Altman's clearest explanation of his social and political philosophy.

The Altman world is a hostile one whose forces are
distant, omnipotent, and indifferent to the individual.
The institutions of government, religion, and family that
normally are thought to buffer the harsh and invisible
realities of life are empty forms that are used by the real
powers, the corporations. The individual's allegiance to
these archaic institutions foster a false sense of security
and priorities that themselves further, stabilize, and per-
petuate the status quo.

Although we are destined to be born, live, and die
alone in such a bleak environment, we also have the potential to create true, if temporary, beauty, meaning, and
happiness. Since our power as individuals is limited by
the composition of the world, Altman says, we are freed
from any compulsion to act like heroes and thus are freed
to be people. So although we are unable to create per-
manence and although we live in a world of false institutions and hostile parameters and although we are destined
to have unhappy endings, we do have continual opportunities
to create spontaneous, intense, and beautiful experiences,
regardless of how long they last.

McCabe and Mrs. Miller can be thought of as Altman's transitional movie. As in the traditional film, there are few loose ends. The characters are purely functional; the values are explicitly explained; the identifications unambiguous. Although there is the potential for subtleties, Altman loses confidence in them and, by the end of the film directly explains them. The music works in the same way; the movie is a gentle, quiet one that develops its own moods. Leonard Cohen's dirge-like and distractingly beautiful ballads are obtrusively heavy. Rather than complement or help the moods, they push and determine the moods. Altman's following films, at least until Nashville, will avoid being so pointed and will require more from the individual viewer.

McCabe is also related to many of the other Altman movies in its thematic preoccupation with roles. Like Marlowe, Charley, Bill, and the MASH and Nashville gangs, McCabe is playing a role. This time, the role is a businessman. McCabe, however, never successfully throws himself into the role. Because he mixes his public persona and his private feelings and needs, he is never fully convincing in or understanding of the role. This leaves him unable to anticipate the role's demands. Thus, he does not understand the importance of the deal and acts improperly; he not only fails to make the deal, but also offends the principals. Because he does not know the script, then, he sets in motion the events leading to his own destruction.

While the other Altman characters define themselves so totally in terms of their roles that we never really know them beyond their roles, McCabe does not play his well enough and thus dies.

McCabe is like the later films in its visual beauty and its strong emotional impact. This is the first of his films that are like paintings; it is a film that can be watched simply as a procession of beautiful colors and visual images.[4] The film's beauty, however, is not functional since it does not really complement the theme or the story. Instead, McCabe uses its beauty as its own justification for its existence. After all, McCabe is a moving picture and thus can be looked at simply as a series of moving photographs. There is no reason, then, not to have those pictures be as beautiful as possible.

McCabe and Mrs. Miller, then, is a comprehensive socio-political statement about a younger but not very different America, a beautiful and tender love story, and a stunning visual experience. It also is Altman's last explicit and thus traditional movie; those that are to follow will be much looser and more open-ended. But since all the movies he will make will return to McCabe's core values, McCabe can be thought of as Altman's key movie, his cinematic home.

Notes

[1] Huston made this statement on the December 9, 1975
Tomorrow Show on ABC.

[2] McCabe is not the first, but only one of a number
of revisionist westerns, including Johnny Guitar, Little
Big Man, Bad Company, and Doc. In my opinion, McCabe
is the most sustained and most successful.

[3] In "Robert Altman's Anti-Western," (Journal of Popular Film, Fall, 1972), Gary Engle concentrates on the lack
of heroism in McCabe's final acts. I recommend the article,
which focuses on the social comment McCabe makes.

[4] Altman has made several statements about wanting to
make a movie like a painting, but I cannot locate them. I
think the remark was in an interview in Genesis, in Boston's
The Real Paper, and in Films and Filming. Unfortunately,
I cannot find the quote anywhere and thus cannot present
it with the significance and authenticity it deserves. He
also alludes to the remark and concept in the July 17, 1975
Rolling Stone article, "Bob Altman's Nashville," by Chris
Hodenfield.

CHAPTER 6
IMAGES

Images opened in 1972 to almost unanimously poor reviews and dismal box office grosses in its first few en-
gagements. The results of its first runs were so disappointing, in fact, that the film was withdrawn and never
received national distribution. This is unfortunate because
Images is one of Altman's most interesting movies.

Like the other Altman films, Images reworks a familiar
film genre. This time Altman is working with the subjective
suspense thriller. In these films, we see the movie directly through one of the character's eyes. In some movies,
like the 1947 Humphrey Bogart-Lauren Bacall Dark Passage,
the subjective viewpoint is introduced as a gimmick; we
literally must see through Bogart's eyes and wait until a
mirror or a pane of glass reflects the character's physical identity. Because of its obvious and mannered look,
this type of subjective approach quickly becomes annoying;
when it is dropped after about twenty minutes in Dark
Passage, the movie becomes easier to watch and more effective. There is another, less obvious way to incorporate a
subjective point of view into a movie. A successful example of the more subtle subjective film is Roman Polanski's
Repulsion.

In Repulsion, Polanski deals with the breakdown of a manicurist named Carol. Rather than give the audience an objective, nonthreatening vantage point, Polanski forces the audience to see the world through Carol's distorted eyes. Thus, the rooms of her apartment become increasingly elongated, twisted, blurred, and surreal; her fantasies become increasingly strong and vivid enough to intertwine themselves with reality; her outside and inside worlds coalesce and become terrifying and dangerous.

Throughout the film, as the camera slowly becomes Carol's eyes, we in the audience are denied any substantial explanation of the reasons behind Carol's problems. There are some hints: the photograph of her family, the religious references, her relationship with her sister. The clues never assume any definitive significance because the information that would make sense of them is withheld. This lack of information guarantees the audience's inability to understand the reasons behind Carol's breakdown and our resulting inability to objectify her experience.

Polanski deliberately denies us the information. By not being able to understand Carol's behavior intellectually, the audience's tendency to treat her clinically as a case study of madness is hindered. Without this more distant vantage point, we are forced to look at Carol on a less analytical, more emotional level. Because the details and objectivity that differentiate us from Carol are minimized, we are thrust into her experience. Rather than watch

Carol's madness, we are encouraged to feel and experience it.

Polanski achieves this emotional involvement by carefully structuring the film. The first part of the movie moves slowly; Carol goes about her daily routines. There are, however, many hints of her impending breakdown. She moves about in a daze, twitches her nose, is repelled and fascinated by the noise of her sister's lovemaking and by any male intrusion into her life (Colin's kiss and Michael, her sister's lover's toothbrush), and her inability to concentrate at work. This part of the movie is shot objectively; although we do not understand why Carol is getting more disoriented and distracted, we still are watching her from a rational, somewhat removed position.

Polanski begins to change this with the mirror scene. As Carol turns around, she imagines a man in the corner of her mirror. His momentary appearance in the mirror is as startling, disorienting, and frightening to us as it is to Carol; it is not an hallucination of madness, after all, but an ordinary fantasy that many of us have had. This is the first time the audience has been manipulated into having the same emotional response as Carol's. The transition into her point of view continues until Colin bangs the door of Carol's apartment down. The only sympathetic character in the film, he seems genuinely attracted to and concerned about Carol. When he comes to her apartment, however, we see him through Carol's eye, the hole in the door that distorts his face. He, like the audience, barges into Carol's world; when he breaks down the door and enters her apartment, he enters her jurisdiction. And since he is threatening to her, Carol brutally kills him with all the love/hatred she has. From then on, the camera does not leave the apartment or Carol's point of view.

After she kills Colin and, later, the landlord, Carol's breakdown intensifies; the cracked walls crack even louder and more severely and become more curved and elongated. They also get softer and more aggressive; hands reach out of them and try to grab Carol. The apartment becomes darker, gloomier, more shadow-filled. There are no objective shots and no relief; the audience is forced to see the world through Carol's eyes and, at least to some extent, is forced to undergo her experience.

For all Repulsion's subjectivity, however, it is an unambiguous movie. Because so much time is spent with Carol at the initial stages of her breakdown, the audience gets to know her environment and her situation. The more subjective part of the film can thus be identified and at least minimally analyzed. Because we have seen the cracked walls and the dimensions of the apartment in the objective part of the film, we know that the more startling cracks, the twisted walls are imaginary ramifications of the objective world. Since we are able to make this judgment, we also can unambiguously identify the men in her bed and the hands in the walls as figments of her imagination. This lack of ambiguity gives us at least some understanding and intellectual distance and thus undercuts our disorientation.

In the film's last scene, the subjectivity is dropped altogether. Carol's sister and Michael return from their holiday, find the two bodies and Carol, who is catatonic and under the bed. Michael picks Carol up and carries her past the crowd in the apartment building and the audience into the street. The camera follows them out and then returns to the room, which is disordered but restored to its original dimensions. Slowly the camera pans to the photograph of the family and zooms in to Carol's eye, separating and objectifying the audience and reestablishing the distance between character and audience. The movie and the experience over, Polanski eases us back into our own worlds.

Images does not give us this security of an objective framework. Operating without any framing devices, Images maintains its subjectivity throughout the entire film and thus demands a more active and more flexible audience. From beginning to end, Images thrusts us into a schizophrenic experience; not once does it compromise its structural design of subjective point of view and audience disorientation.

Schizophrenia, popularly thought of as the phenomenon of a split personality (a notion popularized by countless films and television programs), is more correctly defined as a split from reality.[1] As Images begins, Kathryn, a

children's book author, has already started to break away
from objective reality. There have been three men in her
life. Rene was the first, a lover who was killed three
years ago. Because she put him on a plane that crashed
and because she "miscarried" his child, she has never been
able to rid herself of that relationship's guilt. The second is Marcel, a promiscuous artist who lives near her
country home. She slept with him once the previous year
and still is both tantilized and repulsed by their brief
sexual encounter. The third man is her current husband,
Hugh. An ineffective, insensitive person, Hugh has none
of the sexuality of the two others but does offer her the
stability and security of a "good" marriage.

Kathryn's chief problem we quickly discover, is that
she cannot keep the people in her life straight. In the
middle of a kiss or a sentence, Hugh will become Rene who
will soon turn back into Hugh. When Hugh leaves the room
to get the quail, for example, Rene appears to talk, tease,
and abuse her. When she hits him, Rene bleeds all over
the carpet, even though Hugh does not notice the blood when
he comes back inside, possibly because his finger is bleed-
ing all over the carpet too. Kathryn is then forced to
deal with an imaginary Marcel who makes passes at her even
when the real Marcel is in the next room talking to his
daughter, Susannah. Then Kathryn is drawn into a strange
and special relationship with the twelve year old Susannah,
who looks mysteriously like Kathryn. Finally, there is

Kathryn's alter-ego, a woman who looks just like Kathryn and who Kathryn often sees standing in the distance watching and, perhaps, waiting.

In addition to making the country estate quite crowded, the presence and rapid interchanging of personalities are confusing and upsetting to Kathryn. Even more frightening are the ensuing events. Kathryn stops fighting Rene's and Marcel's advances and indulges in a particularly satisfying lovemaking session. She is, however, unable to tell which, if any, man was her partner.

Terrified, she confronts Rene. Realizing he must be dead because she saw him get on the plane, she asks him why he cannot be a "good ghost and stay dead." He then tells her that he is a product of her imagination who can be exorcized by a ritual act of murder. If, he tells her, she herself kills him, he can no longer bother her. With this advice, Rene hands her a loaded shotgun, which she uses. His advice apparently works, for he does not trouble her again - even if his bloody body does lie on the floor for the rest of the film. No one else notices the body although they do hear the gunshot and see the still camera of Hugh's that the blast has destroyed.

If she can kill Rene, she reasons, she can also kill the imaginary Marcel. During her first attempted murder of Marcel, however, Hugh interrupts her. She then waits until Hugh is called out of town, makes sure the real Marcel is occupied with a woman from town, and calmly hacks the imaginary Marcel to death. The next day, Susannah comes without her father; Kathryn has some nervous moments over whether she killed the right Marcel. But the real Marcel, she discovers when she takes Susannah home, is very much alive. Relieved, she turns the car around and starts home. On the ride back, she sees her alter-ego begging her for a ride. Ignoring her, Kathryn speeds home, only to be unnerved by the two bloody corpses and empty house. Deciding to join Hugh in London, she gets back into her car and is again stopped by her alter-ego, who begs for help and professes love for Kathryn. Suddenly Kathryn realizes that she can kill the alter-ego as easily and finally as she has Rene and Marcel and runs her off the cliff. With all her ghosts laid to rest, she drives to her London apartment and finds an already steamy bathroom. She gets into the shower and waits for Hugh. When the door opens, however, it is not Hugh, but her alter-ego, who is smugly laughing. Confused, Kathryn's mind is thrown back to the cliff. At the bottom of the cliff lies a bloody, very dead Hugh.

Kathryn is suffering, then, from schizophrenia because she is unable to differentiate between the real world and her imaginary one. The inability to differentiate forces her to act in a private world that is a unique combination of actual and illusory realities. Denied the benefits of a constant, objective reality, she is a disoriented kaliedoscope of moods: bewildered, confident, frustrated, desperate, sensual, frightened, rational, irrational.

To communicate her experience, Altman has designed a film so harrowing and so disorienting that we are immediately thrust into Kathryn's world. Unlike Carol in Repulsion, we do not see Kathryn in her early, slower stages of her breakdown. The first time we see Hugh, he turns into Rene; fifteen minutes into the film, Kathryn and her alter-ego become inexplicably intertwined. Without any previous information, we are expected to handle characters and plot shifts that we are not equippped to deal with. Like Kathryn, we are çonfused and frustrated; denied even the slender emotional distance Polanski allowed, we have no more idea which character is who or what really happened than Kathryn does.

The deeper we become involved, the more confusing and ambiguous the film becomes. When Kathryn is driving to Green Cove that first day, for example, she gets out of the car and stands on a hill to catch the first glimpse of her house. As she watches, to her horror, she sees her car drive up to the house and sees herself get out of it, look toward the hill she is standing on, and then go into the house. Then there is a shift to the Kathryn inside the house, who can see the Kathryn on the cliff who is still watching. This happens several more times - although Kathryn's relationship with her alter-ego becomes more ambivalent as her alter-ego becomes more aggressive, we can never really know which Kathryn was the one we met first. Any effort to untangle the two Kathryns leads to

an insolvable, frustrating maze that further disorients
the audience. This disorientation becomes a mirror of
Kathryn's mental state; we feel with her rather than intellectually understand her position.

Other insolvable puzzles and intentional ambiguities
abound. Regardless of how many times the scene with Hugh,
Marcel, Kathryn, and Susannah talking after dinner is
watched, the tracing of who is laughing and kissing Kathryn
and who is sleeping is impossible. Also untraceable are
the characters and events of the love scene. Was it mas-
turbatory and illusory or real? Was it one of her ground-
less fantasies or was it Hugh or Marcel? Like Kathryn herself, we have no way of knowing; also like her, we want,
even need, to know. Because we cannot, our own feelings
of frustration, dislocation, and confusion are further intensified.

Probably the film's major ambiguity concerns the identity of the body at the bottom of the cliff. Altman has
carefully allowed for two possible interpretations. The
first, the rational interpretation, is that Kathryn has
had a breakdown. Her confusion over her sexual feelings
and desires, her frustrations with her artistic career, and
her resentment over her contradictory need for the security
promised by a traditional marriage all lead to her subconscious taking control. Once in control, the subconscious
tricks her into killing Hugh.

Justifications for this interpretation include the shot of Hugh's train returning and someone, presumably Hugh, getting off the train; Kathryn passing the land rover that Hugh was to ride home on had he returned early; and Kathryn's alter-ego sounding more like Hugh than Kathryn with all the "Jesus Christs" and "Goddamns." Also used as evidence of Hugh's death is Kathryn's final phone call to Hugh in London; although she talks to him, he has never answered the phone. Throughout the conversation, the phone keeps ringing - as it must since Hugh is dead at the bottom of the cliff. Perhaps the final evidence for Hugh's death is the genre Altman is working in. Hugh's death makes sense and gives the film its twist and irony necessary for a strong conclusion. With this ending, Images becomes a clever reworking of Repulsion.

Ths interpretation is accepted, however, only by ignoring contradictory evidence. We cannot be sure, for example, that the person getting off the train is Hugh; the camera is too far away and the focus is too soft to make any identification. Also, shortly after the train shot, Kathryn declines Marcel's dinner invitation because she has "something very important to do," thus indicating a foreknowledge of her run-in with Hugh/her alter-ego on the cliff. But since she does not and cannot know about Hugh's return, she must have imagined the train shot and therefore also imagined the meeting on the cliff. Also, when the imaginary Marcel asks how she will manage to be alone with him, Kathryn answers, "I'll simply think him (Hugh) away, just as I thought you here." Shortly thereafter, Hugh is conveniently called away. Hugh's riddles are further proof that he is not really dead. "What is black and white, black and white, black and white?" he asks. "A nun falling down the stairs," is the grisly answer. And later, the alter-ego/Hugh falls down the cliff - and the film shifts from color to black and white. Neither the alter-ego nor Hugh are nuns but both may be figments of Kathryn's imagination and therefore "none" (nothing) in the physical sense. Hugh's last riddle continues the veral pun. "What's the difference between a rabbit? None, one is both the same." If Hugh is not down at the bottom of the cliff, nothing and no one is. He, then, is no more real than the alter-ego.[2] Still more confusing is Kathryn's speech before running the body off the cliff. Since "Hugh" and "you" are homonyms, we can never be sure what she is saying; is it "I know it's you (the alter-ego) but I found out I can get rid of you," or "I know it's Hugh but I found out I can get rid of Hugh"? Since the two characters speak their lines interchangeably, the scene may very well be an extension of Kathryn's imagination. Finally, when Kathryn enters her London apartment, the bathroom is filled with steam. If Hugh had been killed and since the alter-ego is a creature of the mind, the bathroom could not have been used. Since someone has been in the bathroom and since Kathryn has just arrived at the apartment, it is unlikely that anyone but Hugh, still in London, could have steamed it up.

There are, then, two equally plausible explanations, that the real Hugh was killed and that no one really was killed. If the real Hugh were killed, the movie is a chilling, if familiar, psychological suspense thriller. If he were not really killed, the terror remains the same but focuses on the horror of Kathryn's madness. _Images_ then becomes more like a nightmare, equally upsetting but less tangible.

To decide which of the two is the correct interpretation is futile because both are included in the film's design. Unlike _Repulsion_, which grounds itself to objective reality, _Images_ cultivates its subjectivity and ambiguities. If one and not both of the interpretations is true, we will know what really happened and will leave the theatre secure and confident. If, however, we are not sure, we will leave the film confused, disoriented, frustrated. Because _Images_ never endorses or returns to objective reality and because its ambiguity insures our dislocation, _Images_ remains consistent to its metaphor of schizophrenia, a split from reality.

The maintaining of ambiguities and insolvable puzzles in _Images_ is consistent with the schizophrenic metaphor in another way. Because emotions are so important to this film and because Kathryn's moods are so changeable, she and the film have no one constant emotion. Similarly, we can never know if Hugh was or was not killed; Altman is forcing us to have an ambivalent emotional response.

Depending on our own mood, our reaction to this variable
film changes each time we see the film. One time we may
be struck by the horror of Hugh's death; another time we
may be drawn more to Kathryn and the power of her madness;
still another time we may just be carried by the beauty of
the film's craft and colors and be oblivious to the drama
of its content. Like Kathryn, we can pick, choose, and
react to whatever we want. All the ambiguities and irra-
tionalities invite and demand our active emotional participation.

Images, then, is carefully structured to simulate a
schizophrenic experience. It demands an intense personal
involvement from its audience and rewards this involvement
with confusion, ambiguities, insolvable puzzles, and frustration. Especially frustrating is the desire for a rational coherence and a definite conclusion; the more we
want to know and try to find out what really happened, the
more frustrated and disoriented we become - and the deeper
we are drawn into the schizophrenic experience.

As emotionally powerful and perplexing as the final
confrontation in the bathroom and the flashback to the
cliff are, they are not the film's last moments. After
Kathryn screams and her alter-ego moves towards her, the
credits appear over the jigsaw puzzle that has been worked
on throughout the film. The missing pieces have all been
found; the puzzle is of Green Cove, Kathryn's country home,
and has a unicorn standing by it. Rather than with the

music or abstract sounds of the rest of the film, _Images_
concludes with the ending of the children's book Kathryn
has been writing. This time, however, the words are read
not by Kathryn, but by young Susannah. By ending with
this transformation, Altman underscores the importance of
their relationship to the film.

From the beginning, Kathryn and Susannah react to each
other intensely, instinctively, and non-verbally. Primarily because we do not enter into the relationship, it does
not seem intellectually or rationally motivated. For example, the first time Kathryn sees Susannah, the girl is
hiding in the cupboard, Kathryn assumes she is just another
ghost and shuts the door on her. When Susannah is finally
let out of the cupboard, she is understandably irritated
and sticks out her tongue at Kathryn, who surprisingly
sticks her tongue out too. Although this may not seem
proper behavior to us, Susannah understands and accepts
Kathryn's action. Next, Kathryn asks how old Susannah is
and learns that she is twelve and a half. Susannah then
asks how old Kathryn is; "Thirteen and a quarter," is
Kathryn's answer. Although we may be surprised by the in-
appropriateness and strangeness of her remark, Susannah
again understands instinctively. Altman allows the two
characters to indulge in almost a private joke and sets
the tone for their ensuing relationship. Throughout the
course of the film, the two become increasingly close, but
the nature of the friendship and their underlying motivations are never explicitly developed.

We do know that they closely resemble each other; the physical similarities are startling enough for Marcel to take special notice of them. Kathryn's concern for Susannah's feeling and welfare quickly replace her initial surprise and ease Susannah's initial hostility; when Susannah asks her to be her best friend, Kathryn is delighted. Because of their friendship, Susannah stops caring about a visit from her former best friend, a fifteen year old city girl. Susannah wants to know if Kathryn looked like her when she was younger because "when I grow up, "I'm going to be exactly like you." Later, when Susannah asks what Kathryn did as a child, Kathryn answers that "I used to go for walks, tell myself stories, play in the woods." Then Kathryn asks Susannah what she would do if Kathryn had to go away. Susannah calmly answers, "I'd tell myself stories, play in the woods. I'd make up a friend."

We see them drifting closer and closer to each other, merging their individual identities. Our suspicions and their verbal exchanges are, however, inadequate preparation for the final shot of the two of them together. Kathryn drops Susannah off at Marcel's and is about to drive away. She looks at Susannah through the glass car window; Susannah looks at her. They do not speak, for they already have said good-bye, but their faces become superimposed onto each other. In what is almost a freeze frame, the physical blending completes the mental merger; the two have entered into a chilling communion.

As Susannah reads the book's words, we see the unicorn superimposed over the puzzle and learn that the name of the book is In Search of Unicorns. The unicorn, a mythical beast, can be fed, as the legend goes, only by a virgin. Kathryn not only is no virgin, but is a repository of unresolved sexual conflicts; she cannot feed or even find the unicorn. She can, however, find Susannah, a virgin who can feed it. At the end of the film, Kathryn has mystically transmitted her identity to Susannah and has thus initiated Susannah into a circular process that will someday see Susannah become a Kathryn in search of her own Susannah.

The idea of a circular process is reinforced by the artistic circle of Images. The film opens with the camera looking through the window at Kathryn while the opening of the book is being read aloud. At the end, the unicorn replaces the camera and looks through the window at exactly the same angle. The constantly searching camera finally rests on the object of its search, the unicorn. The rest is, however, deceptively temporary; soon Susannah will grow up to be just like Kathryn, will lose her ability to feed the unicorn, and will reenact the story of spiritual possession.

Because Kathryn knows about the pain, confusion, and terror that eventually will descend upon Susannah, she is clearly apprehensive and upset over the transmission of identities. Whenever Susannah makes a verbal or an emotional progression into the merging of their identities,

Kathryn reacts with a look of anger, unhappiness, and warning. When Susannah tells her that she is going to grow up to be just like her, that she does not need any other friend besides Kathryn, and that she will behave just like Kathryn used to, Kathryn does not look pleased, but worried and frustrated. However troubled Kathryn is, however, she does nothing to stop Susannah's increasing involvement; it is almost as if Kathryn is a powerless bystander watching an irreversible process. And after the two faces merge in the car window, the symbolic merger of their two identities, Kathryn speeds away, her face contorted and grim.

The idea of possession is primal and familiar. Although the idea is not intellectually frightening because it is so improbable, it is emotionally terrifying on a non-rational, non-verbal level. Similarly, we can experience the bizarre side to Kathryn and Susannah's relationship without knowing why intellectually. In review after review, Altman was criticized for not sufficiently, or more properly, intellectually and rationally developing their relationship. This criticism, like the complaint that Images is too subjective, seems invalid because it stems from a failure to understand and accept the film on its own terms; we cannot understand the relationship, but can feel it. And feeling, not understanding, is what Images is all about.

A classic symptom of schizophrenia concerns a faulty perception of stimuli that lead to responses that are

inaccurate.[3] In other words, the schizophrenic takes ordinary stimuli, perceives them differently than a non-
schizophrenic does, and thus behaves differently than a
non-schizophrenic. Because Kathryn perceives the world
differently, she can look at a room and conjure up ghosts
that seem real or can listen to Hugh and suddenly turn him
into Rene, Marcel, or her alter-ego. Misinterpreting her
environment, she turns the mundane into a grotesque private
world.

We in the audience have a difficult role in Images
because we are expected to enter Kathryn's private world
and experience with her. Because her world is not based
on rationality but instead relies so heavily on her moods,
predispositions, and emotions, her world is disorienting
to us. As we sit through the film, we logically try to
make some sense out of Kathryn's actions and look for
some pattern that we can use to understand what is happening. Because we are trying to filter this grotesquerie
into our more mundane, non-schizophrenic value systems, we
are bound to be frustrated. After all, these values are
unable to translate, much less explain, the irrational
components of Kathryn's world. More important than the
frustration and the futility of our efforts is the ironic
reversal Altman plays on us; he gets us to exhibit a
schizophrenic reaction similar to Kathryn's. Although she
takes the mundane and makes it grotesque and we take the
grotesque and try to make it mundane, both are taking

stimuli, misinterpreting the context, and then acting according to the resulting false perceptions. Although we may be irritated, then, we must admit that Altman has moved us one step closer to Kathryn's schizophrenic experience.

Images embodies another symptom of schizophrenia, loose association.[4] Suspense and horror films are noted for their relentless pacing that keeps us on the edges of our seats. Repulsion, for example, builds from a slow first third to an increasingly quick rhythm. To help the faster pace, Polanski relies almost entirely on the straight cut, the fastest editing device. Images, however, goes against this pattern, using non-functional transitions like superimpositions, wind chimes, and hanging mobiles. Although they form a pattern of visual consistency and are beautiful, they are distracting because they slow down the film and draw attention to themselves, not to Kathryn and to the events. Also, the camera wanders over the rural landscapes for no other reason than the countryside's beauty, thus distracting from the functional rhythm normally associated with the genre. This dreamy, non-direct style breaks the continuity and pacing necessary to generate sustained suspense.

Altman undoubtedly knows this. He also knows that the faster moving, more linear style that would achieve a superficial suspense would sacrifice the film's subjectivity. By employing a loose style, he is using the camera as Kathryn's eyes; he is making us see the world in the same loose associational way she does. In this way, he successfully intertwines Image's theme and style.

The final symptom of schizophrenia that Altman incorporates into the design of the film is the loss of ego. A non-schizophrenic has no trouble distinguishing between himself and other people and objects; he knows where his body ends and where some other one begins. A schizophrenic, on the other hand, cannot.[5] Thus, Kathryn's ego perception becomes so disoriented that she sees her alter-ego, an extension of herself, watching her actions and trying to integrate into her ego. Kathryn is also confused enough to be unable to separate her husband from her alter-ego and her other male fantasies. Because she cannot tell who is real and who is not, we cannot either. As we wonder which one is real, we experience a similar, if less immediate, loss of ego boundaries and are forced to deal with one more aspect of schizophrenia. Even more than that, however, the loss of ego boundaries is the bridge between schizophrenia and Altman's idea of the artistic experience.

Kathryn's ability to detatch and watch herself is not much different from the detatched way we watch movies; there is always a separation or distance between film and audience. This distance inhibits a complete integration with the film and, as a result, inhibits the ability to feel and experience the film. Since there is this distance and lack of total involvement, there is a shift from feeling to understanding, which is an intellectual concept requiring some differentiation between the screen and the audience.

Placed in this context, Altman's desire to make a movie like a painting that is looked at and emotionally responded to becomes especially important; his use of schizophrenia as a metaphor for the artistic experience seems inspired. If, like the schizophrenic, we can be disoriented and separated from our objective reality, then we can be shaken loose from our rational vantage points, can minimize the inherent distance between us and the movie, and can feel the film.

The demand that we feel, rather than understand, Images motivates the film's design. Had Altman wanted us to know what really happened or why Kathryn was sexually frustrated and schizophrenic, he would have told us. Instead, he has built a series of insolvable puzzles and ambiguities that prohibit a rational, definitive interpretation. And since we cannot react securely and rationally, we are forced into an emotional response.

Altman purposely confuses the conventional relationship between film and audience even further by intertwining the reality of his actors' lives with their characters' lives. As the movie begins, develops, and ends, Kathryn is writing a book called In Search of Unicorns. The book was actually published; its author, a woman named Susannah York, who is also the actress who plays Kathryn. In addition, Kathryn's young friend, called Susannah in the movie, is played by Kathryn Harrison. Rene Auberjonis plays Hugh; Hugh Millais plays Marcel; Marcel Bozzuffi plays Rene. Roles, reality, and illusion are thus blurred and eventually indistinguishable; a rational response to the movie is made even more unlikely.

The first and the final clue to the film is in its title, Images. Altman gives us a series of images that ultimately must be taken as their own reality. He uses glass, mirrors, lenses, windows, and transparent wind chimes that all make images or reflections of the real world. In Images, however, they have a life of their own; they are transitory devices because they often are used to shift the locale or to indicate movement, but they are not used to establish a pattern or hint that the film or Kathryn is moving from "reality" to "fantasy." Instead, they become beautiful objects that reflect and create images for their own sake and their own justification. When we try to make them replicas of our own lives, the lack of a clear pattern and satisfying purpose frustrate and disappoint us. But when we accept the images on their own terms, forgetting to bend them to our own preconceived values and viewing habits, we are ready to enter the artistic experience. Yes, the men in the film may be real characters in a traditional sense; yes, they may only be images generated from Kathryn's imagination; yes, they can be both real and imaginary. Freed from the false rational need to mean something and be explainable, Altman is presenting a series of images and letting us respond to them. As he says, "I'm not going to tell you anything.... I'm not even going to show you anything; I'm going to let you see something. And if you don't help me, my picture can't be any good."[6]

Images, then, is a uniquely explicit plea for an alert and aware audience. Surrender, it begs us, to the artistic vision; abandon the insistence on the rational and mundane world and revel in the beautiful and horrifying new world of Images.

Just as McCabe is Altman's clearest explanation of his socio-political philosophy, Images is his most overt statement about the film experience. Movies should not have to tie up loose ends or be simple reflections of the outside world; unless they want to, movies should not have to cater to passive audiences. And since Images demands a more active and flexible audience, those not willing to accept their new roles will find themselves shut out and bored by it. But those willing to help, willing to suspend demands for rationality and reality in place of the more individual standards set by the movie itself, may be rewarded by a more expansive, more emotional, and more artistic film experience.

Notes

[1] *Webster's Third New International Dictionary* (Springfield, Mass., 1968), p. 2030.

[2] For a similar discussion of Hugh's riddles, read Mark Falonga's review of *Images* in *Film Quarterly*, summer, 1973, pp. 46-48.

[3] Arieti Silvano, "Schizophrenia," *Encyclopedia Britannica*, 1969 ed., v. 19, p. 1161.

[4] Webster's, *op. cit.*, p. 2030.

[5] *Ibid.*

[6] Terry Curtis Fox, "Nashville Chats: An Interview with Robert Altman," *Chicago Reader*, July 4, 1975, v. 4, no. 39, p. 10.

CHAPTER 7
THE LONG GOOD-BYE

Just as McCabe and Mrs. Miller is Altman's western,
The Long Good-bye is his contribution to the detective film.
And just as Altman did with the western, he examines the
conventions of the detective genre and carries them to their
logical ends.

From the beginning, movie private eyes have dealt with
the seamier aspects of life, regardless of the social class
involved. By necessity, and with the notable exception of
The Thin Man's Nick and Nora Charles, the private detective has been isolated from the rest of society, including
the police and the legal authorities. The world may be
amoral or immoral, but the private eye consistently remains true to his personal, often old-fashioned standard
of morality. Because he is a moral force in a non-moral
world and because of his peculiar occupational demands,
he usually must sacrifice a traditional lifestyle and must
exhibit a healthy disrespect for conventional social behavior, especially behavior revolving around the nine to
five, forty hour a week job. This helps explain the typical private eye look - the rumpled, unshaven, chain smoking, rough talking, smart alecky, solitary outsider.

Although rarely wealthy, he is attractive to women, especially those of high breeding, who do not often meet a man of such honesty and masculine sexuality. And like the best whores, the best private eyes hide a sentimental streak behind their cynical, hard exteriors.

The prototype private detective is unquestionably Humphrey Bogart; the definitive movie, probably The Maltese Falcon; the key scene, the one where Sam Spade (Bogart) refuses to listen to Bridget's plea for love and mercy and turns her in to the police. Yes, he admits, she is the only woman for him; yes, he does love her - but she has killed his partner and "that has to count for something." Also, if he lets her go, she can use his action against him whenever she needs to. His combination of cynical awareness and moral considerations leaves him no real choice; he must make a personal sacrifice and report her. Although he is composed and determined when he makes this decision, he is honest enough to admit to the loneliness and pain he will feel because of it.

If The Maltese Falcon is the most popular detective movie, the most beloved cult private eye film may be The Big Sleep. Bogart moves easily from Hammett's Sam Spade to Chandler's Phillip Marlowe. Although he plays basically the same role in both, the two films are totally different.

Where The Maltese Falcon is tight and fast, The Big Sleep is incoherent. There were many scriptwriters, including William Faulkner and Leigh Brackett (who wrote the

screenplay for The Long Good-bye), who worked on The Big
Sleep. The result is a plot that is unusually indecipher-
able. Characters drop in and out of the movie as fast as
the bullets fly; complications develop without regard for
length, theme, or story; one liners exist independently
from the rest of the film. The brilliance of some of these
scenes and the undeniable chemistry of Bogart and Bacall
make the film memorable; over the years, the film's confusion has even attained a reputation for uniqueness and
charm. Indulge, its devotees say, in its obtuseness; get
lost in its meanderings. Thirty years later, Altman would
take this looseness and intentionally incorporate it into
his thematic design.

In addition to the Bogart Marlowe, there is another
Marlowe from the forties. Two years before The Big Sleep,
Dick Powell played Marlowe in a film called both Farewell
My Lovely and Murder My Sweet. Although not widely remembered, it is arguably a better film than The Big Sleep.
Complicated but reasonably coherent, it is important here
because it offers Powell's personal brand of befuddlement
instead of Bogart's gutsy persona. Under Altman's guidance,
the two Marlowes would eventually coalesce into a peculiar
alliance. For as he did with the western, Altman has un-
sentimentalized the detective genre and has taken its traditions to their logical conclusions.

We first meet Altman's Marlowe in his typical private
eye apartment. Framed by a wall scarred with the residue

of struck matches and by a bed with dirty, crumpled sheets, Marlowe is pried out of his bed by his cat, who is hungry but particular. Regardless of the hour, the cat will eat only Curry Brand Cat Food, which, of course, Marlowe does not have. After a futile search at an all night grocery store for the obscure brand (they all taste alike anyway, the stock boy tells him), Marlowe returns home to meet a scratched Terry Lennox.

In terms of the plot line, the cat episode is meaningless; the film really begins with Lennox's request to be driven to Mexico. It is, however, an extremely funny and original sequence. In addition, it subtly establishes several important motifs. First, it begins the pattern of Marlowe being inconvenienced and used by others; the cat is just the first of many to ask him for a favor. It also introduces the idea that Marlowe is a loser; not only does he fail to find the cat food, but ultimately cannot even keep the cat. Finally, Altman sets up the first parallel between Marlowe and Lennox. Despite Marlowe's apparent loyalty and generosity, which later seems to distinguish him from Lennox, both have been scratched on the face; Marlowe by his cat, Lennox by his wife.

The meeting with Lennox not only sets the plot in motion, but also demonstrates the importance Marlowe places on friendship. In the middle of the night, Lennox asks Marlowe to drive him to Tiajuana. Although Marlowe is understandably unhappy about the long drive, he feels his friendship with Lennox obligates him to drive Lennox to Mexico, which he does, no questions asked.

When Marlowe returns to Los Angeles, the police are waiting to question him about his role in the Lennox affair. The police are thugs with badges who thrive on the abuses of authority and brutality that their role can encompass. As such, they do not understand or believe Marlowe's refusal to pry into Lennox's situation just because the two were friends. So the police bully Marlowe in an ineffective search for some answers. But partly as a result of Marlowe's distaste for the way they ask questions, partly because Lennox is not there to defend himself, partly because of Marlowe's ignorance, and partly because of his professional ethics and reputation, Marlowe refuses to answer their questions. Rather than be intimidated into disloyalty and submission, he breaks into an Al Jolson routine and gets thrown into jail.

Although Marlowe's use of fingerprinting ink for black-face and his choice of Jolson as a role are original, Marlowe's behavior is conventional movie private eye behavior. He distrusts cheap force and corrupt authorities and refuses to be intimidated by them. Regardless of his own comfort and situation, he remains loyal to his friend. And, perhaps most of all, he has a sarcastic and irrepressible sense of humor that complements his courage and stamina. Because Marlowe has so much humor and the others have no sense of humor at all, he is the only one who can laugh and not take himself seriously. Because he is more likeable and more refreshing than the other characters, he wins our sympathy and emotional identification, just like Bogart's did.

Marlowe not only demonstrates a fidelity to many of his role's traditional values, but also maintains its traditionally high standard of professionalism. When he accepts the assignment of locating Eileen Wade's missing husband, Roger, he quickly finds him even though he has only one obscure clue.[1] Roger Wade, it turns out, is a patient-prisoner at Dr. Verringer's private sanitarium; after Marlowe finds Roger, he then must rescue him. Which Marlowe easily does.

Marlowe not only succeeds in rescuing Roger, but also succeeds in not being overwhelmed by this oversized, hard living man. Although Wade is more famous, more imposing, more financially successful, and more complicated than Marlowe, Wade is unable to awe or manipulated Marlowe into becoming Wade's servant. Wade does extract Marlowe's promise to return to the writer's home, but he fails to convert Marlowe into another parasitic and slavish hanger-on. Marlowe never surrenders his integrity and functions humanely, responsibly, and as his own man.

From Wade, Marlowe moves to another set of characters, Marty Augustine and his ecumenical gang of hoods. Marty, a very rich and powerful gangster, threatens Marlowe and gets the same bravado that the police got. Although

Augustine hits harder and plays more dangerous games than the police, Marlowe still refuses to be intimidated. He must accept some physical pain here but uses his wit to beat the gangster at his own game. Marlowe's eluding of Harry, his inept tail, his own effortless success at following Augustine, and his refusal to cower further emphasize Marlowe's self-confidence and agility.

In addition to the traditional private eye character, Altman gives us the traditional complications of the private eye film. First, Marlowe, who has never accepted the labeling of Lennox's death as a suicide, gets a $5,000 bill from Lennox. He learns that Lennox was Augustine's delivery boy; he catches Eileen Wade lying about her relationship with Lennox and about her husband Roger's possible relationship with Lennox's wife; he finds out that the Wades and Augustine are involved in a dispute about money; he witnesses the mysterious return of Augustine's money and the horrifying suicide of Roger; he finds that Eileen has disappeared. Each complication intertwines Lennox's fate with the other characters' activities; Marlowe's concern for Lennox's reputation and his substantial commitment of time and emotions continue to draw him deeper into the mystery. Though everyone else is satisfied, Marlowe takes his obligation to his friend and to the truth more seriously. Even without a client, Marlowe is determined to finish the investigation.

His path leads, of course, back to Mexico and to Lennox.
With Lennox's $5,000, Marlowe buys the necessary information.
Lennox, who is Eileen Wade's lover, killed his wife. Roger
Wade, however, was convinced that he killed her in one of
his drunken rages; Eileen and Lennox use this belief to
drive Roger to suicide. With the spouses out of the picture, Eileen and Lennox planned to meet and live in wealthy
anonymity in Mexico. Armed with this information, Marlowe
is realy to confront Lennox.

In their meeting, Lennox is unable to understand Marlowe's anger. Lennox was in trouble, knew Marlowe was
there, planned to pay him well for the inconvenience, and
so had used him. "After all," he asks, "what are friends
for?"

Marlowe sees it differently. Friends, he says, are
"To turn to, Terry. Not to use. You put my neck right
under the ax. What's worse, you lied to me."

Lennox justifies his actions by telling Marlowe that
Marlowe is out of the mainstream of contemporary ethics.
"You're always going to be disappointed in people. In this
world, you've got to look out for number one, and that's
something you've never learned. I guess you never will
learn."

Marlowe's answer and reaction is surprising. "Just a
born loser, that's me. I even lost my cat. (Produces a
gun) Terry, there's such a thing as being too damned smart.
(Shoots and kills Terry)"

Marlowe kills Lennox, then, but not because Lennox has brutally killed his wife. Instead, the real reason he has to die is because he abused Marlowe's friendship and violated Marlowe's code of conduct. Marlowe's murder of Lennox recalls an earlier speech given by the gangster, Marty Augustine. "He was a criminal. He murdered his wife. (But) That was just a minor crime. A misdemeanor. The real crime was that he stole my money. The penalty for that is capital punishment." For Marlowe, money is not that important; his standard of conduct, however, is. When Lennox violates this code, Marlowe is as personally offended as Augustine is over the theft of his money. And when Marlowe executes Lennox, he is acting no differently than Augustine would - or than Lennox did. Marlowe has placed his own value system over every other standard and thus feels totally justified in punishing the offender. That the punishment is motivated by revenge and involves muder does not matter. In Augustine's words, Lennox deserves capital punishment. And if Marlowe does not administer the penalty, who would?

With this scene, Altman has taken the private eye's glorification of the righteous individual to its logical conclusion.[2] Marlowe is the only positive force in the movie - likeable, witty, secure, competent, loyal, dedicated. He is also smart, much too smart to believe that our existing institutions would effectively and impartially administer justice. So if morality and justice are to be

upheld, Marlowe himself must be the avenger, the hand of
justice. Thus, Marlowe, a decent man, seems to act out of
decent and moral motivations. He is so convinced of the
moral correctness of his stance that he calmly executes a
once good friend. And after administering the punishment,
he feels so cleansed that he dances down the street. Unlike Sam Spade and his sleepless nights, Marlowe will sleep
soundly, untroubled by any twinge of conscience. By making
Marlowe a vigilante capable of murder and by thus identifying him with all the other characters, including Lennox and
Augustine, Altman has shown that the private eye is really
no different than any of the others and that the moral superiority, integrity, and heroism of the private eye is
just another myth.

The characterization of Marlowe as a self-styled agent
of justice is not only the film's radical departure from
conventional private eye movies, but also the structural
device that gives The Long Good-bye its coherence. Like
the other Altman films, The Long Good-bye appears to be
loose and non-linear a la The Big Sleep. Characters wander
in and out of the film with little apparent reason; the
episodic pace of the film continues oblivious to the more
central concerns of the plot. Thus, such loosely related
characters like the cat, the yoga ladies, and Dr. Verringer
find their way into the film, adding depth and atmosphere
even though they do not further the story line. Upon
closer examination, however, the episodes and characters

are all directly related. No matter how subtle the connection, each character and each episode reiterate the film's
major concern, the unrelenting pursuit of one's own desires,
regardless of the needs of and cost to others.

The opening episode with the cat is a good example of
this. Even if it were saying nothing about the rest of
the film, it would still be an excellent first scene because it is very funny and arresting. No one sitting in
the audience would be confused or thrown off by the scene,
even if the more subtle nuances were missed. Although the
movie could have begun with Lennox barging into Marlowe's
apartment, the cat scene works cinematically. In fact,
however, it also immediately defines Marlowe's relationship
to the outside world. Throughout the film, people will use
Marlowe for their own purposes, regardless of the inconvenience to Marlowe. Despite Marlowe's efforts, he is unable to successfully interact and maintain relationships
with his cat or with his other characters.

Marlowe's next door neighbors, the candlestick ladies
who prance around nude in a yoga-drug induced state of
mindlessness, are another example of a set of characters
that seem unrelated to the rest of the film. They play no
part in the plot; as Marlowe says, "They aren't even there."
Concerned only with their own pleasures, they do not hesitate to ask Marlowe to buy them groceries even though they
never do him a favor in return. But the ladies are never
unfairly used by Altman; there are no cheap or prurient

zooms in on their naked bodies. Although they are pursuing
their own desires more obviously than any other character,
they are not criticized for wasting their lives nor are
they extolled for having fun without hurting anyone else.
Instead, they are used because they are visually interesting and amusing, because they elicit some very humorous
and immature reactions from the male characters, and because they further the film's concern with the pursuit of
personal pleasure.

Dr. Verringer, the quack who is treating Roger Wade,
also has little to·do with the film's story line, especially
since his original importance as Wade's alibi has been cut
from the film. But like the others, he adds depth and atmosphere to Marlowe's story while remaining an independent
cinematic character.

While Verringer's hospital is obviously comic, his
final confrontation is unsettling and strange. The unusual
little doctor wanders into Wade's party, demands his $5,000
(curious how this sum keeps popping up), and slaps Wade on
the face. We are still reeling from the film's first slap,
Augustine's Coke bottle scene, so we empathize with the
stunned Wade, who obediently writes the check. Verringer
demonstrates the way of the world; like Marlowe, Lennox,
Augustine, and Eileen, he feels he has been abused and feels
justified in behaving insensitively, forcefully, and self-
fishly so that he can regain what he feels is his.

Since we are shown Verringer's behavior but are not given the information necessary to understand it, Verringer is a typical Altman peripheral character. Because of a lack of background information, we are forced to respond to the character instinctively, emotionally, but not intellectually. Because most movies are artifically closed and omniscient, we are not used to this less rational style of film-making. But as Citizen Kane warns us as it fades out on a "No Trespassing" sign, movies do not always succeed in getting inside and revealing a character. The Long Good-bye does not even try. Thus, we are amused and then as shocked and confused by Verringer's behavior as the guests at the party are. And Verringer leaves as quickly as he came, answering no questions, adding emotion and mystery to the film but prohibiting a safe intellectual response.

Although Wade is slightly different because he is totally unsuccessful in getting what he wants, he does try to inflict his problems and needs onto everyone else. Afraid that he can no longer love and write, he tries to bully his wife and intimidate Marlowe into being his servant. When neither of these efforts works, he surrounds himself with his eager army of parasitic freeloaders. Underneath his brash facade, however, he is alone and afraid. When he is publicly assaulted and humiliated by Verringer, Wade cringes and cries. He does not have the self-assurance and toughness of Verringer or Eileen; he

cannot cope with their sense of purpose and tactics so he
writes the check and he commits suicide. More than anyone
else in the film, Wade is the victim, the weak prey who
cannot survive in The Long Good-bye's harsh, egocentric
world.

Like the other characters, Wade is developed enough
to make the plot line intelligible but not enough for us
to respond intellectually. We know that he is a heavy
drinker who is subject to amnesiac blackouts, that he loves
his wife and threatens to commit suicide to keep her love,
that he is afraid he has killed Lennox's wife and lost his
talent. We know he is a loud coward, full of meaningless
sound and fury. We do not know enough about him, however,
to really understand the private Roger Wade, who remains
enigmatic and distant. His role in the film is frustrating because he is a potentially interesting but undeveloped
character. By dying before we really get to know him,
Wade intrigues, fascinates, and involves us on an emotional,
not a rational, level. Altman thus insures our freshness
and our interest.

Augustine and his gang of hoods are more engaging than
Wade, but not as challenging. As respectable hoods, they
offer the obvious commentary on success in the seventies.
Augustine, the head hood, is rich and acceptable enough to
live next door to Richard Nixon. Like the other characters, Augustine is eccentric, affable, and even benevolent
until his interests are threatened. Then he is capable of

casual and extreme brutality. His willingness to scar his lover so that Marlowe would take him seriously and his speech labeling the theft of his money as the real crime are the two most explicit explanations of The Long Goodbye's world, especially since the acts are juxtaposed against Augustine's normally ridiculous and seemingly harmless personality. Had his capacity for cruelty and violence remained undeveloped, his obsession with physical fitness and his clumsy, inefficient gangsters would remain clever satires about California society. But Augustine and the others in the film only appear harmless and humorous when their self-interests are not threatened. As soon as someone takes something from them that they value, they are capable of any cohesive action to retrieve the object and are brutally able to punish the offender.

Like Augustine, Lennox is a familiar and superficial character. More than any other, he exists to give the plot direction; his murder of his wife, his escape, and his fake suicide motivate the entire movie. Marlowe's efforts to say good-bye to him, to clear, explain and finally get even with him provide the framework for the film. And Lennox is probably the purest representation of the film's theme. When asked to justify his unnecessarily brutal beating of his wife, he tells Marlowe he had no choice. She threatened to turn him in to the police, scratched him, and made him lose his temper. In other words, she inconvenienced him and interfered with his pursuit of the good

life. Because she caused him trouble, she deserved to be
eliminated from Lennox's point of view. When he killed her,
then, Lennox had no guilt feelings or pangs of regret.
People, after all, are there to be used. And Lennox, like
all the other characters, do not mind using them.

Perhaps the most inscrutable character of all is
Eileen Wade. She is beautiful, cunning, and ambiguous. A
quick but not totally convincing liar, she claims to love
Roger and be terrified of his violent and erratic behavior.
At the same time, she seems malevolently manipulative, cold,
and unforgivingly judgmental. She is suggestively teasing
and helpless around Marlowe (except domestically) and is
constantly using her sexuality as a tool to get information.

Her amorality is frightening; because she loves Lennox,
she is able to forgive his brutal beating and killing of
his wife and is able to help push Roger into suicide.
Eileen, like the others, is interested in getting what she
wants. In her case, it is a life with Lennox. To realize
her ambition, she is pragmatic, ruthless, and aware. To
achieve her happiness, she is willing to use Marlowe and to
destroy her husband.

All the characters, then, act on the assumption that
their immediate desires and values deserve primacy and fulfillment, regardless of the cost to others. On a first
viewing of the film, the tendency is to separate Marlowe
from the rest; Marlowe seems more like a refugee from a
forties detective movie than a contemporary of the other

characters. He almost could have gone to sleep thirty years ago, woke up, and was then forced to deal with the more cynical and egocentric world of the seventies. When Marlowe kills Lennox, then, Hollywood and justice seem to triumph.

Unfortunately, however, Marlowe is no different from the rest of the characters. Because The Long Good-bye is Marlowe's movie, we see the events from his perspective; by the end, we not only like him but accept his actions as proper. When viewed from a less personal, more objective perspective, however, his uniqueness fades. His bemused tolerance that lets him shrug off all weirdness with "It's okay by me," applies only when his self-interest is not directly threatened. More than a bemused tolerance, his reaction is more properly an indifferent passivity. As soon as his interest is involved, however, he becomes as cold and vengeful as the others. He may have more charm than the rest of the characters, but his persistence in tracking the truth and his happiness when he avenges it prove that he is no different than any of the other characters.

The Long Good-bye may be thought of, then, as McCabe and Mrs. Miller told from Butler, the hired killer's, point of view. Rather than the warmth and tenderness that emanates from real human interaction in McCabe, The Long Good-bye is cold and cynical. There is no sincere interaction between people, only continual manipulation and game playing aimed at self-maximization.

The movie's cynicism is structurally reflected in its most brutal and striking scene. Augustine's mistress, JoAnne, walks in on his effort to scare Marlowe and asks for a Coke. One of Augustine's hoods gets the only Coke in Marlowe's apartment; it is almost empty, warm, and flat. The state of the Coke triggers an Augustine monologue on the general state of Marlowe's apartment and on JoAnne's beauty. As Augustine is talking, he quickly and unexpectedly smashes the bottle into her face. As we watch in slow motion, the bottle breaks into her skin and flies off her face. Like Marlowe, we are totally unprepared for this violent intrusion; even though we have no personal investment in JoAnne, we are sickened by the senseless and horrifying brutality. Marlowe is surprised and stunned by the sudden cruelty, as we in the audience are; Altman has acted with the same mentality as Augustine. First, he has disarmed us by showing the ridiculous, seemingly harmless antics of the zany hoods. Then, without warning, Altman thrusts a minor character forward and mutilates her in slow motion. The action happens so quickly and is so skillfully suspended by the use of the slow motion that the moment becomes hypnotizing and compelling; we cannot look away. So we sit there, cleverly manipulated and coldly exposed to the same ugly and dangerous violence that Marlowe sees.

The camera work also integrates style and content. This movie does not try to penetrate the minds of its

characters; it is not a film fraught with psychological insights. Similarly, it is not a movie that is interested
in absolute value judgments; people are out for themselves
as a matter of fact, not a matter of morality. Some are
likeable, some are not; still, their appeal and fate have
little to do with abstract moral evaluations. Lennox, for
example, is a negative character because he is vain, overly
self-confident, and boorish. Augustine, on the other hand,
is much more brutal but is likeable because he has so many
amusing eccentricities. The technical reflection of this
lack of moral absolutes is the film's constantly moving
camera. As if to avoid any definitive or judgmental comment and to keep the movie outside the characters, the
camera never settles on one object or perspective. In addition to the constant motion, the film is shot in pastels,
which are neutral colors that also work against any overt,
definitive statement.

Like Altman's other non-linear films, The Long Good-
bye sacrifices a tight plot for a more episodic pace. Because the movie seems to ramble, its events are not
enough to generate continuity and consistency. The use of
pastels and the moving camera help for they tend to blend
one scene into the next. Perhaps more important for the
film's continuity is the thematic similarity of all the
characters and their overwhelming concern for their respective desires. Even more significant, however, is
Altman's use of movie allusions and music.

The movie allusions first. There are several reminders of Altman's own films. The death scenes of Terry Lennox and of McCabe's cowboy are shot the same; both show the victim's same look of surprise, they both fall into the water and turn over in slow motion the same way. Also, the cowboy's death and the Coke bottle scenes come at the same time in both movies and evoke the same stunned response from us. The sunset in the Mexican mountains recall the sunset shots in McCabe and Images, while the soft focus colors when Marlowe chases Eileen are reminiscent of Kathryn's ride back to London in Images.

Even more noticeable are Marlowe's allusions to other films and the Malibu Colony guard's impersonations. The guard spends his entire day and role imitating famous movie stars like James Stewart and Walter Brennan. Although everyone else is puzzled by the guard, Lennox and Marlowe are immediately appreciative of the guard's act (still another connection between Lennox and Marlowe). Marlowe puts on blackface from the fingerprint ink and breaks into an impromptu tribute to Al Jolson, the first talking film star. Then he meets Asta, the dog from the non-Marlowe type Thin Man detective series, who will not get out of Marlowe's car's way. There is also an hilarious encounter with the Invisible Man, a curious metaphor for Marlowe who can be both invisible and highly visible. "Loved all your movies," Marlowe casually remarks.

These allusions do more than draw attention to Altman's previous efforts, favorites, and influences. Instead, by constantly drawing attention to the movies as an art form, he is telling us that we are watching a movie. Thus, he reminds us that The Long Good-bye is not an imitation of life or literature, but its own art form. For the first time, Altman lets his allusions emerge full screen. They are no longer left in the corner of the frame as a flapping movie poster, nor are they thinly disguised. Now the allusions are an integral part of the movie, confident with being self-conscious. Because of their presence, the allusions naturally help create the boundaries and character of the movie.

Even more important is the way Altman establishes overt continuity within his diffuse, non-linear framework by the use of music. The only music in the film is the song "The Long Good-bye"; no matter what scene, character, or setting is on the screen, the accompanying music is a recognizable variation of the song. It plays, for example, on the car radio as an easy listening song; a Musak version hums through the supermarket; a Mexican funeral band plays it as a dirge; a bartender tries to learn it for the lunch trade; people dance to it at the Wade's party; even a doorbell chimes the song's first three notes. The song weaves in and out, giving unity and coherence to the diverse, episodic parts. Using the theme this way, Altman is cinematically coherent in a non-literary, non-visual, non-linear, and artistically exciting manner. Tying all the parts together, the music gives The Long Good-bye the style and identity that Altman was so self-consciously striving for in Images. He has finally made the movie that is conscious but not self-conscious about being a movie.

With this in mind, the ending of the film with the song "Hooray for Hollywood," the only time the music is not a variation of "The Long Good-bye," has several implications. As already mentioned, it is a sign of Marlowe's exhuberance over his retribution. Also, Hollywood is an easy target whose faults are widely known and accepted; the swipe at it here is cliched and jaded enough to be in keeping with the film's cynical mood. At the same time, "Hooray for Hollywood" is an extremely appropriate song for Marlowe to sing; after all, the role of the self-sufficient vigilante has been endorsed and popularized by countless American movies. Finally, and somehow simultaneously, "Hooray for Hollywood" has another dimension. The movie is over, Elliot Gould is pulling out of the role of Phillip Marlowe. And so, to leave The Long Good-bye and the world of the movies, he does a little song and dance, a cinematic curtain call, that takes us out of Hollywood's reality and puts us back into our own realities.

The Long Good-bye, then, is a sustained, original, and complete work. When grouped with McCabe and Images, it represents Altman's achievement of a personal film style and forms a body of work that justifies his status as one of today's more prolific and more important auteurs. Also, after The Long Good-bye, Altman has produced a wide enough range of films to begin drawing more from himself and his films than from any other source. Which brings us to Thieves Like Us.

---

[1] Interestingly, a scene in both the novel and the screenplay had Marlowe going to a central information-type agency and buying a computer analysis of his clues and finally of Verringer's whereabouts. This omniscient, invisible agency certainly is consistent with Altman's pressentation of omnipotent corporations in McCabe and could easily exist in The Long Good-bye's world. Its omission, for whatever reason, strengthens the impression of Marlowe's professional competence and self-sufficiency.

[2] Actually, the idea that the private eye would actually give up his quarry to the legitimate authorities at the end of the movie was always illogical. For almost the entire movie, the police would be seen as ominous, corrupt, inept, interfering; the private eye, who was honest, persistent, and dedicated, was harried and hassled by them. At the very end of the film, however, the police would suddenly become friendly rivals with the detective and responsible administrators of blind, fair justice. Even in the context of these original private eye movies, the concept of benevolent authority that the ending depends on seems inconsistent; in Altman's world view, the idea has no place whatsoever. All Altman has done, then, is remove the inconsistency; the law as administered by the legal authorities is as arbitrary and corrupt at the end of the movie as it is at the beginning. Since Marlowe cannot trust or interest the police at the beginning, there is no reason why he should do so at the end.

CHAPTER 8
THIEVES LIKE US

Thieves Like Us draws from many sources, including the 1937 Edward Anderson novel of the same name; the 1948 Nicholas Ray film adaptation, They Live By Night; and the 1967 Arthur Penn film, Bonnie and Clyde.[1] As he does in McCabe, Images, and The Long Good-bye, however, Altman personalizes and demystifies its film genre. More than just another gangster picture, then, Thieves becomes an examination and restatement of those films. In addition to this redefinition of the genre, Thieves also puts Altman's film style in a new perspective. Following three of Altman's most sustained and influential films, Thieves works within a familiar visual style. As we shall see, it demonstrates both the strengths and weaknesses of that style.

Before Thieves can be considered, however, its relationship to Bonnie and Clyde must be noted. Bonnie and Clyde turned insignificant and unfulfilled characters into romantic and mythic heroes. Both Bonnie and Clyde were poor, restless, and anonymous. Realistically perceiving that their conventional futures looked bleak, they became bank robbers. In their increasingly violent exploits, however, they found fun, fame, and riches. Especially when contrasted to the blandness of Eugene and Vilma and the evilness of Malcolm and the law, Bonnie and Clyde became "somebodies," heroes of the people.

Thieves Like Us does not share this romantic view of crime. The gangsters here never seem to have as much fun robbing banks as the Barrow gang did, nor do they find the same fame and fulfillment. Instead, Thieves paints a darker, less glamorous picture. Rather than depict the relentless pursuit of the authorities, Thieves concentrates on the more mundane, commonplace pressures that lead to the gang's destruction. Bowie, Chicamaw, and T-Dub are not destroyed because they are romantic outlaws that threaten society, then, but instead are governed by the same conditions of existence that constrain all of us.

The first sound in the film, the call of a bird over the United Artists logo, establishes the film's context. In addition to capturing the sound of a Mississippi swamp, it also suggests Brewster McCloud and his unsuccessful attempt to break free. The film's first shot, an excurciatingly long pan shot, picks up this comment; its seemingly circular motion foreshadows the group's ultimate inability to escape, even as it prepares us for the scene's unexpected humor. For despite the tension of this first shot, this scene is comical. Chicamaw explains that Jazzbo, who they will kidnap, sells marijuana to the prisoners; we see Jazzbo swerve across the road and hit a "pothole" in the road. T-Dub buys size 14 shirts ("Do you think we're midgets?") and size 46 overalls ("Do you think we're giants?") for their getaway outfits. Even Jazzbo tells a joke about a little boy who gives his turtles blisters by rubbing their feet on a table. Even more than the jokes, however, Jazzbo's character provides much of the scene's humor. Like many other peripheral Altman characters, Jazzbo's obesity makes him instantly identifiable, as does his whining fear of personal harm. As the three fugitives leave his car, which has a blown out tire and a flat spare, the camera zooms in on Jazzbo's face and hands and the soundtrack captures his bizarre and terrified assurance that he will follow Chicamaw's instructions. Although his name is briefly mentioned once more, we never see Jazzbo again. Still, like Verringer, the preacher, and the other peripheral Altman characters, Jazzbo's unusual physical appearance and personality develop his character effectively and efficiently.

Other Altman-esque details abound. The overlapping soundtrack, even more inaudible than usual, offers a direct commentary on the film's action. T-Dub reveals his amateurism not only by counting the number of his bank robberies, but by exaggerating the number of them. He begins by saying, "This will be my twenty-eighth bank." The next bank job, however, will be his "thirtieth"; the following one, his "thirty-third." T-Dub's tendency to exaggerate is further compounded by his counting the hold-up game at Mattie's as a real bank job. More importantly, the first two bank robberies are accompanied by radio soundtracks of old Gangbuster programs, which make the three's operation seem ridiculous and juvenile. The context of the broadcasts also warns of their eventual destruction; "they blazed their way across the state before being brought down by the guns of the law," the radio blares. The connection between the soundtrack and the characters is further emphasized by the leader of the radio outlaws being called the Octopus. Shortly thereafter, in Mattie's house, Lula tells T-Dub, who functions as the group's leader, that he is an "octopus."

Equally obvious is the "Romeo and Juliet" broadcast. Keechie and Bowie have been growing increasingly close; as they make love for the first time, the radio blares out "thus did Romeo and Juliet consummate their first interview by falling madly in love." Although Altman may have been trying to foreshadow the disintegration of Bowie and Keechie's relationship by contrasting them with the most romantic, most idealized love affair in history, the verbal intrusion seems cynical and distracting. Later that evening, when Bowie and Keechie make love twice more, Altman repeats the line from Shakespeare, even zooming in to the radio. The device does not only distract us, but it robs the scene of its dignity. Altman seems unable to humanize his characters and let them enjoy a tender, fulfilled moment.

Altman spends a great deal of time developing Bowie
and Keechie; their unusual physical appearances (so different from the Hollywood glamour of Warren Beatty's Clyde
and Faye Dunaway's Bonnie), their innocence, honesty, and
vulnerability make us respond to them as people, not characters in a film. Unlike the typical gangster movie that
glamorizes gangsters, we see Bowie and Keechie as people,
not as the gangster or social problem and his gun moll.
Unlike Clyde, who totally defines himself through his occupational role of outlaw, Bowie's and Keechie's love has
nothing to do with his being a thief. Similarly, Keechie's
objections to Chicamaw and T-Dub have little to do with the
morality of living outside the law. Instead, she seems
jealous of the times and loyalties the men share. Since
this human dimension of the characters is crucial to the
film's success, Altman should be maximizing, rather than
minimizing our relationship with Bowie and Keechie. In
the Romeo and Juliet sequence, however, Altman's insecure
and insensitive use of the soundtrack makes fun of their
innocence. For the first time since McCabe, Altman lets
his self-conscious, highly visible style separate himself
from the characters. As the result, he degrades them,
cheapens the scene, and, at least momentarily, undermines
his film's effectiveness.

Thieves' camerawork can also be distracting. The
film's dominant camera movement is the slow zoom, which
reflects the use of the camera to direct our attention.

In the scene where the three are reading the account of
the escape, for instance, the camera tells us exactly how to
react. The camera watches Bowie and then Keechie as she
approaches the house; from the beginning of the scene,
Bowie is separated from Chicamaw and T-Dub, allied with
Keechie. Bowie and the camera move into the living room,
just before Keechie, who carries the newspaper. As the
three read about their escape, the camera moves in slowly
until it rests on the three and empahsizes the words of the
article. When it lists the three's identities, Bowie
leaves the room; the camera follows and shows him staring
at Keechie. We only hear the few lines about T-Dub and
Chicamaw; we are more interested in Bowie's longing for
Keechie. When T-Dub reads the longer part of the article
about Bowie, however, the camera moves back to Chicamaw and
T-Dub, who clearly resent the extra coverage devoted to
Bowie. As the article moves back to a description of the
authorities' reactions, the camera cuts to Bowie, who is
still watching Keechie. Then, as T-Dub begins reading the
article's punch line, "If you can't trust a trustee, who
can you trust?" the camera returns to the room and rests
on T-Dub and Chicamaw. Afterwards, Chicamaw and T-Dub
elaborate on their dissatisfaction with the article's treatment of them; as each speaks, he is isolated in the frame
by a still camera.

This scene also illustrates Altman's functional and
thematic use of the camera. The content of the article,

Bowie's leaving the room, and the camera's constant reminder of his physical isolation and desire for the even
further isolated Keechie all cooperate in underscoring the
potential discord between the characters. For an Altman
film, however, the relationship between the camera and the
action is unusually obvious. The trustee line is funny,
for example, but the pointed camera work draws too much attention to it. When climaxed by the set monologues of
T-Dub and Chicamaw, the obtrusive camera movements create
a contrived, stagey impression. Like the gangbusters and
Romeo and Juliet jokes, the obviousness of the camerawork
in this scene distracts us and self-consciously interferes
with the material.

Fortunately, Altman subdues both his camerawork and
stylistic mannerisms in the latter part of the film; the
distractions occur earlier in the film. Rather than a
major problem, they become minor irritations, important
primarily because they suggest limitations of Altman's
style. Except for these few excesses, Altman does restrain
himself; as the film progresses, he drops the artificiali-
ties and contrivances of the earlier scenes and lets the
material present itself.

Except for these earlier lapses, Altman handles his
details and characters with his usual skill. Mattie, for
instance, is seen as the radio plays the introduction to
the Shadow ("Who knows what evil lurks in the hearts of
men?"), but only after the radio has been unobrustively

incorporated into the fabric of her home life. Later, when Bowie and Keechie come to her Pickin Grapes Motel, the radio calls her "the heart of gold." Ironically, Bowie and Keechie turn the radio off. The door falling on Dee Mobley's head as he leaves the wounded Bowie is humorous but will turn on itself as the door to Bowie's cabin falls off during the shootout. Bowie's birthplace in the Ozarks is reflected in the title story of the pulp detective magazine; "Fiend of the Ozarks," the magazine advertizes. And when Mattie decides to let them stay, she gives them cabin thirteen. "It figures," mutters Bowie, whose superstitious nature has been hinted at by his earlier reluctance to meet in a "haunted" house. In addition, Thieves is shot through a filter that effectively captures the feel of the past and the Depression without resorting to the overused and sentimental soft-focus look. The costumes, sets, and objects used in the film add to its authentic appearance; the faded Coca-Cola signs, thirties' radios, and old southern buildings give the film a lived-in air. The soundtrack helps, too. Altman drops the gangster programs and replaces them with political broadcasts; in the third bank robbery, for example, we hear Roosevelt's inauguration and in the train station, a speech by Father Coughlin is broadcast.

More interesting than these details are the minor characters of Thieves; each one is impressed on our memories. Lula, T-Dub's young wife, dedicates herself to cosmetology; she continually redoes Noel Joy's hair, dyes T-Dub's hair, and gives him manicures. When she hands Bowie her marriage certificate, Bowie humorously mistakes it for her beauty school diploma. Although superficial and only shabbily sexy, she radiates warmth; beneath the stereotype of the gun moll lies a likeable and decent person. Less likeable but equally effective is the jail warden. Totally self-centered, he gluttonously eats an enormous meal in front of Bowie. Too rude to invite Bowie to share his dinner, too' lazy to walk a few yards, he reveals the extent of his self-preoccupation during the escape. "This is gonna cost me plenty, boys, this is gonna cost me plenty." A reflection of the world of The Long Good-bye, all that matters is his own welfare. Dee Mobley also impresses us with his negative quality. A drunk who does nothing without some sort of renumeration, he appears menacing but is more sound than fury, easily handled even by Keechie. He becomes important, however, because he foreshadows Chicamaw's mental deterioration; when Chicamaw brings the wounded Bowie back to Dee's, Dee explodes that he has never enjoyed the benefits of fame and fortune. An uncharacteristic outburst for a worthless drunk, it lifts Dee out of his stereotype and gives him a measure of humanity. Even more memorable are Mattie's two children, Noel Joy and Bubba. Noel Joy is a strange, passive girl, chained to Mattie's rules of training that will supposedly mold her into a model southern woman. Her strikingly different face

and her sadly docile manner help her tap dance her way
into our hearts. Bubba is more familiar and more entertaining; he has the face of an old man and the mind of a
master criminal (a fate he may be destined for). He plays
with firecrackers, incessantly lights matches (a habit that
humorously pays off when he alone can give T-Dub a match),
blows ashes all over the table, and jumps in puddles when
dressed in his Sunday best. All of Mattie's determination
and punishments cannot tame him.

However effective and interesting Jazzbo, Lula, the
children, Dee Mobley, and the warden are, they remain minor
characters. Although they provide atmosphere and depth to
the movie, they cannot carry the film. This task belongs
to the major characters, Bowie, Keechie, T-Dub, Chicamaw,
and Mattie. We spend more time with these people than with
the others; because we know them better, we feel their degeneration more.

Altman deals first with Chicamaw, T-Dub, and Bowie.
Prisoners and later criminals together, they compare themselves to the three musketeers; "There'll never be another
group like the three of us," T-Dub constantly repeats.
Despite this boast, however, they rarely function as a
unified group. In the beginning, Bowie's youth, inexperience, and notoriety sets him apart from the more seasoned
older men. Chicamaw and T-Dub laugh at his naivete and
even throw a petrified bat at him. When they pull their
first job, they force Bowie to drive the car; after all,
"he don't know how to rob a bank."

The alliance, however, soon shifts. When Mattie goes to the railroad station and leaves the three alone, T-Dub and Bowie dream of a more normal life. Although not ashamed of their actions, they realize the risks they run. "I made my mistake when I was a kid," T-Dub decides, "I should have been a doctor or a lawyer or run for office and robbed people with my brains instead of a gun." He dreams of a farm in New Jersey, where he can put mistletoe on his coat-tails and let the world kiss his ass. Bowie does not dream of a farm, but of pitching pro ball. He too has no illu-sions about the romance of robbing banks. Chicamaw inter-rupts this reverie by pushing his hung-over head out the window and turning them back to the business of robbing banks. Just as Clyde in Bonnie and Clyde cannot envision any other occupation than bank robbery, Chicamaw can think only of drinking, loving, and robbing banks. Because of this inability, Chicamaw cannot share T-Dub and Bowie's dreams of a different future.

This difference is accentuated by Chicamaw's problem drinking, his violent personality, his increasing resent-ment of Bowie, and his total dedication to his role of a thief. The scene where Chicamaw, T-Dub, Noel Joy, Bubba, and Lula play bank robbery reveals Chicamaw's dependence on his role and his potential for violence. Noel Joy plays at being a teller and Bubba makes a very funny porter, but T-Dub plays only so he can frisk Lula. Lula wants no part of the game, thinking it "dumb," until Chicamaw screams that she had better take it seriously. He scares her into submission, showing how dangerous he can be. His behavior also demonstrates how deeply engrained his role is; unlike the others, he cannot play-act or have fun with the game. Instead, he takes his role so seriously that it has already begun to destroy him.

Despite the friction and differences between the three men, they do have a relationship that demands Bowie's loyalty. Because he feels an obligation to his partners, he returns to Yazoo City over Keechie's objections. After T-Dub dies, Bowie privately grieves, movingly saying good-bye to T-Dub as he stokes the fire. And he calls Chicamaw his only friend and hopes to get to Mexico with him.

Although the partnership elicits a loyalty and gives the three the means to live, it fails to satisfy their personal needs. T-Dub wins Lula, who loves the luxuries money buys and thus offers no real resistance to the demands of the three's association. Bowie, on the other hand, must deal with Keechie's insistence that he "go straight." Less realistically and materially motivated than Lula, she hates Chicamaw and has little use for money. Bowie, as a result, is torn between Keechie and the two men. Chicamaw, denied the benefits of a love relationship, becomes the most unsatisfied and least stable. Resentful of Bowie's charm and competence from the beginning, Chicamaw has no other source of satisfaction outside the group. When this does not fulfill him, he degenerates into a psychopathic rage.

When Bowie smoothly frees him from prison, Chicamaw explodes. Bowie makes him "look like thirty cents. It just
rips my guts out."

By the end of the movie, then, their relationship has
become destructive and debilitating. T-Dub is dead, possibly because his love for Lula made him put his real name
on the marriage license; Bowie's attempt to save Chicamaw
provides the excuse and rationale for his death; and Chicamaw's rationality has been destroyed by his jealousy. As
in all Altman relationships, then, what seemed beneficial
and positive turns out to be destructive and dangerous.

This depiction of the disintegration of the gang in
Thieves makes it a much less romantic movie than Bonnie
and Clyde. Throughout Thieves, T-Dub and Bowie have shown
that they are not ashamed of their work; Bowie's only regret was getting $19,000 instead of $100,000. Keechie does
not object because Bowie is a thief, but because he must
divide his attention between her and the boys. Although
devoted to form, Mattie does not mind when T-Dub reads a
newspaper account of their robbery at the dinner table.
Even there, they treat their occupation matter-of-factly;
the discovery that they are wanted dead or alive has a
sobering, but not a moralistic, effect on them. And, unlike Bonnie and Clyde, the law does not play a very visible
role in the film; the gang does not seem to be chased at
all. Rather than focus on the spectacular and dramatic,
Altman concentrates on the more banal, ordinary events of
their existence.

The film neither condemns nor glorifies them, then, for being gangsters living outside the law. As bank robbers, they steal and kill, but only Chicamaw seems to enjoy the violence. (T-Dub tells Bowie that the money is insured and the bankers just hand it over, steal some themselves and thus turn a personal profit; "It's like a piece of cake," he says.) Although they take more risks and are more visible, then, they are no different from lawyers, doctors, politicians, gasoline attendants. Unlike Bonnie and Clyde, who become mythic heroes destroyed by the forces of society, T-Dub, Chicamaw, and Bowie remain "thieves like us," ordinary people who are defined and destroyed by desires, pressures, and conflicts common to all human relationships and occupations.

Mattie, Bowie's agent of betrayal, specifically reflects the film's unsentimental approach to gangsters. When T-Dub, Chicamaw, and Bowie celebrate their first bank robbery and plan for their future, Mattie refuses to join in the euphoria; "It'll take more than money to get Bud out of jail," she tells them. Still, even with that awareness, she accepts T-Dub's $12,000 motel. When Bowie begs to stay there, she simply tells him that T-Dub is dead and no longer matters. Bowie cannot understand her attitude, especially after T-Dub financed the motel and called her "real people." Mattie, however is pragmatic; with T-Dub only a memory, continued association with his gang could only hurt her husband's chance for parole. Bowie's forceful insistence eventually wins him cabin 13; as he will soon learn from Chicamaw, however, no honor exists among thieves.

Although Mattie reluctantly allows Bowie to stay, she quickly turns his presence to her advantage. Presumably to hasten her husband's release from prison, she betrays Bowie's presence to the police. In the name of love, and for her own self-interest, she accepts responsibility for Bowie's and Keechie's murder - although Keechie saves herself by wandering over to Mattie's to get a Coke just before the gunfight. Mattie's tears at the gunfight and her sincerely solicitous concern for Keechie during the shooting show that she understands her role and condemns herself to a life-long guilt. Consistent with other Altman characters, then, she is driven to an abominable and destructive act so that her role in a permanent relationship could be maximized. More important than Mattie, however, is Keechie's final reaction.

Rather than blame Mattie, Keechie blames Bowie; he has crossed and lied to her "once too much." Keechie feels that Bowie has chosen the men over her. Like Mattie, she has defined herself totally through her relationship to Bowie; had the roles been reversed, she would have acted just as Mattie did. As in the other Altman movies, the love relationship raises expectations that cannot be fulfilled and leads to destruction.

When we first meet Bowie and Keechie, they are both young and immature. Bowie (his name even sounds like "boy") has bangs that accentuate his baby face, appears gangly, clutches his baseball glove, adopts a stray dog, and misses his mother. Keechie is unkempt, has straggly hair, wears ill-fitting clothes, and does not inhale her cigarettes. They cannot meet each other's gaze and shyly refuse to commit themselves to an acknowledgement of their feelings. "I have a watch for you, if you want it. Do you want me to have it? I guess so. Well, I guess I want it then."

Gradually, however, they become more adult; she cuts her hair while he combs his more stylishly, wears flattering suits, and gains more assurance because of his material success. After she cares for his wounds, they make love. And although they exhibit a winning ignorance about sex as they wonder how many times to make love and if they should during the day and although they still talk in juvenile cliches ("I like you a million, billion, trillion bushels full."), Bowie can now simply tell Keechie that he loves her. The transition from the awkward, evasive, and euphemistic baby talk to Bowie's simple, sincere, and committed statement of love gives this moment and scene a rare beauty and poignancy.

After this scene, Bowie and Keechie are quickly propelled into adulthood. Keechie loses her passivity and reticence by demonstrating a surprising self-assurance. She tries to make Bowie choose between herself and the gang, claiming that Chicamaw is no good and that she does not care about money. Bowie, however, sees their plight

more realistically. Besides being a fugitive with no means
of support, he has an obligation to his friends. His continued identification with the gang is hinted at by his
use of Chicamaw's "Keechie Keechie Koo" after they sleep
together. Keechie, who is ignorant of the origins and
sexual implications of the remark, answers with her own re-
frain, "Bowie Bowie Boo." Rather than the private bed talk
that brings the two closer together, this verbal exchange
foreshadows the inevitable friction that will separate
them.

When Bowie goes to Yazoo City, Keechie feels betrayed.
Instead of trying to understand and help Bowie, she acts
selfishly and shrewishly. She accuses him of lying to her,
using her, and choosing his friends over her. The difference between the easily satisfied and easy going Keechie
of the film's first part and the new Keechie is emphasized
by a startling shot of the distorted reflection of her face
in a warped mirror. No longer the sweet innocent, Keechie
has become twisted and ugly. As if realizing the change,
Keechie runs to Bowie. Since she has nothing without
Bowie, she convinces herself that Bowie, who has been so
stunned by the day's events that the cannot even speak,
would never let her leave. Instead of leaving him, she
throws herself onto him.

This sequence illustrates the relative immaturity of
both Keechie and Bowie. Although they are forced to deal
with the adult world and although they are no longer the

youthful innocents of the first part of the film, they
cannot cope with their problems. Thus, Keechie childishly
expects Bowie to devote all his time to her and to magi-
cally establish a conventional existence. Even though
Bowie has a more realistic perception of their future and
thinks more about Keechie's welfare than his own, he also
fails to act maturely. When faced with Keechie's tantrum,
he is rendered speechless. More importantly, he cannot
imagine getting to Mexico by himself; this lack of faith
in his own abilities makes him free Chicamaw, which in
turn results in Bowie's death. Had Bowie been more self-
reliant and more willing to act on his own, he might have
survived. Their transformation into adulthood is not complete, then. They lose their innocence; they gain little
beyond the beauty of their initial sexual experiences.

Although Keechie agrees to stay with Bowie, her feelings of rage and betrayal return all too soon. Sick because of her pregnancy, she does not realize that he freed
Chicamaw so that she could escape to Mexico and have the
normal family life she wants so badly. Instead, she interprets Bowie's escape plan and death as a further betrayal
of her. This feeling motivates her final bitter and chilling action.

Earlier in the film, when Bowie is playing catch with
Alvin, a young boy, Keechie brings up the possibility of
their having a baby. Bowie says he heard that children are
important because they are the way men become immortal;

although he cannot imagine having a child immediately, he wants one sometime in the future. When Keechie tells the woman at the train station that her husband died of consumption (one of Altman's more ironic jokes) and that she hopes her baby will be a boy "who will not be named after his daddy," she shows her deep hatred for Bowie. Rather than mourn his death, Keechie feels sorry only for herself. And to pay Bowie back, she plans to punish him horribly - by denying him his chance for immortality.

The impact of this action, intensified by the film's final shot of the crowd of passengers moving slowly up the stairs, going nowhere "for a long time" and swallowing Keechie up, is even more devastating when compared to McCabe and Mrs. Miller. The two couples undergo similar fates; they fall in love, are driven apart by societal presures and occupational roles, and end with the men being murdered and the women surviving. Of the two women, Mrs. Miller is better off. She never defined herself totally through McCabe, understood McCabe's death, and could support herself. Keechie, on the other hand, cannot understand Bowie's death and feels betrayed. Even worse, she is pregnant and consumed with hatred. Her bitter and aimless emotional state, soon to be coupled with the demands of parenthood, makes Keechie's situation unpleasant and pathetic.

Keechie's depressing end indicates a darkening of Altman's vision since McCabe, then, because she proves that love is not only an impossible emotion to maintain, but leads to betrayal and hatred. <u>Thieves</u> also suggests inherent limitations to Altman's self-conscious style of film-making; at times, his allusions and mannerisms distract us from the movie and undercut the actions of his characters. The gangbusters and Romeo and Juliet radio broadcasts suggest a separation of Altman from Bowie, Keechie, T-Dub, and Chicamaw. The devices are unsuccessful because they throw us out of the film and undermine our relationships with the characters. Altman has built into his film style an inherent limitation; too much omniscence, self-consciousness, and distance from his material guarantees a noticeable failure. Unfortunately, Altman will not learn his lesson; he makes the same mistake and suffers the same failure, on a larger scale, in <u>Nashville</u>.

---

[1] For a sustained comparision of <u>Thieves Like Us</u> and <u>They Live by Night</u>, read Robert Kolkers "Night to Day" in the Autumn 1974 <u>Sight and Sound</u>. Also recommended is Marsha Kinder's "The Return of the Outlaw Couple" (<u>Film Quarterly</u>, Summer, 1974), which concentrates on the relationship between <u>Thieves</u> and <u>Bonnie and Clyde</u>.

CHAPTER 9
CALIFORNIA SPLIT

By the time Altman made California Split, he had already developed a noticeable array of personal trademarks: overlapping dialogue, episodic pacing, pessimistic endings and optimistic moments, sudden appearances of superficially unrelated and intellectually undeveloped characters, a preoccupation with whores and gamblers, frequent allusions to other movies, and a reworking of a genre. And California Split has them all. Its genre seems to be the gambling movie but, like Thieves Like Us, it is more a commentary on the other Altman movies than on the broader genre. It is more about McCabe and Mrs. Miller and The Long Good-bye, then, than The Lady Gambles, The Lady Eve, The Cincinnati Kid, The Hustler, and The Sting.

California Split is basically the story of two men, Charley and Bill, who are classic opposites. Charley is spontaneous, sloppy, free, irreverent, and self-confident. Whether he is being mugged, playing poker, or getting drunk, he never breaks character or stops his brash, witty, and colorful mutterings. An exciting personality, Charley operates on his dynamic and irresistible energy. Bill, on the other hand, is middle-class, successful, bored,

146

repressed, and rational. Unlike Charley, who trusts and acts on his instincts, Bill needs facts and justification before he can act. After a race that ends in a photo-finish, for example, Charley dances to the ticket window before the winner is announced; he just knows he has won. Bill cannot understand how Charley knows and looks worried and apprehensive. Only after he sees that they officially have won does he celebrate. Not surprisingly, Bill is fascinated by Charley, who seems to be the ideal person to teach Bill how to enjoy life.

The interactions between the two not only constitute the film's major plot line, but also determine the film's structure. The first part of the movie is shot from Charley's point of view and is consistent with his person-ality; it is fast paced, carefree, and constantly alert to the humorous absurdities inherent in the film's events. The second part of the film belongs to Bill; instead of the humor, there is an underlying desperation and ugliness. The final part of the movie is a mixture of the two points of view; Charley's humor is present but seems empty and false when framed by Bill's more serious needs.

Because Charley focuses on the humorous possibilities of every incident, the first part of California Split ig-nores the latent ugliness of its characters and settings and favors their lighter elements. The first scene at the poker palace, for example, is played for laughs; the poker players are grotesque or nondescript in a harmless,

good-natured way. The woman with the bulldog face who
thinks she is an expert gambler is not ridiculed but presented as a peripheral, eccentric, fleetingly revealed,
and refreshing personality. We do not make fun of her;
she is absurd but we like her. Even Lew, the thug Charley
fights and is later mugged by, is so obnoxious, so big, so
boorish that he is almost a caricature of a movie villain.
He is so mean and so broadly drawn, in fact, that he loses
his reality; in keeping with Charley's attitude, he is too
much. He thus becomes an absurd annoyance, rather than a
serious danger.

The fight at the poker table lets us know that Altman's
world view has not changed. As the two men accuse each
other of cheating and begin fighting, no one else gets involved. Instead, they avert their eyes and complain about
the interruption of their game time. Even Bill gets involved only reluctantly, gets punched by Lew, and quickly
escapes by crawling away from the table. Charley, however,
does not hid from the fight or bemoan the failure of the
others to get involved. Rather than moralize about the
incident, Charley's constant chatter is fast and energetic
enough to dispel any unpleasant implications of the fight.
Because of Charley's reaction, the game remains very amusing and non-threatening; the fight seems only a calculated,
safe, and playful risk on Charley's part.

Later, Charley pushes on to a topless bar. Here he
overhears a conversation between a waitress and her girl

friend, who presumably is a junkie in need of thirty dollars. The waitress, with Charley's unasked for support, borrows the money from the cash register and leaves the film. The character is as curious as any other incompletely overheard and incompletely explained conversation. Although she remains an unsolved little mystery, the waitress benefits from Charley's benign tolerance and ability to accept people on their own terms, devoid of any overbearing moral judgments. The sordid potentialities of the two women's relationship are thus downplayed in favor of a more amused, indifferently curious, and mysterious presentation.

The bar scene is crucial to the development of Charley's and Bill's relationship. Bill is characteristically sitting at the end of the bar, hugging anonymity. Charley pushes himself on Bill, who, despite himself, responds to Charley's charm and warmth. Almost immediately, they are happily drunk, betting on the names of the seven dwarfs (an allusion to Marlowe's betting on the dollar bills' serial numbers), singing, dancing, and getting mugged. For the first time, Bill looks relaxed and happy.

Even the mugging is not allowed to destroy the film's light mood. We hear Charley and Bill being kicked, beaten, and robbed by Lew. Since the scene is shot in very dark, blue on black tones and is very short, however, the beating is relatively bloodless. Altman thus insures our sympathy for Charley and Bill and our continued disgust for Lew, but minimizes the pain of the mugging.

The jail sequence reestablishes the film's light mood. Charley and Bill are bailed out by Charley's friend, Barbara. This scene is stolen, however, by a white, middle class family who has mistakenly been hauled into jail. Although the family mutters unintelligibly and is never visually placed in the foreground, their looks of bewilderment and their appearances in their bathrobes make them absurdly funny. They reinforce the negative portrayal of the police, who have also mistakenly picked up Bill and Charley, the victims of crime, rather than the perpetrators of it. The family makes a point, then, but does so without forcing a seriousness or preachiness onto the movie.

Charley's and Barbara's home is seen through this same perspective. Although the dishes are dirty, although Charley's relationship to Barbara and her roommate Susan are never explained, although breakfast is Lucky Charms cereal and a bottle of beer, although the furniture is lumpy, the apartment is warm and comfortable and the people who live there care about each other. When Susan, the younger prostitute, comes in crying because the man she "loves" has left her, Charley and Barbara help her get over the rejection. Charley does not give advice or moralize; instead, he tells her about the weight of the tongue of the great white sperm whale. And even though Susan can see through his transparent attempt at cheering her up, she responds to his silly, irrelevant, but sane approach to life and laughs. Ignore the problem at hand, focus on something more amusing, and watch the problem disappear, says Charley. At least temporarily, his strategy works.

Barbara's, Susan's, and Charley's home is not at all usual, but is consistent with the film's point of view. A dirty apartment of a gambler and two prostitutes could easily have been treated as immoral, degenerate, unhealthy. Instead, however, their home is stable, zany, and humane. Its inhabitants are generous, uncomplicated, concerned, and honest. Because we are seeing the film through Charley's unconventional, spirited, and relaxed eyes, the apartment seems secure, warm, and even beautiful.

When Bill leaves the apartment to go to work, he is still under Charley's influence. So although Bill's attitude towards his work is reflected by the magazine's working cover, rows and rows of identical graves in a California cemetery ("Who in his right mind would put a cemetery on the cover of a magazine called California?" his secretary Barbara mutters off camera), the death-in-life theme is casually and ironically treated and then obscured by some other activity. Only when Bill assumes control of the movie will observations like this be allowed to linger and be emphasized.

The differences between Bill and Charley are made explicit in this scene. Unhappy about being in his office, Bill calls Charley. While Bill is neatly dressed and surrounded by the superficially romantic glamour of a magazine writer's existence, Charley is relaxing in his bathrobe, picking his teeth. Charley, who is answerable to no one, feels like going to the race track and invites Bill along. Although Bill wants to go just as badly, he owns his time only after hours and must lie like a schoolboy to go.

The following scenes on the bus and at the track are among Altman's most comic and rhythmic. On the bus to the track, Charley meets an avid, superstitious woman who is betting on the horse Egyptian Fem because she bet on her last year, lost, and feels that the horse owes her money. Charley uses every rational reason he can think of to convince her to change her bet because the horse is a loser. At the track, however, he decided to bet on the horse too. When the astonished Bill sees Charley so confident, he demands an explanation for the strange bet. "She owes me money. She owes my friend money," Charley answers. After the race, before the official results are in, Charley runs to the ticket window. Bill cannot believe Charley's assurance; Charley tells Bill he can feel the win. Bill remains unconvinced but finally, after he has proof of the win, he too becomes exhuberant. "We won! We won!" he screams. "No foolin'" is Charley's deadpan reply, "Where've ya' been?"

The difference between the two's approach to winning is the clearest proof yet of the fundamental differences between the two. Charley is not just an instinctive gambler, but also has fun gambling. Totally at ease and at home at the track, he belongs there because gambling seems a natural activity and a celebration for him. Bill, on the other hand, gambles as if he were slumming; gambling seems exciting to him because it is risky and unsafe. Lacking confidence in his own instincts and feelings, Bill never looks like he is having a good time. Thus, he needs written assurances that he has won; once certified, he then allows himself to have fun. Because of his repressions and caution, he never really integrates into the spirit of the track.

At the end of the scene, Bill once more shows that he is on strange territory. The girl on the bus, who has taken Charley's advice and bet on another horse, sees Charley at the winner's window, realizes that he bet on her horse, and screams and yells at him. Then she begins throwing oranges at the fleeing couple and finally hurls her purse at them. Charley is naturally amused and just grins; Bill, on the other hand, overreacts and throws one of the oranges back at her. Typically, the orange does not come near the girl. "You can't even throw, you asshole," she yells.

Wanting to celebrate their win, Bill and Charley return to Barbara's and Susan's. To their disappointment, they find out that the women have already agreed to go to dinner with one of their regular customers, a transvestite called Helen. Imitating the police in The Long Good-Bye, Charley and Bill wait for Helen, announce they are the vice squad, intimidate and frighten Helen away, and salvage their evening. Despite the prankster humor and the unerring accuracy of their vice square routine, their behavior is cruel, unpleasant, and self-centered. This is still Charley's scene; the other characters stifle laughs and allow themselves to be carried by Charley's force and intensity. Although still light, this scene is the first in which Charley intimidates and victimizes a helpless person for sport. There is, then, an undertone of cruelty that is a foreshadowing of the film's later mood.

The unpleasant undertones vanish, however, as the movie moves to its most touching scene. The four go to a boxing match; they become two couples on a pleasant double date. Even if Susan cannot bear to watch the boxers hit each other, she cheers with the rest of the crowd. The arena is alive and active; strangers are betting both on the fight in the ring and on the fights that have broken out in the audience. "I'll bet five on the man in the suit," laughs Charley as they are leaving the auditorium. Comfortable and happy with each other, the four are having a good time; because the four are so likeable, we too have fun watching them.

Their happiness is unexpectedly cut short in the parking lot, where Bill and Charley are again mugged. Once more, Charley takes control and salvages the situation by his fast thinking and faster talking. Even in this confrontation, which is potentially the most dangerous and most unexpected, Charley proves his ability to instinctively control events and to maintain his healthy sense of humor.

Although they come away from the mugging unharmed and relatively unfazed, Charley's and Bill's luck begins to turn. Charley and Bill return to the poker casino. This time, however, Charley and Bill are playing at different tables and are adrift in a sea of matronly ladies. Earlier in the film, Charley had explained that he likes the casino because the players there are suckers who think they are good gamblers. "Boy," he says, "do I love to beat those suckers!" Now, however, Bill and Charley are being beaten by those same suckers; none of their fast talking is able to minimize their losses. Charley's arrogant attitude and boasting has backfired; for the first time, we sense a superficiality behind Charley's routines.

The film's transition from Charley's to Bill's point of view continues with Bill's call from Sparkey, his angry and unpaid bookie/loan shark. Under Charley's supportive gaze, Bill puts on a fake show of bravado and succeeds in postponing the payment deadline. Even though the delaying tactic is successful, it is the first ugly and real challenge of Bill's responsibilities to Charley's more spontaneous lifestyle.

In the first part of the film, Altman has intertwined the characters, moods, and events. Charley's light, playful, and impulsive personality dominates and determines the perspective by which the events are presented. Thus, the ugliness of the confrontation between Charley and the other poker players is glossed over by Charley's fast wit and by

Bill's comical escape; the first mugging is softened by the preceding warm drunk scene and following comic jail scene. Charley's, Barbara's, and Susan's unusual home life is framed by the concern each has for each other and by the sanely eccentric and child-like quality of their behavior. The Egyptian Fem sequence is so well paced, comic, and good natured that it buffers the nastiness of the encounter with Helen, leaving only a hint of the imminent mood shift and ultimate reassessment of Charley's character. At least in the first part of the film, then, the sheer force of Charley's personality puts everyone, including the audience, under his dazzling spell.

As soon as Charley leaves, however, the mood of the film changes. With Charley gone, Bill becomes the film's controlling force. And from the first moment, the shift is noticeable. In an especially degrading scene, Bill meets Sparky, the loan shark, and grovels for more time. We watch Bill plead, beg, and endure Sparky's insults and contempt. Had Charley been in the same situation, his ability to fast talk may have made the scene funny. Bill, however, lacks his charm and instincts; his inadequate attempts at hustling are ugly and unpleasant to watch.

Bill's efforts to raise the money display none of the film's earlier compassionate and gentle humor. Harvey's ESP flash about Bill's need for some new house paint is more ludicrous than funny, especially when juxtaposed with Bill's real needs. Had Harvey been introduced earlier and been seen through Charley's sense for the absurd, he may have been genuinely funny and likeable. Appearing in Bill's segment, however, he loses the element of respect and healthy humor and becomes instead a character to laugh at, not with.

Failing to get money elsewhere, Bill goes to a poker game held in a dirty building in a decaying neighborhood. To enter the game, he has to walk through a dark, cluttered apartment where he is jadedly propositioned by a black whore. In the room adjoining the game, there are an expressionless woman and baby. The contrast between this house and Barbara's and Susan's home is striking; instead of warmth, light, and love, there is only squalor, poverty, and broken people.

The disintegration of a healthy environment is continued in the film's second bar sequence. Bill is drinking alone in a bar much like the bar he met Charley in. But there is no conviviality here, only an abusive drunk woman who, like Bill, has run out of luck. Although her clothes and appearance indicate a former dignity, she is now shrill, embarrassing, and depressing. She dominates the scene, making it as uncomfortable for us as it is for the bar's patrons. The humor, good will, and optimism of the first part of the movie are now totally absent.

Bill goes back to Barbara's and Susan's house in the hopes that Charley has returned, but finds Susan alone. Bill is still reeling from the increasingly difficult

demands being placed on him; Susan is still in between re-
jections; both, then, are in need of genuine human contact.
When Susan tells Bill that she finds him sexually attractive, he awkwardly explains that he has no money. Since
even McCabe had to pay for Mrs. Miller, there is some tension hinging on Susan's reaction. Susan, however, is no
Mrs. Miller; she smiles, tells Bill that she really likes
him, and will do it for free. Despite or perhaps because
of her sincerity and tenderness, Bill is embarrassed and
clumsy. As they try to struggle out of their clothes and
get comfortable, Barbara comes in and further embarrasses
Bill into leaving. As he leaves, he becomes one of the
many men who have broken Susan's heart. As he shuts the
door, the camera moves in on Barbara's tear stained and
suddenly old face; she clings to Susan and tells her of
the two men they are going to Hawaii with the next day.

Susan and Barbara do not return to the film; they
leave California and our field of vision. Their exit is
to be followed by Charley's return and thus is the final
segment of Bill's segment of the movie. Despite their
relatively early departure from the film, however, Susan
and Barbara are very important characters.

Susan is a painfully naive, vulnerable, and open person. She is more a child than a woman, wearing silly pa-
jamas, exhibiting a very short attention span and an un-
limited gullibility, vacillating from deep depression to a
joyous belief that her "lover" will become her husband.

Barbara, on the other hand, is older and wiser. She is the
one who copes with the daily living requirements, from bail-
ing the men out of jail to managing the evening with Helen
to setting up the Hawaii trip. Although she tries to keep
Susan hopeful, Barbara's eyes and face show that she knows
Prince Charming will pass them by.

Like Mrs. Miller, Barbara probably would not give her
body, her livelihood, away for nothing, which perhaps explains the lack of physical intimacy shown between Charley
and Barbara and also their separate sleeping quarters. Despite this similarity, however, Barbara lacks Mrs. Miller's
self-confidence, business mind, and foresight. Where Mrs.
Miller takes a book to bed, Barbara takes the TV Guide.
Both women are approaching their last years of active whoring, but Barbara seems financially and mentally unprepared
for the transition to a future means of support. In fact,
Barbara seems more like one of Mrs. Miller's whores, a decent, sensitive "class girl" who lacks Mrs. Miller's strong
survival instinct and ambition.

Although Barbara and Susan do not have a bright future
or a permanent love relationship with a man, they do have
each other's respect and love. They have a home, complete
with Christmas tree lights, and are committed to each
other's welfare. Barbara offers Susan physical, nonsexual,
and psychological comfort; in the rarer instances when
Barbara herself is in need of reassurance and affection,
Susan is capable of providing it. At first glance, their

relationship appears to be a reversal of the Altman pattern of the isolated individual incapable of sustaining a permanent relationship.

Upon closer examination, however, and despite Barbara's and Susan's genuine and deep concern for each other, their relationship is incomplete. It is based upon their lack of sustained relationships with men and the more practical need of having someplace to live. Given the chance, each would choose a relationship with a man. Since there is no man, they rely on each other. Thus, regardless of how functional or comforting their relationship is, it still is a substitute for a totall fulfilling one.

Unlike Susan and Barbara, Bill and Charley choose to be together. Charley thinks Bill is a good gambling partner; Bill expects Charley to help him loosen up and enjoy himself more. But like Susan's and Barbara's relationship, there is an incompleteness and quiet desperation to their friendship. When Charley gets back from Mexico and they become partners again, there is an unresolvable tension between Charley's absurd, fast talking style and Bill's more sober, more troubled needs. Because of the conflict between the two moods, the last part of the film is a mixture of both; we still laugh but it is no longer funny.

When Charley appears in Bill's window, complete with Mexican hat and paper bird, Bill is organizing all his pawnable goods. Bill is hurt by Charley's abrupt departure and feels left out. Rather than deal honestly with

Bill's emotional, if neurotic, reaction, Charley characteristically reverts to the crudely funny one-armed piccolo player joke. Bill laughs too long, too loud, too hysterically to be laughing at the joke; he is also exhibiting relief at the reestablishment of their relationship.

Partners again, the two set out to raise as much money as they can so that they can enter a big poker game in Reno. While Bill pawns all his possessions, Charley resorts to street hustling, beating cocky young basketball players and mugging Lew, who he runs into at the track. And although we still sympathize with Charley and still laugh at his efforts at hustling, the humor is more forced. Even though he still is likeable, he no longer seems as harmless and healthy as he did in the earlier part of the movie.

As soon as they get the money, the two go to Reno. Bill tells Charley he feels like he is going to win everything and must play the hands, listens to Charley's instinctive and correct assessment of the other payers, and then kicks Charley out of the room. From this point, the humor stems from Charley's efforts to keep busy and pass the time while Bill plays. After a slow start, Bill becomes the big winner at the poker table. When he exhausts that, he turns to twenty-one, roulette, and craps. His streak holds; he finally stops, after winning eighty-two thousand dollars. Understandably ecstatic, Charley is already making plans on which tracks to spend the next months at. Bill, however, is strangely subdued. "Do you always take a big win so hard?" jokes Charley. "I lied," Bill admits, "there was no special feeling." Charley looks at him disbelievingly; "I know that," he answers, "everybody knows that." This is not enough for Bill, who stares at Charley. Finally, realizing he must say something, Charley fumbles with his money and then looks at Bill. "It don't mean a fucking thing," he quietly says.

A knowledge of The Hustler helps make Bill's disillusionment over the absence of a special feeling more understandable. In that movie, Sarah tells Eddie, a pool hustler who loves the game, that he is a winner. Even though he has no money and no security, he feels magical when he picks up the pool cue. Because he loves what he is doing, because he is one with the pool cue, he has something much more valuable than material success. That feeling distinguishes him from the other characters; since they have no activity that they can feel at one with, they are losers. This is the same feeling that Bill hopes to find in gambling.

Bill, an educated, conventionally successful person, is unhappy with the routine banalities of the middle class world. He is irresistibly drawn to gambling, but is too cautious and reserved to be secure in the gambling world. Charley seems to be his perfect mentor. Despite a streak of cruelty and overpowering self-centeredness, Charley is fun loving, street smart, impulsive. Having no job, no family, no real home, Charley is free of all traditional responsibilities. Most importantly, Charley appears to work purely by instinct and feeling, rather than reason. His ability to enjoy himself and control any situation suggests that he has captured the essence of gambling.

Because so much of Charley's appeal to Bill stems from his spontaneity and naturalness, his admission that people only act as if there is such a feeling is particularly damaging. In a world of increasing standardization and distrust, Charley's honesty and integration of his public and private selves are refreshing and rejuvenating. His admission of only acting like there is a special gambler's instinct is also an admission that he is playing a role. This undercuts the concept of Charley as a spontaneous and natural person, acknowledges a gap between the public and private Charley, and raises the question of Charley's posturing. He did not know, then, that Egyptian Fem had won before the results were posted, but only acted as if he knew. In his own way, he is just as studied, mannered, and confined to a role as Bill is. His role may be more attractive, mainly because it passes itself off as an instinctive non-role, but it is a role nonetheless.

If Charley can convincingly act out a special feeling that he does not feel and use the feeling as the cornerstone of the core activity of his life, he can also act out the more peripheral roles. His talent for conveying a role explains the zeal and effectiveness he brings to his police impersonation, the success and ease he has in hustling the kids on the basketball court and handling the black mugger. Charley is as convincing in these roles as he is in his performance of a gambler. His entire act rests upon the premise that he moves naturally and instinctively, that gambling is right for him because it feels right. Without that instinctive feeling, the role of the gambler becomes kin to that of a con man. It is no longer a question of feeling, but of giving the impression of feeling.

The realization that there is no special feeling or instinct to gambling has important implications to Bill. Instead of an exhuberant and spontaneous activity, gambling is merely another game that does not "mean a fucking thing." At the beginning of the film, there is a machine that flashes a still from McCabe and tells whoever puts a quarter in (Charley, in this case) that the film will teach him how to play the game. And at the end of the movie, Bill has learned to play with style. But he still does not feel anything; he has merely escaped from one rat race into another.

At the end of the movie, then, Bill sits alone at the bar. He has absorbed everything he could from Charley; he has learned all the moves and has learned them well. And he has won. But the winning has been devoid of the feeling, the excitement, the emotion; this emptiness negates the win and makes it a far more serious loss.

So although Bill has won a great deal of money, he
has spent many agonizing and joyless hours winning it. And
in spite of the money, the personal pain and disillusionment that he has undergone make him a loser. There is no
special feeling, Bill finds out, only a manufactured sense
of false excitement that cheapens and degrades gambling
and gamblers. Had Bill lost the money, there would still
be potential winners; by making him such a big winner and
still a loser, Altman shows that there are no winners in
the gambling world.

This comment is reiterated and underscored by two
beautifully understated details. The first occurs when
Charley and Bill are about to enter the Reno poker game.
They stop to pet Dumbo, an ivory statue that recalls the
film's first bar scene and the flowering of their friendship, for luck. As they do so, a player that has just been
beaten walks out of the poker game they are about to enter.
Although Bill and Charley do not notice him, they have seen
him before.

In the film's first scene, there is a collection of
individual types playing poker. One man is middle-aged,
mild mannered, white collared, and Jewish looking. Although he does nothing distinguishable, he is memorable
principally because he looks like Bill's father and just
like what Bill will probably look like in twenty years.
When he walks out of the Reno game Bill is going to walk
into, the implication is that Bill will not disassociate

himself from the gambling world he finds so little satisfaction in. Even though it is not satisfying, gambling is a habit that is hard to break.

This detail is further amplified by the movie's final shot. While the singer sings, the credits pass by and over a spinning wheel of fortune. About two-thirds through the credits, the credits begin to follow the wheel's rotation until they are picked up and roll with it. The film ends, then, on a circular motion - everyone is where they began. Some are a little more disillusioned, all are a little older, and all are still on the circular treadmill. Once on, there is no getting off.

As the film ends, Charley and Bill, like all the other characters, are alone. Bill shakes his head; "I'm going home," he tells Charley. "Oh, yeah," Charley snaps, "Where do you live?" Bill sadly smiles; he cannot tell Charley where because he himself does not know. So instead, he just says "I'll see ya'." The camera pulls them apart and the deeply depressed and disillustioned Bill leaves. Charley is more resigned to life's lack of meaning and is more comfortable in his role; he bounces back much faster. Thus, after Bill leaves, we see Charley give the wheel of fortune its final spin and then hear him banter and sing with the Reno singer. "It's the story of my life," he tells the singer as she begins to sing "Bye Bye Blackbird," a bittersweet song of endings. "Pack up all my cares and woes, here I go, singing low. Bye, bye, blackbird," they sing. The next line is even more appropriate. "No one here can love or understand me." Even though he has perfected the role to the point where it seems natural, it is still a role; we do not know the real Charley who is behind the role. And since we cannot know him, we certainly cannot love or understand him.

Altman has, of course, been dealing with the essential isolation of the individual in all his movies; the movie allusions in California Split help remind us of this running concern. Although there are several references to Disney films, including Snow White, Dumbo, and Bambi, and to The Cincinnati Kid, the majority of the allusions are to The Long Good-bye and McCabe. More than entertaining trivia, the allusions are used to establish contexts, depth, and comments on the characters and events of California Split.

The still from the gambling scene in McCabe and the verbal cue that the movie will teach how to play the game is in the first scene. This is especially interesting because McCabe died because he could not play the game and could have used the lessons. The next scene also uses an allusion, this time to The Long Good-bye. Bill and Charley bet on the seven dwarfs, just as Marlowe and Lennox bet on the three brothers and on the dollar bills' serial numbers. Soon thereafter, in both The Long Good-bye and California Split, the male leads are thrown into jail. And when Charley imitates the cops in Helen's scene, he is imitating the ones who shook Marlowe down.

The allusions go beyond specific references; the characters themselves allude to and define themselves in reference to the other movies. Susan and Barbara, for example, are directly contrasted with Mrs. Miller. When they cling to each other, they do so against Mrs. Miller's question, "What do you do when two whores get sweet on each other?" Whey they take down their Christmas lights and plan for next year's display, they recall Mrs. Miller's observation that "a good whore with time on her hands will turn to religion nine times out of ten." And when Susan offers herself to Bill, she does so against Mrs. Miller's insistence that McCabe pay. The association with Mrs. Miller gives us an immediate context for Susan and Barbara. When taken alone, Barbara and Susan appear to be unable to satisfactorily shape their lives. But when the religion they turn to is dime store Christmas lights and when they cannot even get genuinely sweet on each other or even begin to manage their future, they show that they are in need of a woman (or man) like Mrs. Miller to take care of them. Without seeing McCabe, the same observations could be made; a knowledge of the comparison between Mrs. Miller and Susan and Barbara, however, makes Barbara and Susan even more poignant and more vulnerable.

Although Images' Kathryn and The Long Good-bye's Roger Wade are writers, Bill does not share their creativity or their colorful nature. Instead, Bill's inability to fit comfortably into his chosen role, his relationship with

Susan, and his final losing in winning all suggest a kin-
ship with McCabe. McCabe spends his time trying to become
a respectable middle class businessman; Bill, on the other
hand, tries to disassociate himself from its repressive
role demands and wants to capture the more immediate emotional intensity and romanticism of the gambler. Neither,
of course, can succeed. Although McCabe has Mrs. Miller
and thus, however temporarily, achieves a beautiful and
intense emotional relationship, he never learns his role.
Bill, on the other hand, has Charley and learns his role
well. But he learns that gambling is a role, not a spontaneous or instinctive activity. At least McCabe has his
misguided adherence to the empty code of heroism; Bill
knows that his dreams of gambling as a meaningful lifestyle are empty. Bill is also less enviable than McCabe
because he is denied even the few moments of life and love
that McCabe gets.

Charley is a more obvious continuation of an earlier
character, Phillip Marlowe. Partially because they share
the same actor, the two share a tendency to mumble, a
touch for the absurd, an affinity for gambling, and a potential for violent and egocentric behavior. Both are engaging and magnetic; both are their films' most charisma-
tic figures. And most importantly, both delineate the
world in which the films move.

Charley defines California Split most clearly when he
mugs Lew, gets his money back, and gets to beat him up.

Although Charley is unnecessarily brutal and is obviously enjoying himself, our sympathy remains with Charley. Lew has, after all, beaten and robbed Charley and has gone unpunished. If he is to be punished, Charley must be the agent. So once more revenge becomes necessary and acceptable. Nothing has changed; it is as if Marty Augustine was in the background screaming that the man "took my money" and therefore deserves "capital punishment." And since the principle of self-maximization of personal interest is still operative, Charley's mistreatment of Helen, his unannounced departure to Tiajuana (still another allusion to The Long Good-bye), and his hustling all seem understandable and justifiable.

These comparisons and refinements do not mean that California Split is no more than The Son of McCabe Meets The Long Good-bye. Although it does deal with the same themes and character types as the earlier Altman movies, it expands the vision to the contemporary American middle class. It also is the first of his to explicitly detail a character's moment of realization that his dream is empty. And most importantly, California Split finds still another way to attain continuity.

Relatively early in the film, we and Bill become aware of the large number of women characters named Barbara. At about the same time we notice it, Bill remarks, "I'm meeting an awful lot of Barbaras these days." He is right; the female lead is Barbara, his receptionist is a

Barbara and is played by an actress named Barbara (Colby),
a writer at his magazine is Barbara, as is a waitress.
When Bill is in need of assurance at the beginning of his
Reno fling, he sees a female casino employee's name tag -
Barbara. Bill smiles, having found his sign and his courage. Then, as the film ends, comes the final Barbara.
"For Barbara," the credits read. Barbara, then, ties together all of the film's episodes because the name enforces
a continuous thread. It gives Bill critical comfort and
gives Altman a heightened personal involvement; the film
is special because it is for her. And because we too can
discover all the Barbaras with Bill, we are also participants and beneficiaries in the device.

California Split is, then, a derivative work. Even
if it does not have the originality of McCabe, Images, or
The Long Good-bye, it is a sustained and complex film.
There is the totally new method of continuity here and
there are more major and better developed characters. Also,
there is a more varied emotional range and mood shift in
California Split than in the other Altman movies. His funniest and warmest comic moments are here, along with some
of his quietest and most effective tragedy. Unfortunately,
in his next movie, Nashville, Altman will strive for even
greater range, but will sacrifice the depth and humanity
he achieves in California Split.

CHAPTER 10
NASHVILLE

Since Nashville is the first Altman film since MASH
to receive widespread media attention, it may be remembered
as the movie that brought him back into the public eye. It
also may be remembered for its kaleidoscopic motion and
intertwining of its characters' lives. It will not be remembered, however, for its thematic depth or its well drawn
characters.

When Altman decided to make a two-and-one-half hour
movie about twenty-four characters (or a little more than
six minutes for each one), he had to resort to caricatures,
stereotypes, and simplifications. Since there simply is
no time to effectively develop so many characters, Altman
utilized these devices in order to tell the story.[1]

Several character types exist in Nashville. Perhaps
most striking are those characters that are least developed
but original, like the Tricycle Man. He never speaks, but
appears mysteriously throughout the movie, doing his magic
tricks, giving characters silent support, or just moving
through the frame. Although his role cries out for interpretation, no clues are given to his identity and he remains an entertaining visual mystery. The soldier is

another unusual character. Since his mother saved Barbara
Jean's life years ago, the soldier has been raised in awe
of Barbara Jean. Rather than enjoy her music, he hovers
respectfully around her, a frightening representation of
the total fan. Rather than enriching himself, his slavish
devotion to his idol has dehumanized him.[2]

Lacking the intellectual information necessary to
categorize these two characters, we can only respond to
them emotionally. Just the opposite is true of several
other characters. We know too much about them to react
emotionally, but not enough to react intellectually. Lady
Pearl, for example, seems gracious and competent, but is
also tearful and withdrawn as she reminisces about the Kennedy boys' Presidential campaigns. Although her preoccupation foreshadows the film's climactic assasination and contrasts the Kennedy charisma with Hal Phillip Walker's anonymous media politics, Pearl's inability to adjust to the
present conflicts with the rest of her personality. Since
we do not know enough about her to reconcile her two sides,
we fail to believe in her.

Like Lady Pearl, Barbara Jean is incompletely developed
and, as a result, ineffective. Although we can see her in-
stability and fragility, we cannot understand her nervous
breakdown. Although her eager acknowledgement of the fans
at the airport and the hospital suggests her happiness with
the role of a star, the private Barbara Jean cannot mentally
withstand its demands. Again, we do not know why. We are

always kept on the outside of Barbara Jean; we watch her collapse and get murdered, but never get to know or understand her. As a result, we never develop a sustained identification or personal relationship with her. Had our involvement with her been more deeply cultivated, her murder and the film's ending would have had more of an impact.[3]

Other stereotypcial characters are merely trite. Triplette, for example, is Nashville's company man. Anonymously good looking and innocuous, he sneaks into hotel and hospital rooms, quietly pursues his interests, and perseveres. All image and no substance, Triplette is one of the film's most dangerous and negative characters because he packages the events and climates of the times. His facelessness and reliance on superficiality and style make him a familiar evil of our age.

Kenny, the assassin, is another stereotype. A "tourist-drifter," he is polite and nondescript.[4] One of those quiet losers of life, we only see him at a distance: his car blows up in the traffic jam; he gives Mr. Green comfort and sympathy; he talks to his mother on long distance and assures her he has not picked up a fungus from the rooming house's sheets; he fails to attrack L.A. Joan's interest. At the end of the movie, when he shoots Barbara Jean, he becomes another of those repressed individuals who uses violence to gain attention. Unfortunately, Altman uses the cliche without illuminating, refining, or explaining the stereotype. Because Kenny remains a stereotype, our

reaction to the murder is dulled; we have seen too many
similar situations to respond to Barbara Jean's murder in
a less jaded way. Although our reaction reinforces Nashville's criticism of America as violent and egotistical,
the reaction is obtained cheaply and deceptively. Had
Altman developed Kenny and Barbara Jean as people, our
reaction to the assassination would have been more telling.
But by keeping us so distant from both characters, Altman
creates and guarantees a detached audience response.[5]

Although most of Nashville's characters are stereotypical, Sueleen Gay, Wade, and Linnea Reese transcend their
types and become real people. Sueleen, a talentless singer
who dreams of being a star, demonstrates the strength of
her dreams. Even after being ridiculed and forced to strip
at the smoker, she still hopes for the big break. More
promising than her show business future, however, is her
friendship with a loud, crassy co-worker, Wade. Because
he really cares for her, he tells her that she cannot sing
and tries to get her out of Nashville. We do not find out
if he succeeds or even if she could be happy without her
dreams; we do not even know enough about Wade to substan-
tiate our positive response to him. But Sueleen's refreshing innocence and Wade's honesty and insight into Nashville's false values, when added to the human affection
they demonstrate towards each other, give them a dimension
of humanity and individuality missing from Nashville's
other characters.

Linnea Reese is perhaps the film's most intriguing, most complex character. An outsider within Nashville's power structure, she is the only white gospel singer in a black choir and goes to the black church. Seemingly un-impressed by the false tinsel of show business, she is happiest when at home with her two deaf children. Quietly dissatisfied with her marriage, however, she uneasily goes to Tom's motel room. After they make love and she begins to leave, Tom calls another girl. Despite Tom's insensi-tivity, Linnea smiles, kisses him, and tells him in sign language that she is happy to have met him. Because she seems so giving, so vulnerable, and so unhappy, Tom's shallowness and callousness angers and embarrasses us. Unlike the other characters, Linnea seems to deserve much more.

We see Linnea one more time, at the finaly rally. There too she differentiates herself. After Barbara Jean is shot, Linnea alone acts humanely. Realizing that a life has just been taken, she "stands devastated, somehow unable to reconcile any of it with the song."[6] Linnea, unlike the others, recognizes the value of life; she needs, respects, and strives for genuine human interaction. Although we do not spend much time with her, Linnea projects a troubled but alive presence that makes her unique and effective.

Even though Nashville has twenty-four major characters, it is more a socio-political statement about contemporary America than a character study. Although the nature of society has not changed since McCabe, although America is still ruled by invisible corporate powers, the ordinary people have changed. In McCabe, people were sufficiently selfless, albeit misguided, to work together so that the church, the symbol of civilization, could be saved. By the nineteen-thirties and Thieves Like Us, people had lost the ability to work together; the question was no longer the survival of society but of the individual. In addition, McCabe's and Mrs. Miller's love had been replaced by Keechie's ultimate hatred for Bowie. In today's society, even this hatred, a deep and personal emotional commitment, vanishes. Instead, Altman finds modern America composed of individuals uncommitted to another person or a social group. The concept of social responsibility has been re-placed by the carnival-like megaphone of Hal Phillip Walker, who himself is invisible. Triplette understands that poli-tics and show business have become indistinguishable. Thus, Haven supports the rally because he has been tantalized with the promise of Tennessee's governship. Bartlett, Barbara Jean's manager-husband, thinks that Walker is an unaccept-able candidate, but hopes Barbara Jean's appearance at the rally will make up for her cancelled concert. People in Nashville are, then, no different from those in The Long Good-bye; in both, they act only out of self-interest.

Although both Nashville and McCabe end in scenes of public crises, the endings are only superficially similar. In McCabe, the townspeople, who know each other, respond

selflessly to save a common symbol of their lives. In
Nashville, the anonymous crowd cares only about hearing a
concert. When Barbara Jean is killed, the human impulse
is to panic and run. As soon as Albequerque gets control,
however, the crowd calms down, cooly accepts the shooting,
and joins Albequerque in singing "It don't worry me."
Rather than affirm the resilience of the human spirit and
the ability of people to work together in a crisis, the
ending ironically and depressingly comments on the lack of
human feeling in today's world. Unlike McCabe, Nashville
shows us a faceless crowd interested only in self-survival.

This comment on America is not new; Altman made it in
The Long Good-bye and, to a lesser extent, in California
Split. Los Angeles, gambling, and sleuthing are, however,
idiosyncratic and specific worlds that do not easily gen-
eralize to the rest of America. With Nashville, Altman is
able to be more comprehensive and inclusive.

Nashville is the center of the new South, a place
where the traditions of the past blend with the optimism
and material prosperity of the present. Although it, like
Hollywood, is a dream factory for those who want to be show
business stars and although it revolves around its success
stories, the dream and the stars seem more accessible, more
human, and more committed in Nashville. The heroes, including Haven, Linnea, and Tommy Brown, sit in the same bars
that the locals do and drive the same types of cars. They
all go to neighborhood churches, sing in local choirs and

live in comfortable but modest homes. Uninsulated from the outside world, they deal with the more ordinary people, including lawyers, doctors, nurses, farmers, tourists, waitresses, chauffeurs, patients, soldiers. When Barbara Jean is in the hospital, for example, she sings in the church choir and cares about Mr. Green and his sick wife. She is not a prima donna or temperamental star, then, but an interested person too. When Tom wants to call Linnea, he does not have to go through personal secretaries and answering services; he just picks up the phone, dials her number, and talks to her. Nashville, then, is not just about a rich and atypical group of country-western stars, but about us all. The characters in the film encompass every economic, occupational, and social group; if someone is not in Nashville, he or she is probably not in America either. So when Joan Tewkesbury, the scriptwriter, says that "All you need to do is add yourself as the twenty-fifth character," she is explicitly including us as a vital part of Nashville.[7]

This inclusion goes beyond the usual Altman demand for an active viewer. This time, Altman is making a political statement about America today. As American viewers, we are a part of that statement. What is said in the movie, then, is applicable to us as well. By using Nashville and such a broad range of characters, then, Altman has obtained maximum generalization; he has forced us to confront ourselves in the film.

As the twenty-fifth character, we are not spared from the film's climax. We may get caught up in its pageantry, may be shocked and sickened by its sudden violence, may be bored by it, or may even try to analyze and thus detach ourselves from the ending. Ultimately, however, we will return to our own more egocentric and private interests. The problem of the quality of American life and the enormous task of reform is too big for our individual abilities; we will retreat into our smaller, more manageable private lives. In the end, then, "it don't worry us" either.

Nashville is not at all a pleasant movie. Its humor is often ironic and sordid; its characters, petty and negative stereotypes; its events, bleak and degrading; its possibilities for solutions and hope, minimal. Cold, cynical, impersonal, it offers little to laugh about or identify with.

Despite Altman's comment that he and his lack of knowledge and superiority are represented by Opal, the BBC reporter, Altman seems very sure of himself in Nashville.[8] There is no debate in this movie; it shows us the way things are in Nashville, Tennessee, the South, the United States of America. It knows America is a dismal place and demonstrates this point by moving twenty-four characters, without true human complexity, through situations that prove their emptiness and lack of fulfillment. Despite all the improvisation that went on before and during the filming, the characters remain puppets who reinforce a pre-determined political statement.

Rather than unfamiliar or shocking, Nashville's message is not a hard one to argue against. Since the message, although not palatable, is not troublesomely offensive, since the twenty-four characters keep the film moving breathlessly, since the acting and technical skill behind the film are uniformly excellent, and since the advance publicity, critical acclaim, and extensive advertising all suggested a major blockbuster, why was Nashville a financial failure?[9]

Failure is an ambiguous term unless its criteria are adequately established. Although some reviews of Nashville were ecstatically favorable, many, especially the non-Eastern and later reviews, have been unfavorable. Many in the Altman cult have been disappointed by the stereotypes and superficialities of the movie, especially after viewing it more than once. But as Altman taught us in Images, we must let the movie generate its own standards. For Nashville, that criterion does not seem to be critical acclaim, but box office receipts.

From the moment that Nashville began becoming the new media event (a phenomenon helped by Pauline Kael's obnoxiously self-confident advance rave), Altman made no secret that he hoped that Nashville would make millions. He thought it would "clean up. I think it's going to take all the money in the world. But then," he added, "I'm pretty

naive about commercial success."[10] To this end, he, the
producer, Jerry Weintraub, and Paramount agreed to promote
the film without any quote ads or "highbrow appeal. Adver-
tise it as an event, not as a film." Thus, Nashville was
not "an orgy for movie-goers," but "the damndest thing you
ever saw."[11] So with almost the entire East Coast critical
establishment, a cover story from Newsweek, and a broadly
based advertising campaign, 1975's biggest movie was
launched.

Even if unaware of their commercial hopes for the film,
the opening sequence makes Nashville's ambitions clear.
The soundtrack album spins towards us, accompanied by the
voice of a late night television salesman.

> "Now - after years in the making....Robert Alt-
> man brings you the long awaited Nashville -
> with twenty-four, count 'em - twenty-four of
> your favorite starts." The music comes in,
> loud, seguing from one song to the next, and
> he continues with a hype on each until every-
> thing has whirled and spun and played through
> your senses. "And along with the magnifi-
> cent stars - the magic of stereo sound and
> living-color picture - right before your
> very eyes, without commercial interruption
> ....Nashville.[12]

A satire, of course, but also an accurate representation
of the movie. Like MASH, this one is a commodity, a
packaged piece of merchandise.

Nashville is a kaleidoscope, a blur of characters and motion. Like Charley in California Split or like its own Triplette, it is a movie that has replaced substance with style; in an appropriate cliche of the times, "what you see is what you get." But while this lack of depth may cause resentment from the relatively small group of intellectual film goers and would be a possible cause of their disappointment with Nashville, the general public in the year of Jaws would not be adversely influenced by a superficial but exciting movie. No, Nashville certainly did not fail because it substituted flash for intellectual depth.

The key to Nashville's limited appeal may instead be in its unique focus for audience identification. Unlike an Airport, which offers familiar stars like Burt Lancaster, Dean Martin, and Jacqueline Bisset and immediately lovable old ladies like Helen Hayes, Nashville offers actors familiar primarily to Altman fans. Not only are there no stars, there are also no enviable or instantly attractive roles to identify with. Unlike the other multi-character movies that deal in stereotypes, there are no pre-established audience favorites or larger than life super-heroes or villains. The "ordinary" viewer does not get immediately rewarded, nor does he have enough time with a character to develop an emotional relationship beyond the stereotype or exterior. As a result, he becomes bored, lost, and confused.

For Altman fans, however, there is an instant target
of identification with Altman himself. We have been following most of the actors for nine films now and have a
surprisingly deep affection for them. As veterans of the
Altman scene, we are able to welcome his newest discoveries
because we are old members ourselves. Too, we know about
his tricks; we are attuned to the constant verbal action,
are primed for his cinematic moments, and share or at least
are comfortable with his values. Instinctively, then, we
relax and let the movie happen; we sit with Altman above
the characters and share in his vision of <u>Nashville</u> and
movie-making. Because of this, <u>Nashville</u> becomes almost
like an in-joke or an exclusive and self-congratulatory
secret.

The in-joke is typified by the cameo appearances of
Julie Christie and Elliot Gould. Elliot Gould comes to
Haven's party; we hear his unmistakable voice and then we
see him. When asked why he is in Nashville, he mumbles,
"I'm just coming to a party....I'm promoting a movie, not
making one."[13] Then Julie Christie wanders into a bar;
Haven welcomes her to Nashville, the others wonder about
her. "Is she the one that got off the train in the snow?"
Del whispers to Triplette. Although most of us who have
seen <u>McCabe</u> smile at the unmistakable reference, the walk-
ons, even to those of us in the know, seem distracting,
self-conscious intrusions.

As with all in-jokes, _Nashville_ becomes an elitist film. Since the identification is made with the director and since that identification is derived from a foreknowledge of Altman or an extremely heightened cinematic perceptivity, most people in the audience will not be able to make the connection. Since the events are disconnected and only superficially developed and since the characters are so shallow and unattractive, the more casual viewer has nothing to engage him. Similarly, the more serious viewer cannot enjoy _Nashville_ in the challenging, inexhaustible way he can some of the other Altman films; he does not bring anything new out of the theatre. So while _Nashville_ cuts itself off from the traditional, admittedly small, Altman audience, it also fails to be acceptable to the general public as well.

Since 1968, Altman has turned out an amazing, probably unparalleled body of work. Since _MASH_, he has mastered his craft and has directed movies of extraordinary range, depth, and beauty. His lack of commercial success is not his fault, but the American movie-going public's. _Nashville_ was Altman's attempt to woo the public, to out-MASH _MASH_. The result, however, is his least successful movie, both from an artistic perspective and from its own financial criterion. Perhaps the failure stems from the knowledge Altman has gained from the last eight movies; _Nashville_ is Altman slumming. Unlike the others, which appear to be personal movies conceived, filmed, and edited with an artistic and a private purpose, _Nashville_ seems like it

was edited for what he thought other people, the American
public, wanted. And for the first time, Altman seems detached, uninvolved, mechanical.

Nashville, then, is a turning point for Altman. It is
his culminating political statement. It updates his political concerns and broadens his message to specifically
include us all. Because he has now presented the socio-
political vision so completely, he has exhausted the issue;
it is now time to move on to new issues. If he does not,
he risks repetition and stagnation. Also, Nashville has
given him a much greater degree of visibility; instead of
just a brilliant cult director, he is now an authentic
celebrity. As such, he has the status to assume total control over his career; he does not have to worry that the
movie companies will mishandle and then quietly drop his
movies, as they have done since MASH. But he has also
alienated many of his old fans, who hate the idea that
"their" film director has gone public or who simply did
not like Nashville. For the first time, then, many are
skeptical, uncommonly critical, and hostile. Altman is
confronted with an uncertain audience and is entering a
new stage in his career. He can learn from Nashville and
can continue to develop artistically, hoping one day to
receive the popular acclaim that he deserves. He can
stagnate and remake his old movies until he runs out of
money and syncopants. Finally, he can continue to go
after the broader commercial market. His past record and

artistic awareness give us hope that he will continue to artistically grow; although current accounts of his associates indicate that he is already surrounded by people who shield him from criticism and negative comments that are necessary for artistic growth.[14] His upcoming Buffalo Bill and the Indians offers stars like Paul Newman, Burt Lancaster, and Joel Grey; adopted from Arthur Kopit's Indians, it may be a political diatribe, a fine movie, or another commercial attempt. His plans to film the mediocre but popular Breakfast of Champions with an all-star cast and Ragtime, with an even bigger cast, indicate he still wants that big movie. Thus, he can go in any direction; the only certainty is that the choice is his.

---

[1] For an interesting account of Nashville's shaping, read Jack Viertel and David Colker's "The Long Road to Nashville," in the June 13, 1975 New Times.

[2] The information about the soldier's background does not appear in the movie, but appears in the screenplay. It is unclear how much background information Altman assumes the viewer gets about each character. In any event, when information is drawn from the screenplay, I have footnoted it.

[3] Albequerque is another character whom we cannot believe in. Since she carries the ending and becomes a star, she is working within the Ruby Keeler mold. She seems too vacant, too stupid, and too lucky for us to believe in her or disbelieve in her enough, however, to give the ending the power it deserves.

[4] Joan Tewkesbury, Nashville (New York, 1976). (There is no pagination in the screenplay.)

Notes (continued)

[5] All of the characters are stereotypes; I did not develop each because the point had been made. Tom is the typical rock star; L.A. Joan, the typical groupie. Mr. Green exists only to suffer. Del conforms so predictably to the stereotypical perception of the new southern lawyer that he loses his believability. Typically prosperous-looking in his well tailored but pedestrian suit and his pot belly, he is superficially a pillar of the community. Thus, he goes to church each Sunday and appears to be a devoted family man. His private behavior is much different, however. After the smoker, he realizes Sueleen's vulnerability and uses his position to gain a sexual favor. More importantly, he has never even bothered to learn the sign language of his children, who are deaf-mutes, in order to communicate with them.

To make the point of the successful yet hypocritical professional, Altman milks the stereotype, strips Del of his humanity and believability, and robs him of his effectiveness. He seems to like his children and be conventionally interested in his wife; he would have had to make a deliberate effort not to learn how to sign speak in twelve years. Although Altman seems interested in underscoring the hypocrisy and inhumanity of Del's stereotype, he has overdrawn it instead. And as a result, Del becomes unbelievable, contrived, and ineffective.

[6] Tewkesbury.

[7] Ibid.

[8] Terry Curtis Fox, "Nashville Chats," Chicago Reader, July 4, 1975, p. 1.

[9] Nashville, at last report, had made about one million dollars profit. In light of the hopes for the movie and the spectacular profits reaped by the big hits of 1975, Nashville remains a box office disappointment, in spite of its modest profit.

[10] Jack Viertel and David Colker, "The Long Road to Nashville," New Times, June 13, 1975, p. 56.

[11] Ibid., p. 59.

[12] Tewkesbury.

[13] Ibid.

[14] Chris Hodenfield, "Bob Altman's Nashville," Rolling Stone, July 17, 1975, p. 31.

CONCLUSION
THE AUTEUR

Although the nine films from That Cold Day to Nashville hopefully represent only the first part of Altman's
film output, they constitute an already impressive body of
work. Because they share a coherent socio-political philosophy and an evolving visual style, they prove that Altman is a true auteur, a director whose command over his
medium and his material is strong enough to make each film
a personal statement. From these nine films, then, we can
extract both the intellectual and artistic framework that
guide his movies.

Perhaps most constant in the nine films are Altman's
beliefs about society. From the beginnings of modern America, he tells us in McCabe, the individual has been a helpless, if willing, victim of civilization. As represented
by the church and Ida's empty marriage, civilizations's
symbols are hollow and fradulent, ultimately useful only
to the real winners, the invisible power centers of the
ruthless corporations. Still, the ordinary people believe
in civilization's promise of middle class security and have
no real alternative but to cooperate with the corporations's
demands.

By the time of the depression and Thieves Like Us,
the quest for survival shifts from the survival of society
to that of the individual. By the Thirties, the institutions of civilization are strong enough to exist without
the support of the individual and are indifferent to the
plight of the people. The people, however, need help.
Without any marketable skills or resources and without any
aid from government, big business, or the church, these
people must fend for themselves. Because they are powerless and isolated, they become trapped into miserable,
doomed lifestyles. The invisibility of the power structure
denies them a visible target for their frustrations and
anger. Instead, they turn their rage inward and destroy
their personal relationships, too. Thus, Mattie turns
Bowie in, wins back her husband (for as long as he can stay
out of jail), and adds guilt to the list of hardships she
must endure. And unlike Mrs. Miller, who still loves Mc-
Cabe, Keechie can only feel bitterness and hatred for Bowie,
her dead lover.

Although MASH deals with the Korean War in an adolescent, absurd manner, its humor depends on the same negative
world view. Alone in an inhumane war and world, the MASH
unit establishes a supportive, zany, positive environment.
Sex, drink, drugs, and fun, themselves a juvenile (if in-
viting) concept of happiness, are readily available to its
members. Threats to group stability are either neutralized
and then assimilated, like Hot Lips, or expelled, like

Frank Burns. Because the real world is harsh, dull, and repressive, MASH's own demand for conformity to its norms seems a small price to pay for MASH's appeal. Because the MASH unit looks so implausibly healthy when contrasted with the world beyond the theatre, because MASH functions as a sane reprieve from the outside world's values, MASH depends on the same bleak world of McCabe and Thieves. And, just as the movie must end, MASH exists as a temporary aberration. Dish, Duke, and Hawk-eye must leave Korea and return to their more conventional and ordered American existences. Even in this fantasy, then, the values of the hostile, dehumanizing world intrude and conquer.

Brewster McCloud more clearly illustrates the strength of the real world's hold. Essentially a contemporary retelling of Peter Pan and Daedulus, Altman keeps to the spirit of the fantasy until the film's end. There, he changes Peter Pan's bitter-sweet ending to the sterner, more mythological, and unhappy one. Brewster takes place in the Astrodome, a man-made, controlled environment that ultimately constricts Brewster. Although he does fly, Brewster cannot break out of the dome and escape his earth bound fate. Even in dreams, man cannot free himself from society's boundaries and control. And if he tries to escape, he guarantees his destruction.

The Long Good-bye, Nashville, and California Split bring Altman's vision of America into the seventies. In these movies, the strong emotions of McCabe and Thieves

have been muted by an improved material prosperity and by
the increasingly complex power structure. The social responsibility of McCabe and the rage of Thieves have been
replaced by a pervasive indifference to anything larger
than one's own immediate and individual self-interest.
Thus, until Marlowe's values and self-esteem are questioned,
everything he sees is "okay by me." Charley and Bill
hustle other gamblers and victimize Helen because they need
the money for their big game or want to have a good time.
Tom can casually sleep with women because he is "easy";
Haven can support Walker so that his own political ambitions can be furthered; Barbara Jean can opportunistically
use the rally to make up for a cancelled concert. And when
Barbara Jean is killed, thousands can sing the new national
anthem, "It don't worry me." Until, of course, their self-
interest is threatened.

The pursuit of self-interest has its consequences.
Mrs. Miller explains that if no one else is going to take
care of her, she must take care of herself. Because the
individual's survival rests only on his or her own efforts,
self-reliance becomes necessary. To rely on another person
is foolish; the other person may die, fail, or just leave.
No, in a hostile world, the individual who survives must
depend only on himself.

In such a world, then, isolation is both the natural
and desirable state of the individual. Since the business
or marriage partner will not always have the same interests,

he or she will someday be a liability. When the inevitable conflict occurs, psychic and material loss will result; the individual will be hurt by the partnership. Since they will turn out disadvantageously, long term associations have no place in Altman's world. Their traditionally depicted security and fulfillment never materialize; not one major character in Altman's films is involved in a healthy permanent relationship. Society destroys McCabe and Mrs. Miller, Bowie and Keechie, Duke and Hot Lips, Barbara Jean and Barnett, and even Eileen and Terry. Some relationships self-destruct: Suzanne turns Brewster in, Bill leaves Charley. The other characters do not even have relationships to destroy. For Altman, then, the world is not made up of couples, but of individuals.

To survive in this world of isolated, egoistical individuals, one minimizes his vulnerability by learning and using roles. Without these roles, or prescriptions for behavior, personal problems and needs might interfere with the individual's performance and put him at a disadvantage. McCabe, for example, who does not understand his role fully, permits his trouble with Mrs. Miller to interfere with his dealings with Sears and Hollander. Because he fails to act within his chosen role of businessman, he ultimately dies. No other Altman character will repeat his mistake; at the beginning of California Split, Altman tells us that we "are going to learn how to play the game" and emphasizes the game's importance by showing us a still from McCabe.

The best example of Altman's hiding his characters behind roles is Californa Split's Charley. Through the film, Bill envies his spontaneity and refreshing impulsiveness. When Charley impersonates the vice squad cop or the arrogant, aging, and inept basketball player, he is surprisingly convincing and amusing. At the end of the film, however, Bill is startled by Charley's admission that he has been impersonating a gambler, as well; "Everyone knows there's no special feeling," Charley says, "you only act like there's one." Only then do we realize, with Bill, that we have never seen the Charley behind the roles; the Charley we know is the one he presents for public consumption. That is why Charley succeeds; he has learned the role and game well enough to be resilient, invulnerable, and self-sufficient. Thus, at the end of the film, after their partnership has been dissolved, Charley quickly bounces back. As the singer sings "Bye Bye Blackbird," he is already bantering with her. "That's the story of my life," he jokes.

The realization that Charley is playing a role causes us to re-examine our relationship with the other Altman characters. Those characters who seemed to know what they wanted and how to get it have, we realize, been adept at playing their roles, at presenting public images well. Even those whom we thought we knew well turn out to be intensely private characters; we know them only by observing them in public situations and can only guess at their

innermost nature. Because we see Mrs. Miller's expressive
face and watch her handle McCabe in a variety of situations,
for example, we think we know her. But, as McCabe says, she
"spends more time behind a locked door than any other female." When she retreats into her private drug-induced re-
veries, we too are excluded; her private life and thoughts
remain unknown. Marlowe works the same way; probably because Elliot Gould plays both Marlowe and Charley, the two
characters share many traits. Like the police, we witness
Marlowe's brash impudence; as viewers, we follow his pursuit of the truth and thus deduce his personality. Although at the end we can evaluate his values and his motivations, we know little more about Marlowe than Lennox does.
Like Charley, Marlowe is always acting the role of the
private eye; like Charley, he never lets us get close to
his inner self.

The necessity for roles also explains Altman's unparalleled use of stereotypes. Perhaps no other director
has been able to take a stereotypical character and make
him seem so unusual and original. The entire MASH unit,
Brewster's characters, Nashville's cast, Dr. Verringer,
Marty Augustine, all depend upon our immediate identification with a stereotype. After the initial identification
is made, an individual quirk or trait that gives the character his immediate impact and individuality is established.
Augustine, for instance, depends upon our familiarity with
the successful, respectable, corrupt, and inept nouveau

riche; his amusingly absurd monologues, affectations, and
inept henchman are doubly comical because they are representatives of successful suburbanites. Lulled by the con-
ventionality of the stereotype Augustine is defined by, we
and Marlowe are astonished by his sudden, uncharacteristic,
and brutal smashing of a Coke bottle into his mistress'
face. Especially since he has seemed so absurd and inept,
his unexpected and dramatic display of violence stuns us
into believing his power and status. Verringer uses the
stereotype in the same way; one of the film's most absurd
and seemingly ineffectual quacks, Verringer and his strange
hospital are genuinely funny partially because they reflect
the almost equally absurd faddists of today's society. His
bold entrance into Wade's party and his surprising show of
strength there go against the stereotype; like Augustine,
he reverses his portrayal and establishes a new and credible
dimension to his character. Because they understand their
roles, Verringer and Augustine become successful. They
realize that most relationships are superficial and brief;
conforming to a stereotype or role is essential if the relationship's time is to be used effectively. But to differentiate themselves from everyone else and establish an
individual identity, they use the stereotypes creatively;
they let the type work for them by adding an original and
unexpected twist. Thus, with one well placed move, they
make themselves potent and memorable. They transform their
harmless, amusing eccentricities into serious power bases;

their demands no longer seem annoying trivialities but become unavoidable and formidable.

Those characters who remain stereotypical, who quietly and unimaginatively play their roles, fall flat and fade from our memories. Another set of characters, however, either fail to learn their roles or are unable to find roles that work for them. California Split's Susan and Brewster, for example, are too innocent and unsophisticated to have learned a role. Ignorant of the ways of the world, they cannot function without the maternal aid of Barbara or Louise. We respond maternally to them as well, accepting their incompetence and vulnerability more readily than we do Altman's troubled adults, who have had more time to learn. Frances, of That Cold Day, Wade, of The Long Goodbye, Barbara Jean, of Nashville, and especially Kathryn, of Images, are all too troubled to maintain their roles and thus lose their abilities to function rationally or socially. Totally out of control, they place themselves at the mercies of other people, as Wade does, or of their uncontrolled emotions, as do the women. Losing the ability to cope means losing control over one's existence. As we find out most painfully from Kathryn, who occupies an entire movie with the search for her identity, underneath the roles lie not a healthy and engaging honesty, but a horrifying helplessness and terror. Rather than being more positive and appealing, these individuals that do not hide behind roles are disturbed, depressing, and doomed.

One character does not fit into any of these characters. California Split's Bill is dissatisfied with his ordered, rational, and predictable existence. Instead, he wants to be like Charley, who appears to live by his instincts in a spontaneous, exciting world of gambling. The film is Bill's education; he learns to become a gambler and, under Charley's tutelage, wins thousands of dollars in the big game. He also learns that there is "no special feeling," that gambling too is a role. At the end of the movie, the awareness that even gambling is not spontaneous and genuine leaves Bill stunned and empty; although there are clues that Bill will resign himself to this insight and play the role, we can only speculate on his next step.

Because Bill is the first Altman character to discredit the artificiality of social roles and because he is the first relatively controlled and coherent figure without a role, Bill's future seems especially interesting. Unfortunately, Altman's next installment, Nashville, does not address itself to his predicament. Instead, Altman retreats and reverts to a diverting but stereotypical and superficial collection of character vignettes. Amazingly, then, the nine films do not present a single fulfilled and open individual; all the characters either search for or already have a satisfactory public role. Perhaps Altman feels that the happy individual makes dull art; perhaps he just does not see one. In any case, the person who is free from roles and happy simply does not show up in Altman's movies.

Although the perception of a hostile universe filled
with egoistical role playing individuals is depressing and
pessimistic, it does not eliminate exhuberance, joy, and
beauty from Altman's films. In fact, the realization of
pain and loneliness heightens the films' moments of happiness. The predetermined unhappy ending frees the beginning
and the middle; since the outcome is known, the emphasis on
the climax can be relaxed and the preceding events can become more independent and more valued. Brewster may fall
to the Astrodome's floor, for example, but he does fly to
the dome's top. Even though the flight does not last long,
Brewster experiences life at its most meaningful. Similarly,
McCabe and Mrs. Miller, Keechie and Bowie, Charley and Bill,
Susan and Barbara end up alone, but they all enjoy moments
of communication and fulfillment. And those moments of
beauty, excitement, and love make life so valuable.

This perception of life as a series of moments squeezed
into a finite existence not only motivates Altman's thematic
investigations, but his visual style as well. Underlying
every stylistic trait of Altman's, from his episodic pacing
to his overlapping dialogue to his tangential details and
movie allusions, is this belief in life's little moments.
And since the beauty of these moments heightens the emotional response to other people, to the environment, and
to oneself, Altman cultivates the viewer's emotional, non-
rational reaction.

The episodic pacing in Altman's films is consistent with this philosophy. We know the dimensions of the ultimate ending; the destination becomes less important than the quality of the journey. By slowing the pace down and freeing it from the demands of an unrelenting narrative plot line, Altman gives himself the opportunity to include any shot, object, character, or incident that strikes him as cinematic. These superficially unrelated episodes may be single shots, like the beautiful, nonfunctional sunset scenes in McCabe, Images, and The Long Good-bye, Hugh's gloves in Images, and the old woman's quivering face in Brewster McCloud. On a more extended level, Altman develops entire sequences and characters, including Brewster's lecturer, California Split's Egyptian Fem sequence, and The Long Good-bye's Dr. Verringer and cat scenes. Although their elimination would tighten the plot lines and quicken their films' pace, these sequences, results of Altman's commitment to an unhurried pace, contribute much of the films' humor and originality. To cut them in the interests of a more controlled story line would be unthinkable.

The emphasis on episodic pacing gives Altman the freedom to use tangentially related or even superficially unrelated material. It also gives him a method to effectively minimize our rational distance from his movies and thus force our emotional reactions. Since he can include episodes of varying length, he can control the amount of background information we have. He can quickly present a character or situation about whom we have no intellectual information; denied the rational referential points, we can only react emotionally. Since thinking can do us little good, we are forced to feel the situation. The lesbians in That Cold Day, the cowboy's death in McCabe, the Coke bottle scene in The Long Good-bye, Barbara Jean's breakdown in Nashville happen too quickly and without proper intellectual preparation for us to react any other way but emotionally. Images is the best, most sustained example of Altman's demand for emotional involvement; throughout the film, he carefully withholds information we need to react analytically. Because we are denied the answers to the characters' real identity and to what "really" happened, we are confused, frustrated, and forced into a personal, emotional reaction to the movie. And because we are so used to being told how to feel, we may be uncomfortable with our emotions and with this style of film-making. Are we supposed to laugh at Barbara Jean? Cry? Squirm? That insecurity soon passes; since Altman courts an emotional response, any emotional response is correct. Once the fear of an individualistic emotional reaction is accommodated, the viewer can relax with the film and become totally involved in it.

The alert viewer is not only rewarded with a more intense emotional experience, but with a more complete awareness of the movie's action. Unlike many other directors, Altman keeps subtle, clever, and important details hidden behind the main action. A careful viewer would catch Mrs. Miller peering out of the door at Bear Paw, birds' names on the rest homes and license plates in Brewster, the Art Deco apartment of That Cold Day, the older George Segal look-alike walking out of the Reno casino in California Split, Bowie saying good-bye to T-Dub in Thieves. Although these details are not necessary to the understanding of the films, they greatly increase our enjoyment and appreciation of them and spur us on to even more careful viewing.

This increased involvement greatly enhances the total film experience. Altman's use of multiple levels of dialogue makes it difficult for the casual viewer to understand what is being said. In addition to adding a realistic atmosphere to the film, the overlapping dialogue allows Altman to deal with more than one subject at a time. As with the visual details, the film's general movement can be followed without the careful concentration necessary to catch the words. As soon as they are understood, however, the words add immeasurably to the film. In Brewster, for example, one of the funniest lines, "two big Georges," is almost lost because Wright mumbles it. If caught, it adds dimension to the already comic visual of the old woman trying to embezzle two bills from the miser. On a more serious note, Bowie whispers a moving and private good-bye to T-Dub as he stokes a fire; although it adds a dimension of sincerity and loyalty to Bowie's character, the good-bye is voiced so softly and quickly that it can be easily missed.

The overlapping dialogue does more than add humor or give characters more development, but functions as a creative thematic component. At the end of That Cold Day, for example, Frances' almost inaudible "I want to make love to you," voice-over demonstrates her degeneration and adds impact to the film's final shots of the boy crying. Even more effective are Images' sounds. In addition to the moody abstract sounds of the soundtrack are the faint, eerie, and compelling whispering of Kathryn's name, beckoning her into madness. Perhaps more importantly, at the end of the movie, Susannah, not Kathryn, reads the children's book. Although this concludes a major concern of the film, we hear but do not see the transference. The soundtrack, then, becomes a crucial part of the film. Sound is equally important in the other Altman movies. In addition to placing its climax in perspective, The Long Good-bye's use of varied versions of the theme song gives the movie its consistency. In Thieves Like Us, the radio defines the gangsters' competence, undermines their efforts at professionalism, and distances us from Bowie and Keechie's lovemaking. And in Nashville, the songs, which were written by the non-musician actors, lend a more personal authenticity and realism to the film. Although the inaudibility of much of the sound in an Altman movie may at first seem chaotic, then, it soon reveals itself to be a very carefully and creatively used component of the film. Although, like Citizen Kane, the sound may be too dense to be understood

in a single viewing, it must be fully heard before the movie
can be truly appreciated.

Another favorite Altman device is his frequent allusions
to movies. Like the French New Wave directors, Altman loves
the movies and does not hesitate to refer the viewer to a
wide range of movie jokes and references. From the loudspeaker of MASH, which blares out names, descriptions, and
capsule reviews of old war movies, to Brewster's movie post-
ers to Marlowe's asides to movie heroes of the past, Altman
characters continually remind us of old favorites.

Altman does not use the allusions pretentiously or
self-consciously, however. Instead, they delineate the
boundaries of his works, telling us that we are watching a
movie. Rather than imitate reality, his movies remind us
that movies are a legitimate art form that demands its own
reality. Because movies operate as a unique combination of
reality and illusion, they borrow from both. Altman uses
the actors' real names and Susannah York's real book in
Images; Elliot Gould's real car in The Long Good-bye;
builds a real town for McCabe; and keeps Gould's and Julie
Christie's identities and the singers' real songs in Nashville. And since California Split is dedicated to a Barbara, Altman calls most of its women Barbara and lets Bill
use the name as his good luck charm. He even begins Nashville with a blurb about its being years in the making and
with a satire on the merchandising of its soundtrack album.
At the end of MASH, he uses the loudspeaker to introduce

the cast; at the end of <u>Brewster</u>, he lets the characters change costumes and take bows as part of "The Greatest Show on Earth." Altman goes out of his way, then, to remind us that we are watching a movie, a work of art that determines its own reality.

The allusions serve still another purpose, especially in the later films. Since Altman presents a basically un-changing universe and similar types of characters, each movie plays off the others. <u>McCabe</u>, <u>Thieves</u>, and <u>Nashville</u>, for example, are three separate and independent films. When taken together, however, they show the progression of atti-tudes of the last hundred years and thus help place the in-dividual characters in a more meaningful historical perspec-tive. When the still from <u>McCabe</u> is placed in <u>California Split</u>, accompanied by a verbal explanation that we are going to learn how to play the game, we can immediately understand Bill's predicament and more quickly feel his situation. Also, when we see Barbara and Susan act, we have Mrs. Miller to compare them to; again a context is established that reverberates against an entire network of relationships. Thus, new life is given to the earlier movies and immediate contexts are established for the more recent ones.

The repertory nature of Altman's actors, technicians, and artists also encourages this non-linear, unfinished style of film-making. The reputed degree of openness and improvisation of an Altman set gives Altman's crew a great

deal of individual opportunity and freedom to create. Not
an assembly line film-maker, Altman expects actors to be
on the set the entire time the film is shot. Too, Altman
tries to shoot in sequence. Lines can be written the night
before; the change cannot possibly jeopardize the ending
since it has not been shot. This keeps Altman free to use
unexpected resources and sudden inspirations, like the
circus ending of Brewster. Sensing the possibilities, Altman thought of it while the film was being shot, filmed it,
liked it, and included it.

In addition to the flexiblity, shooting in sequence in
an open atmosphere gives the cast a chance to grow into the
material and into each other. In McCabe, for instance, they
built Presbyterian Church; as the filming progressed, so did
the town. By the end, then, life and art had become so
intertwined that those people did live there. Performing
was made much easier and more natural because of the personal relationship to the sets and to each other; the results show in the finished product.

The improvisation, the episodic pacing, the seemingly
unrelated incidents and characters, the overlapping sound,
the movie allusions might give the impression that Altman
is a loose, undisciplined film-maker whose films consist
of strung together moments, some of which work and some of
which do not. Although he may be that kind of person, however, the amount of improvisation in Altman's movies has
been exaggerated; despite the films' appearances, they are

deceptively tight and structured. Perhaps no other contemporary film-maker pays such careful attention to the relationship of his theme and technique. In an Altman movie, even the most superficially unrelated detail reflects back on the film's main concern. Although more true for the later movies, which show him in a more total and mature control of his medium, even That Cold Day shows his preoccupation with the film's structure. Frances' apartment is a perfect representation of her mental rigidity; the half hour spent in it is a direct clue to her mental state, as is the superficially unrelated and naively amusing sex talk in the gynecologist's waiting room. The random camera work and the transitions on reflective wind chimes of Images ultimately reinforce the emotional experience of schizophrenia and the legitimacy of the artistic experience, while the random camera, pastel colors, and bizarre characters of The Long Good-bye illustrate the breakdown of moral absolutes, which, after all, is what the film is about.

What makes Altman so exciting, then, is not his rejection of disciplined or formal film-making, like, perhaps, Ken Russell. Instead, Altman constantly looks for new ways to unite his cinematic details with his overall, subtle design. As a result, his films demand an open, alert audience. If we in that audience are perceptive enough, we will be rewarded with an emotional and exhilarating experience or, as in the case of Nashville, a disappointing failure. But at least we will have been active; regardless of the quality of the individual film, we will come away from it more demanding, more articulate, and more aware than when we entered.

Perhaps Altma's greatest influence will be this training of a more alert audience. He has reminded film-makers of the power of details and of the ability to rely on atmosphere and theme, rather than narrative. Already, Altman's influence can be seen in films like Taxi Driver (the constant background action and conversations and the soft focus, Images-like colors in the cab) and Don't Look Now (the insistence of an irrational structure for an irrational subject). Even more important, however, is the development of an Altman cult, a small but vocal and demanding group of people who have had their expectations raised and who now will accept nothing less than an emotional, intelligent, involving, and honest film experience - from Altman or anyone else.

Epilogue

Buffalo Bill and the Indians

or

Sitting Bull's History Lesson

The title Buffalo Bill and the Indians or Sitting Bull's History
Lesson tells everything about the new Altman movie. Like the movie itself,
the title is cerebrally amusing and clever; also like the movie, it fails to
emotionally engage us. As such, Buffalo Bill continues Altman's troubling
tendency towards making technically brilliant but ultimately soul-less and
mechanical movies.

Unlike some of the earlier Altman films, especially McCabe, Images, The
Long Good-bye, and California Split, Buffalo Bill is a relatively simple movie.
Despite its episodic pacing (itself an Altman trait), the film directly and
explicitly deals with the making of and living with myths in America. Since
the history of the nation is transmitted through myths that are invented by
slick dime novelists, Buffalo Bill reasons, history and historical figures are
no more than media creations. Annie Oakley, Buffalo Bill, Sitting Bull, and
Grover Cleveland, the biggest star of them all, are no different than today's
rock stars, politicians, or movie directors. They all develop images and then
translate those images into visibilities that bring fame, fortune, and at least
the appearance of power. Because the image or role enacts demands on the star's
personal behavior, it forces the person to publicly become the image. Not only
does this effectively isolate the real person from other people, but it also
eventually leads to an internal confusion between the person and the role.

Although this idea of roles has appeared throughout Altman's work (most
notably in McCabe, California Split, and Nashville), he has rarely been more

209

explicit than in Buffalo Bill. After a quick dedication to the common anonymous settlers who "pave the way for the heroes that endure," we are welcomed
to "the real events enacted by men and women of the American frontier." Then,
in the best Day for Night tradition, the camera pulls back to reveal that we
have been watching and listening to a rehearsal of Buffalo Bill's Wild West
Show. The first title, a self-consciously satiric blurb, "'Robert Altman's
Absolutely Unique and Heroic Enterprise of Inimitable Lustre,'" reinforces the
concern with show business. This jab at Altman's intellectual film audience and
his own reputation as American film's great white hope further establishes
Altman's concern with roles and with art by interjecting a distancing device
into the film. Rather than set up a simple audience relationship to his film,
Altman complicates our role by making us an audience watching an audience,
or at least a rehearsal.

Instead of developing this somewhat traditional concept, however, Altman
uses it only to introduce another idea, the relationship of one's image or
art to reality. Ned Buntline, the novelist and legend maker, tells patrons
of the bar that he plucked William Cody from the (chorous) line, dubbed him
Buffalo Bill, and told the whole country about him, "Sure enough, these
stories....are a big success and the kid comes looking for me, scared to
death about the legends I created but real excited with his new fame." After
Buntline, who clearly enjoys his power to create myths, finishes with a
typically overblown conclusion ("any youngster who figures he's gonna set
the world on fire best not forget where he got the matches."), Altman cuts to the
old soldier, who is telling some Indian children how he himself discovered
Buffalo Bill. The comment is clear; everyone is in show business, everyone
has his or her act. Thus, Major Burke talks in attention--attracting allitera-
tion, Buffalo Bill's groupies interest him by singing arias, Nate dreams of
"Codyfying" the world, Sitting Bull haggles over photographic rights, the

First Lady spreads culture and thinks of herself as a patron of the arts. Everyone, then, is involved in show business, be it behind or in front of the screen.

But although everyone has his part, _Buffalo Bill_ addresses itself more to the pressures, effects, and responsibilities on those at the top, to the stars. Despite William Cody's inauspicious beginnings, his public relations campaign catapults him into a position of visibility and importance. It also forces him to be Buffalo Bill, rather than William Cody. William Cody, for example, may be afraid of caged birds, but Buffalo Bill cannot show that fear. Buffalo Bill, after all, is a star. As a star, he must live up to his image; he must give the public what it wants. To beat the Indians, he makes sure they get slower horses; to sound intelligent and, more importantly, to be quotable, he surrounds himself with glib ghostwriters. At some point, however, William Cody gets lost; even his closest and most loyal associates respond to his image and role, not to the person underneath.

Bill speaks sincerely, then, when he tells Sitting Bull that "it's hard to be a star," much harder even than being an "Injun." Ned Buntline explains further: "Stars spend so much time in front of the mirror, seeing if their good looks and word delivery can overcome their judgement...Once a star.... makes a judgement, it becomes a commitment, and its gotta stick, no matter what the risk. Yessir! Stars are risking a lot more'n ordinary people." The cost of such a risk? Bill describes it to Halsey, Sitting Bull's assistant, "The chief is ready to learn what the show business is all about. And he'll be sorry he didn't do my Custer act, 'cause he's gonna suffer a worse defeat than his. Custer at least got to die. Your chief is gonna be humiliated."

For William Cody, then, the price of being Buffalo Bill comes high; he

must always be on and must always succeed. And because he must live Buffalo
Bill's role, he loses the ability to distinguish between the real William
Cody and the character of Buffalo Bill. He gets rid of Margaret, the Mezzo-
Contralto, by telling her that he cannot deal with her and Sitting Bull at
the same time and still be at his best. Margaret readily accepts his excuse,
begins to sing "Greensleeves," and reveals that even she, his lover, responds
to Buffalo Bill, not William Cody. More importantly, although Bill is really
just making way for the Lyric-Coloratura, his apparently sincere and convincing
explanation of his role's demands demonstrates the ease with which he can
fall into the role and his awareness of its dimensions. When he fails to
perform sexually with the Coloratura, he again retreats into the security
of the role. Sitting Bull and the rest of the dangerous Indians have escaped,
he explains; his fame as a scout makes him the logical and necessary choice for
the leader of the posse. Bill's failure to satisfy the lady and his subsequent
failure to capture Sitting Bull reveal the extent of the discrepancy between
legend and the man. The gulf is so great that when the dejected Bill goes
behind a door and fires a gun, his friends fear that he has shot himself. Bill
does not have that sort of depth and commitment, however, he is merely shooting
(and missing) the Coloratura's pet bird.

More than revealing Bill's ineptitude, this incident shows how dependent
Bill has become on his legend. Bill rushes in to his very real, very eager,
would-be lover, tells her that having her wait for him while he captures the
Indians will make his job easier, and then apologizes: "You know I wouldn't
let anything come between us....except something real like this." Then he
looks around the room. "Where is my real jacket?" he mutters. "Gotta have my
real jacket." The Indians have not, of course, escaped, nor is Bill qualified
to lead the party. But by interpreting real events through his distorted

perspective of the Wild West myth, he misreads the events and acts foolishly. This confusion is heightened by his reaction to his failure; rather than acknowledge and correct his false assumptions, he gets depressed over his inability to live up to his image.

Stardom, then, entails an ambivalent response of anxiety and addiction and results in a blurring of person and myth. Faced with the tremendous pressures and responsibilities of stardom, Buffalo Bill has no one who can understand his dilemma--except another star, like Sitting Bull.

Instead of sympathizing with Bill, however, Sitting Bull and his mouthpiece, Halsey, harass and expose him. From the beginning, Sitting Bull appears to disdain the role of fierce Indian chief; he wanders around distractedly and does not bother to speak English. Although he enters the show only so he can ask President Cleveland for a favor and leaves after he meets him, Sitting Bull has enough star presence to fill the arena and win the initially hostile crowd's approval. And while apparently remaining above petty conventions of show business, he manages to out-negotiate Bill, to expose Bill's use of spraying buckshot (just after Bill's condescending lecture on the true marksman's disdain for the less skillful, less exacting spray), and forces Bill to publicly compromise on his principles and rehire the Indians. And unlike Bill, Sitting Bull seemingly retains his integrity by remaining immune to the lure of show business and leaves after accomplishing his announced purpose.

But although Sitting Bull does not communicate with Bill and seems more real than Bill, Sitting Bull too is a frustrated star. Even if he dies honest, he still dies unnecessarily and futilely. He cannot ask Cleveland the question, much less get the truth about the Indian wars to the public. Not only does the audience still see the same slanted and racist interpretation of the white man's role in the winning of the West, but now watches Halsey, who fits the popular conception of the chief from the film's beginning, play the part of Sitting Bull. With Halsey's participation, Buffalo Bill's version of the Wild West gains even more credibility and force. For all of Sitting Bull's efforts and Buffalo Bill's shortcomings, the power of the myth triumphs over the truth; however inaccurate factually, the film's events have certainly been a history lesson for Sitting Bull. Halsey's participation in the final version of the show, when coupled with his skilled negotiations with Bill and the predetermined and dramatic nature of Sitting Bull's death, makes us realize that the Indians have not succumbed to show business, but have been willing participants from the beginning. The Publicist says it best; if Sitting Bull "weren't in show business, he wouldn't have been a chief."

At the end of the film, the Indian and the white man's sense of history converge as a show business act. The film ends as it began, with the same circus-type music and the same setting of the Wild West show. Although the last close-up of Bill shows the terror, confusion, and lack of control of William Cody and regardless of his dehumanization and of the inaccuracy of the presentation, Buffalo Bill's version is the one that lasts.

The concept of media or myth-making influences on our history has been treated before; The Man Who Shot Liberty Valance and its famous last line, "When the legend becomes truth, print the legend," immediately come to mind. Altman's familiarity with roles and with the relationship between image and reality, however, promised a new, provocative treatment. This expectation, is heightened throughout the movie by the usual striking cinematography, fine acting, and beautiful little moments we have come to expect from an Altman film.

Buffalo Bill is packed with these rewarding and memorable characterizations.

The pregnant girl's relationship with Frank, the old man's insensitive retelling of the myths, the inability of Grover Cleveland and Buffalo Bill to speak without their speechwriters, Buffalo Bill's unconscious racism (especially in his dealing with Dart, his black servant and actor), Bill's concern with his wig, Nate's misuse of language, Buntline's dramatic pretension, the First Lady's immature tendency to attach a -y or -ie to people's names ("Grovie" and "Buffalo Billy"), Nate's entrance and costume's subtle resemblance with McCabe's, and the satire of Nashville's "I'm Easy" in the scene where Nina serenades Buffalo Bill's reception for the President combine with the fluidity of the editing and the originality of the story to represent film-making at its most intelligent and skillful. Somehow, however, the whole of Buffalo Bill is considerably less than the sum of its parts; it simply does not generate the intensity and excitement that make great, or even successful, film-making.

Perhaps the trouble with Buffalo Bill revolves around its failure to involve us with the characters. Neither Annie Oakley nor Ned Buntline emerge as fully developed characters; we know Buntline's story and recognize his function as a Greek chorus and can guess at Annie's past, but we do not really care about them as people. Sitting Bull too is treated with reserve and distance; we may respect his dignity, but do not get inside him either. As a result, his fake assassination attempt and his confrontation with Grover Cleveland are neither funny nor shocking; the announcement of his death and the heavy-handed shot of his smouldering bones leave us curiously unmoved. And, more seriously, we never identify with Buffalo Bill. We are given some information about the real William Cody. He is cowardly, pretentious, ignorant, inept, and racist, in addition to being confused and trapped by his role as a star. Rather than bring us closer to him, however, our inside information serves only to further distance ourselves from the character.

This distancing in turn encourages our lack of involvement with his plight and undercuts the film's impact.

Although our ultimate inability to respond to Bill as a person mirrors the reaction of the people around him and seems thematically to strengthen Altman's observations about stardom, it also suggests a self-defeating weakness in Altman's presentation. As the title indicates, this is a film about ideas more than it is about story or people. As such, Altman has padded the movie with scenes and speeches that insure that even the slowest of audiences will catch his message (even though the general movie going public has not expressed much desire in Altman's style or ideas about movie-making sinch MASH). Most of Ned Buntline's speeches, for example, directly comment on the meaning of the film's action. We see Bill (and Ned) look into the mirror, talk about and to himself, and worry about the responsibilities of stardom. Buntline's simultaneous explanation of Bill's actions seem not only unnecessary, but also annoyingly condescending. In his speech about Indians' dreams, the problem becomes more serious and complex. Again, the relationship between Bill and Bull is quite clear; the idea of Bull's dreaming and then waiting for reality to catch up is unique and striking. Buntline's sociological discourse on the cultural implication of dreams, however interesting, saddles this episode with intellectual and self-important meaning. Rather than let the event determine its own effect, Altman underlines it and forces a symbolic importance onto it. This heavy-handedness also mars one of the film's climactic scenes, Buffalo Bill's encounter with Sitting Bull's ghost. Although this scene utilizes the film's flashiest editing and cinematography, no new information or insights are revealed. Instead, the scene functions as a summation of the film's themes. We know that Buffalo Bill has degenerated into a confused, troubled, and lonely man, but the rambling monologue sounds and looks too prepared, calculated, and pat to be convincing and spontaneous. Rather than bring us closer to the man, this scene functions as Altman's last chance to get his ideas across. Because it uses the character solely as a vehicle of the theme, this scene and ultimately the movie itself become didactic. Buffalo Bill may, then, be ambitious, intelligent, and serious; somewhere along the line, however it stops being fun.

Like Nashville and like Buffalo Bill himself, Buffalo Bill and the Indians suffers from too much style, too much pretension, and too little genuine substance. The self-depracating blurb and the playful music at the beginning of the film indicate Altman's awareness of his tendency towards self-importance. Unfortunately, this awareness disappears as the film progresses; the increasing seriousness and constant repitition of his theme suffocate the film's vitality and greatly undercut the film's impact. And since Altman is one of, if not the, most gifted of our film-makers, his films' increasing lack of humanity and increasing subordination of character development to a statement of a sense of style becomes our problem, as well as his. Maybe he should make a silly little comedy, a suspense thriller, or a light musical--a lark that would enable him to escape from another serious reworking of his more abstract and, I suspect, played out thematic concerns. At any rate, until Altman returns to making movies about people, he probably will continue to make movies like Buffalo Bill--technically unparalled, occasionally brilliant, but ultimately unaffecting.

NOTES

Gene Siskel, <u>Chicago</u> <u>Tribune</u>, July 2, 1976.

Since my study includes only THAT COLD DAY through
BUFFALO BILL, the filmography excludes the television
work, the James Dean documentary, and 1967's COUNTDOWN,
which is available only in heavily edited versions.

THAT COLD DAY IN THE PARK (1969) - screenplay by Gillian
    Freeman; produced by Donald Factor and Leon Mirell;
    presented by Commonwealth United Entertainment.
    Cast: Frances Austin, Sandy Dennis; the boy, Michael
    Burns; the girl, Susanne Benton.

MASH (1969) - screenplay by Ring Lardner, Jr.; director
    of photography, Harold Stine; producer, Ingo Preminger;
    music, Johnny Mandel; released by 20 Century Fox.
    Cast: Hawkeye, Donald Sutherland; Trapper John,
    Elliot Gould; Duke, Tom Skerritt; Hot Lips, Sally
    Kellerman; Burns, Robert Duvall; Dish, JoAnn Pflug;
    Vollmer, David Arkin; Me Lay, Michael Murphy; Pain-
    less, John Schuck; Dago Red, Rene Auberjonois.

BREWSTER MCLOUD (1970) - written by Doran William Cannon;
    director of photography, Lamar Boren and Jordan Croneneweth;
    music, Gene Page; producer, Lou Adler; released by
    M-G-M.
    Cast: Brewster, Bud Cort; Louise, Sally Kellerman;
    Shaft, Michael Murphy; Weeks, William Windom; Suzanne,
    Shelley Duvall; Lecturer, Rene Auberjonois; Abraham
    Wright, Stacey Keach; Johnson, John Schuck; Daphne
    Heap, Margaret Hamilton.

McCABE AND MRS. MILLER (1971) - Produced by David Foster
    and Mitchell Brower; screenplay by Robert Altman and
    Brian McKay; photographed by Vilmos Zsigmond; music
    by Leonard Cohen; released by Warner Brothers.
    Cast: McCabe, Warren Beatty; Mrs. Miller, Julie
    Christie; Sheehan, Rene Auberjonois; Butler, Hugh :
    Millais; Lawyer, William Devane; Ida, Shelley Duvall;
    Sears, Michael Murphy; Smalley, John Schuck.

IMAGES (1972) - script by Robert Altman; produced by
    Tommy Thompson; photographed by Vilmos Zsigmond;
    released by Columbia.
    Cast: Cathryn, Susannah York; Hugh, Rene Auberjonois;
    Marcel, Hugh Millais; Rene, Marcel Bozzuffi;
    Susannah, Cathryn Harrison.

THE LONG GOOD-BYE (1973) - screenplay by Leigh Brackett;
    produced by Jerry Bick; executive producer, Elliot
    Kastner; director of photography, Vilmos Zsigmond;
    editor, Lou Lombardo; music, John Williams; released
    by United Artists.

Cast: Marlowe, Elliot Gould; Eilleen, Nina van
Pallandt; Roger, Sterling Hayden; Marty, Mark
Rydell; Dr. Verringer, Henry Gibson; Harry, David
Arkin; Terry, Jim Bouton.

THIEVES LIKE US (1974) - screenplay by Calder Willingham,
Joan Tewkesbury, and Robert Altman; produced by Jerry
Bick; executive producer, George Litto; director of
photography, Jean Bouffety; editor, Lou Lombardo;
released by United Artists.
Cast: Bowie, Keith ·Carradine; Keechie, Shelley Duvall;
Chicamaw, John Schuck; T-Dub, Bert Remsen; Mattie,
Louise Fletcher; Lula, Ann Latham; Dee Mobley, Tom
Skerritt.

CALIFORNIA SPLIT (1974) - screenplay by Joseph Walsh;
produced by Robert Altman and Joseph Walsh; executive
producers, Aaron Spelling and Leonard Goldberg;
director of photography, Paul Lohmann; editor, Lou
Lombardo; distributed by Columbia.
Cast: Bill Denny, George Segal; Charlie Walters,
Elliot Gould; Barbara Miller, Ann Prentiss; Susan
Peters, Gwen Welles; Lew, Edward Walsh; Sparkle,
Joseph Walsh; Helen Brown, Bert Remsen.

NASHVILLE (1975) - produced by Robert Altman; executive
producers, Jerry Weintraub and Martin Starger;
screenplay, Joan Tewkesbury; director of photography,
Paul Lohmann; musical director, Richard Baskin;
released by Paramount.
Cast: Tricycle Man, Jeff Goldblum; Albequerque,
Barbara Harris; Star, Bert Remsen; Kenny, David Hay-
ward; Kelly, Scott Glenn; Triplette, Michael Murphy;
Del, Ned Beatty; Linnea, Lily Tomlin; Bud, Dave Peel;
Pearl, Barbara Baxley; Haven, Henry Gibson; Barbara
Jean, Ronee Blakely; Barnett, Allen Garfield; Tom,
Tim Brown; Connie, Karen Black; Tom, Keith Carradine;
Mary, Cristina Raines; Bill, Alan Nichols; Norman,
David Arkin; L.A. Joan, Shelley Duvall; Mr. Green,
Keenan Wynn; Sueleen, Gwen Welles; Wade, Robert Doqui;
Frog, Richard Baskin; Elliot Gould and Julie Christie
as themselves.

BUFFALO BILL AND THE INDIANS (1976) - screenplay by Alan
Rudolph and Robert Altman; produced by Robert Altman;
executive producer, David Susskind; a Dino De Laurentis
production; distributed by United Artists.
Cast: the star, Paul Newman; the producer, Joel Grey;
the publicist, Kevin McCarthy; the relative, Harvey
Keitel; the sure shot, Geraldine Chaplin; the Indian,
Frank Kaquitts; the interpreter, Will Sampson; the
legend maker, Burt Lancaster; the President, Pat
McCormick; the First Lady, Shelley Duvall.

BIBLIOGRAPHY

Burgess, Jackson. "McCabe and Mrs. Miller." Film Quarterly, Winter, 1971-72, pp. 49-53.

Byrne, Connie, and Lopez, William O. "Nashville" (An Interview Documentary). Film Quarterly, Winter, 1975-76, pp. 13-26.

Cutts, John. "MASH, McCloud, and McCabe." Films and Filming, November, 1971, pp. 40-44.

Engle, Gary. "Robert Altman's Anti-Western." Journal of Popular Film, Fall, 1972, pp. 268-289.

Falonga, Mark. "Images." Film Quarterly, Summer, 1973, pp. 43-46.

Farber, Stephen. "Let Us Now Praise - Not Overpraise - Robert Altman." New York Times, September 29, 1974, p. 1.

Film Heritage, Fall, 1975. (Entire issue devoted to Nashville.)

Fox, Terry Curtis. "Nashville Chats: An Interview with Robert Altman." Chicago Reader, July 4, 1975, p. 1.

Gregory, Charles. "The Long Good-bye." Film Quarterly, Summer, 1973, pp. 46-49.

Hodenfield, Chris. "Bob Altman's Nashville." Rolling Stone, July 17, 1975, p. 31.

Kinder, Marsha. "The Return of the Outlaw Couple." Film Quarterly, Summer, 1974, pp. 2-10.

Kolker, Robert Phillips. "Night to Day." Sight and Sound, Autumn, 1974, pp. 237-239.

McClelland, C. Kirk. Brewster McCloud. New York: Signet, 1971.

Michener, C., and Kasindorf, M. "Altman's Opryland Epic." Newsweek, June 30, 1975, pp. 46-50.

Quinn, Sally. "Robert Altman is Easy." Midwest Magazine, July 27, 1975, p. 13.

Rosenbaum, Jonathan. "Improvisations and Interactions in Altmanville." Sight and Sound, Spring, 1975, pp. 91-95.

Rosenbaum, Jonathan. "Nashville." Sight and Sound, Autumn, 1975, pp. 204-05.

Rubenstein, Roberta. "Brewster McCloud." Film Quarterly, Winter, 1971-72, pp. 44-48.

Stewart, Garrett. "'The Long Good-bye 'from Chinatown.'" Film Quarterly, Winter, 1974-75, pp. 25-32.

Taratino, Michael. "Movement as Metaphor: The Long Good-bye." Sight and Sound, Spring, 1975, pp. 98-102.

Tewkesbury, Joan. Nashville. New York: Bantam Books, 1976.

Viertel, Jack, and Colker, David. "The Long Road to Nash-ville." New Times, June 13, 1975, pp. 52-58.

Williams, Alan. "California Split." Film Quarterly, Spring, 1975, pp. 54-55.

DISSERTATIONS ON FILM

An Arno Press Collection

Anderson, Patrick Donald. **In Its Own Image:** The Cinematic Vision of Hollywood. First publication, 1978

Bacher, Lutz. **The Mobile Mise En Scene:** A Critical Analysis of the Theory and Practice of Long-Take Camera Movement in the Narrative Film. First publication, 1978

Beaver, Frank Eugene. **Bosley Crowther:** Social Critic of the Film, 1940-1967. First publication, 1974

Benderson, Albert Edward. **Critical Approaches to Federico Fellini's "8½".** First publication, 1974

Berg, Charles Merrell. **An Investigation of the Motives for and Realization of Music to Accompany the American Silent Film, 1896-1927. First publication, 1976**

Blades, Joseph Dalton, Jr. **A Comparative Study of Selected American Film Critics, 1958-1974.** First publication, 1976

Blake, Richard Aloysius. **The Lutheran Milieu of the Films of Ingmar Bergman.** First publication, 1978

Bohn, Thomas William. **An Historical and Descriptive Analysis of the "Why We Fight" Series.** First publication, 1977

Cohen, Louis Harris. **The Cultural-Political Traditions and Developments of the Soviet Cinema: 1917-1972.** First publication, 1974

Dart, Peter. **Pudovkin's Films and Film Theory.** First publication, 1974

Davis, Robert Edward. **Response to Innovation:** A Study of Popular Argument about New Mass Media. First publication, 1976

Facey, Paul W. **The Legion of Decency:** A Sociological Analysis of the Emergence and Development of a Social Pressure Group. First publication, 1974

Feineman, Neil. **Persistence of Vision:** The Films of Robert Altman. First publication, 1978

Feldman, Charles Matthew. **The National Board of Censorship (Review) of Motion Pictures, 1909-1922.** First publication, 1977

Feldman, Seth R. **Evolution of Style in the Early Work of Dziga Vertov.** First publication, 1977

Flanders, Mark Wilson. **Film Theory of James Agee.** First publication, 1977

Fredericksen, Donald Laurence. **The Aesthetic of Isolation in Film Theory:** Hugo Munsterberg. First publication, 1977

Gosser, H. Mark. **Selected Attempts at Stereoscopic Moving Pictures and Their Relationship to the Development of Motion Picture Technology, 1852-1903.** First publication, 1977

Harpole, Charles Henry. **Gradients of Depth in the Cinema Image.** First publication, 1978

James, C. Rodney. **Film as a National Art:** NFB of Canada and the Film Board Idea. First publication, 1977

Karimi, A.M. **Toward a Definition of the American Film Noir (1941-1949).** First publication, 1976

Karpf, Stephen L. **The Gangster Film:** Emergence, Variation and Decay of a Genre, 1930-1940. First publication, 1973

Lounsbury, Myron O. **The Origins of American Film Criticism, 1909-1939.** First publication, 1973

Lynch, F. Dennis. **Clozentropy:** A Technique for Studying Audience Response to Films. First publication, 1978

Lyons, Robert J[oseph]. **Michelangelo Antonioni's Neo-Realism:** A World View. First publication, 1976

Lyons, Timothy James. **The Silent Partner:** The History of the American Film Manufacturing Company, 1910-1921. First publication, 1974

McLaughlin, Robert. **Broadway and Hollywood:** A History of Economic Interaction. First publication, 1974

Maland, Charles J. **American Visions:** The Films of Chaplin, Ford, Capra, and Welles, 1936-1941. First publication, 1977

Mason, John L. **The Identity Crisis Theme in American Feature Films, 1960-1969.** First publication, 1977

North, Joseph H. **The Early Development of the Motion Picture, 1887-1909.** First publication, 1973

Paine, Jeffery Morton. **The Simplification of American Life:** Hollywood Films of the 1930's. First publication, 1977

Pryluck, Calvin. **Sources of Meaning in Motion Pictures and Television.** First publication, 1976

Rimberg, John. **The Motion Picture in the Soviet Union, 1918-1952.** First publication, 1973

Sanderson, Richard Arlo. **A Historical Study of the Development of American Motion Picture Content and Techniques Prior to 1904.** First publication, 1977

Sands, Pierre N. **A Historical Study of the Academy of the Motion Picture Arts and Sciences (1927-1947).** First publication, 1973

Selby, Stuart Alan. **The Study of Film as an Art Form in American Secondary Schools.** First publication, 1978

Shain, Russell Earl. **An Analysis of Motion Pictures about War Released by the American Film Industry, 1939-1970.** First publication, 1976

Snyder, John J. **James Agee:** A Study of His Film Criticism. First publication, 1977

Stuart, Frederic. **The Effects of Television on the Motion Picture and Radio Industries.** First publication, 1976

Van Wert, William F. **The Theory and Practice of the** *Ciné-Roman.* First publication, 1978

Wead, George. **Buster Keaton and the Dynamics of Visual Wit.** First publication, 1976

Welsch, Janice R. **Film Archetypes:** Sisters, Mistresses, Mothers and Daughters. First publication, 1978

Wolfe, Glenn J. **Vachel Lindsay:** The Poet as Film Theorist. First publication, 1973

Zuker, Joel Stewart. **Ralph Steiner:** Filmmaker and Still Photographer. First publication, 1978